# Coaching the Offensive Backfield

# Coaching the Offensive Backfield

Steve Axman

Parker Publishing Company, Inc., West Nyack, N.Y.

© 1979, by

PARKER PUBLISHING COMPANY, INC.

West Nyack, N.Y.

*All rights reserved. No part of this book may be reproduced in any form or by any means, without permission in writing from the publisher.*

**Library of Congress Cataloging in Publication Data**

Axman, Steve
   Coaching the offensive backfield.

   Includes index.
   1. Football--Offense. 2. Football coaching.
I. Title.
GV951.8.A944         796.33'2077        79-11511
ISBN 0-13-139196-8

Printed in the United States of America

DEDICATION

To my wife
Marie

To my daughters
Mary Beth and Jaclyn

To Coach Homer Smith
and to the memory of
Coach Bruce Tarbox

Additional books by the author:

*Attacking Modern Defenses with the Multiple-
   Formation Veer Offense*
*The Pro-Read Option Attack for Winning Football*

# What This Book Can Do for You

*Coaching the Offensive Backfield* is a complete coaching guide that provides a thorough and explicit analysis of every facet of offensive backfield play. From the center-quarterback ball exchange to optioning techniques to backfield pass blocking, you are presented not only with the total understanding of each skill and fundamental but also with an indepth analysis of the coaching points necessary to help produce consistent and precise offensive backfield execution.

When one thinks of offensive backfield play, one immediately focuses on ball carrying. Offensive backfield play is, however, a series of highly demanding psycho-motor skills of which ballcarrying might be only a small part. When the coach grades and/or evaluates his game films, he evaluates and critiques such skills as the ball exchanges, stance, take-off, blocking, passing, pass receiving, optioning, ball security and faking—not just ballcarrying! It is this actual examination of the true roles of the members of the offensive backfield that brings into focus the important and critical effects of offensive backfield play, as well as its needs and priorities.

Emphasizing the critical importance of offensive backfield play is the key. A poorly executed block by a lineman might result in no gain or a short loss of yardage. A poorly executed center-quarterback exchange, a poor pitch or a tipped pass, may all lead to a loss of the ball. A hand-off may seem to be an easier skill to execute than a block. However, the result of a miscue of the so-called easier hand-off skill can be far more catastrophic in its effect on the total play of the offense. For example: the ball is on the 9-yard line going in for a score and a mishandled or poor pitch on an option play turns the ball over to the opposition; a poor hand-off results in a fumble; poor ball security by a ballcarrier results in a fumble or interception—these are but a few of the critical situations the offensive backfield can be faced with every time the ball is snapped. In addition, the critical importance of offensive backfield play execution is not limited to ball exchanges and ballcarrying. A poor dive fake may enable a linebacker to pursue to the outside to shut off the corner threat. Poor passing, receiving, and blocking by the offensive backfield can easily nullify effective offensive team execution.

Unfortunately, concern for the critical aspects of offensive backfield play has not been emphasized enough—not on the practice field, at coaching clinics, or in our coaching literature. This book helps to bring into focus the critical element of offensive backfield play execution as well as to help fill the void that has been left in football coaching literature concerning offensive backfield play.

*Coaching the Offensive Backfield* is virtually a breakdown of every drill and fundamental that offensive backfield play demands. A precise examination of center-quarterback as well as quarterback-ballcarrier exchanges helps develop precise execution in what is perhaps the most critical area of all offensive backfield play. The development of adept ball-handling drills as well as the development of airtight ball security further helps to alleviate a major trouble spot in the execution of the offense. An examination of stance and take-off helps to develop sound execution of the most fundamental aspects of offensive backfield play. An explicit analysis of ballcarrying skills and optioning fundamentals helps to get the ball in motion. An examination of both quarterback passing and backfield receiving helps to analyze and explain the fundamentals necessary for the most explosive part of offensive football—the passing game. Furthermore, an analysis of backfield faking as well as run and pass blocking helps to round out the completeness of this guide to coaching the offensive backfield by helping to create a thorough understanding of the fundamentals and skills most often overlooked in offensive backfield execution. In addition, each chapter concerning the specific facets of offensive backfield play presents you with a series of game-like drills to help you develop precision of offensive backfield skills.

*Coaching the Offensive Backfield* presents you with a complete plan concerning all of the skills, fundamentals and drills necessary to produce a precision-like, explosive offensive backfield. Ball exchanges, stances, take-offs, running skills, ball security, option techniques, passing, receiving, blocking and faking—these offensive backfield topics and more are explicitly analyzed, diagrammed and explained to present you with a *complete* conceptual understanding of offensive backfield play—its teaching, coaching and execution.

Steve Axman

## ACKNOWLEDGMENTS

Much of the material in this book was taught to me by Homer Smith, Head Football Coach at the United States Military Academy at West Point. Coach Smith is a great teacher from whom I have learned much. I am extremely grateful to him for having given me the tremendous opportunity to have coached at West Point.

Very special acknowledgment goes to the memory of West Point's former Offensive Coordinator and close friend Bruce Tarbox, with whom it was my good fortune to have been able to coach for two years. Bruce was a great coach in the truest sense of the word. He aided me as a coach enormously.

Thanks go to Army's passing game Coach Mike Mikolayunas for his assistance with parts of this book. Thanks also go to Sal Polazzo for his photography work. Special thanks to Cadets Greg King, Joe Oliver and Earl Mulrane for taking time from their busy Cadet schedules to pose for the demonstrative photos. Thanks also go to Cheryl Drysdale and Carol Scott for their help in typing the manuscript.

# Table of Contents

What This Book Can Do for You ........................ 9

1. Developing Secure Center-Quarterback
   Exchange Techniques ............................. 19

   Center-Quarterback Stances • 19
   The Center Snap and Quarterback Reception • 21
   Common Center-Quarterback Exchange
      Problems • 23
   "Goosing" for the Football • 24
   Offside Snap • 25
   Wet Ball Snap • 25
   Center-Quarterback Exchange Practice and
      Drills • 27

2. Developing Adept Ball Handling Skills .............. 31

   Specificity • 31
   "The Ball Handling Tricks" • 32
   Ball Handling Practice and Drills • 32

3. Coaching Explosive Backfield Stances and Take-Offs . 38

   Backfield Stances • 38
   Explosive Take-Offs via the Step Technique • 43
   The Dive Take-Off • 44

3. **Coaching Explosive Backfield Stances and Take-Offs**
   *(Continued)*

   The Off-Tackle • 44
   The End-Run Take-Off • 45
   The Counter Step Take-Off • 46
   The Counter Dive Take-Off • 47
   The Quick-Pitch/Swing Pattern Take-Off • 48
   Tailback ''I'' Formation Take-Offs • 49
   Stance and Take-Off Practice and Drills • 51

4. **Developing Secure Quarterback-Ballcarrier Exchange Techniques** .............................. 54

   Quarterback Movement to the Exchange Point • 54
   The Quarterback Hand-Off Technique • 55
   Ballcarrier Reception of Hand-Off • 57
   Quarterback Reverse Pivot Action • 59
   Quarterback Sprint-Draw Action • 61
   Quarterback Counter Dive Action • 62
   The Quarterback and Ballcarrier Techniques on Draw Actions • 63
   The Quarterback Toss/Quick-Pitch • 65
   The Quarterback Option-Pitch • 67
   Ballcarrier Receiving the Toss, Quick-Pitch or Option-Pitch • 69
   The Reverse Hand-Off • 70
   Quarterback-Ballcarrier Exchange Practice and Drills • 71

5. **Coaching the Backs to Run for Touchdowns** ......... 76

   The Dive Concept • 77
   The Freeze Technique • 83
   End-Run Techniques • 85
   Open Field Running • 91
   Dive Jump Technique • 93
   Dive Squeeze Technique • 94
   Spinning Out Technique • 96

*Table of Contents* 15

**5. Coaching the Backs to Run for Touchdowns** *(Continued)*

Dragging or Carrying a Defender • 99
Ballcarrying Practice and Drills • 99

**6. Developing Total Ball Security** .................... **109**

Proper Carry of the Football • 109
The Two-Armed Carry • 111
Changing the Ball from One Hand to the Other • 112
Problem Areas for Ball Security • 113
Ball Security Practice and Drills • 114

**7. Coaching the Backfield Option Game** ............... **119**

The Triple Option Dive Read • 119
The Outside Veer Triple Option Dive Read • 124
The Counter Option Triple Option Dive Read • 125
The Keep-Pitch Read Downhill Attack • 125
Inside Veer Option Action • 131
Lead Option Action • 132
Counter Option Action • 133
Trap Option Action • 133
Outside Veer Option Action • 134
Quarterback-Pitchback Pitch Ration • 135
Backfield Option Practice and Drills • 137

**8. Coaching the Quarterback Passing Techniques** ....... **144**

Gripping the Football • 145
Setting-Up • 145
The Delivery of the Ball • 147
Follow-Through • 150
Passing Trajectory • 150
Passing on the Move • 151
Halfback Option Passing • 153
Quarterback Passing Techniques Practice and Drills • 154

## 9. Coaching Backfield Pass Receiving Techniques ....... 164

Catching Techniques • 164
The Importance of Positioning • 169
Backfield Receiver Separation Techniques • 170
Ball Security and North-South Knifing • 175
Backfield Pass Receiving Practice and Drills • 176

## 10. Installing the Added Dimension of Faking ........... 187

Quarterback Hand-Off Faking • 188
Quarterback Pass Action Faking • 190
Other Quarterback Faking Action • 192
Running Back Fake of Hand-Off • 193
Other Running Back Faking Actions • 194
Backfield Faking Practice and Drills • 194

## 11. Developing Backfield Run Blocking Techniques ...... 197

The Isolation Block • 198
The Lead-Draw Block • 201
The Kick-Out Block • 204
The Fake and Block • 206
The Lead Block • 208
The Arc Block • 209
Backfield Run Blocking Techniques Practice and Drills • 211

## 12. Developing Backfield Pass Blocking Techniques ...... 219

The Cutdown Block • 219
The Pass Pro Block • 224
Pass Pro Blocking a Blitzing Linebacker • 229
Backfield Pass Blocking Techniques Practice and Drills • 230

**Index** .................................................. 237

# Coaching the Offensive Backfield

## one

# Developing Secure Center - Quarterback Exchange Techniques

Nothing is more frustrating than a center-quarterback exchange miscue. At best, the offense recovers the ball, resulting only in a loss of down. Far too often a turnover occurs as the defense pounces on the ball. The center-quarterback exchange, or the snap, is the starting point for every offensive play whether run or pass. It is an offensive action that is far too often overlooked. It is a skill that is taken for granted when there is no obvious execution problem. A focus of attention usually results only when there is a center-quarterback exchange failure or series of failures.

The center-quarterback exchange must be a fail-safe technique. The exchange must be so secure that it actually can be taken for granted that there will be no miscue. However, such an ability to take the center-quarterback exchange for granted can only come about through extensive attention, skill development and practice. It is a skill that must be practiced and coached every day. Such a skill is not a singular concept. Such concerns as quick-count snaps, "goosing" the ball, snapping a wet ball, practicing the reception of poor snaps, late snaps and early snaps must all be incorporated within the framework of developing secure center-quarterback exchange techniques.

### CENTER-QUARTERBACK STANCES

Offensive backfield play starts with the action of a lineman—the center. From his normal blocker's stance, whether it be a three or four point stance, the center grips the ball with a forward passer's grip. Such a grip may vary from center to center due to hand size, arm size and other physiological differences. In general, however, the thumb of the right hand is placed somewhere in the vicinity of the first crossing lace—usually slightly in front of it. Such a grip of the ball will allow the ball to be delivered to the quarterback with the laces up so that the football is positioned for a passer's grip by the quarterback.

The quarterback assumes a slightly flat-footed stance with the emphasis on standing as tall as possible. His heels are slightly off the ground. By standing tall and sticking his chest out, he is best able to study the defense. This also prevents the undesired slouching that cuts down on the important visibility factor. The quarterback stands close enough to the center so that there is a comfortable bend in his arms. He must, by no means, be straight-armed and taut. The comfortable bend will allow for quarterback movement away from the center as the hands are left in their original position to receive the snap. Any straight-armed positioning of the arms results in the inability to leave the hands in a fixed position to receive the snap as the quarterback moves away from the center.

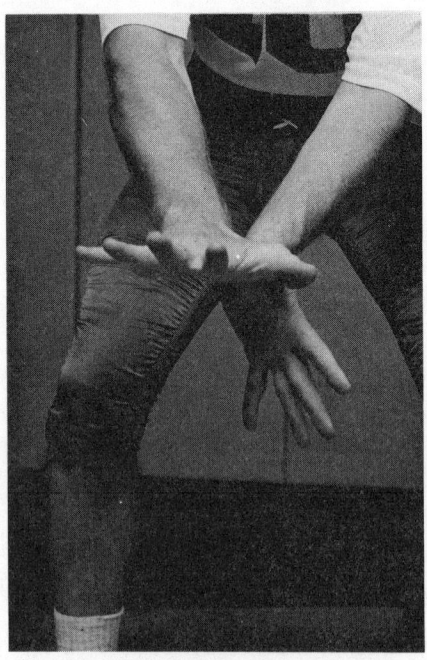

**FIGURE 1-1**
**Quarterback Hand Positioning**

The quarterback's hands fit together to form a 135 degree angle in a two-directional fashion. The top hand presses the middle finger tightly up the seam of the center's pants. Actually, the entire hand presses up against the center's pants with an emphasis that the thumb is in contact with the center's pants. The fingers are spread, extended and taut.

The bottom hand is fitted to the top hand by placing the top knuckle of the bottom thumb in between the two knuckles of the thumb of the top hand. The bottom hand fingers are also spread, extended and taut. The bottom hand attempts to help press the top hand up into the seam of the center's pants. Thus, the two-directional 135 degree angle from the top hand has the bottom hand almost facing down at the football. Although the snap technique attempts to break the "V" of the two hands, as will be discussed later, the bottom hand is in a position to act as a stopper if the ball is snapped poorly and pushed too far to the left. The quarterback hand positioning is shown in Figure 1-1.

## THE CENTER SNAP
## AND QUARTERBACK RECEPTION

The concept behind the snap of the center-quarterback exchange is for the center to break the "V" (the junction) of the quarterback's hands via a pumping action of the ball in an effort to wedge the ball between the heels of the quarterback's two hands. The center cocks his wrist as he pumps the ball towards the heels of the quarterback's hands. By pumping the ball, it is meant that the ball is brought back on a straight line to a spot where the ball can be wedged between the heels of the two hands. Thus, the ball is not swung up to the top hand in a pendulum type fashion via a semi-straight armed lifting of the ball. Instead, the elbow is bent as the ball is, again, brought back in a straight line, or pumped, in an effort to wedge the ball between the two heels so as to break the heels apart. The ball should strike both heels with equal pressure. Thus, the effort is definitely not to lift the ball to the top hand. The center's snapping action is shown in Diagram 1-1.

The center attempts to pump the ball to the delivery point by skidding the ball off his left buttocks just to the left of the seam of the pants. The center attempts to deliver the ball with the right end slightly up or at least parallel to the ground. The skidding action off the buttocks helps the pumping effort and prevents the pendulum-type swinging up of the ball. The aiming point of just to the left of the seam of the pants helps facilitate the positioning of the quarterback's hands. A

Pump back in straight line to break the heels of the QB's hands

Don't swing ball up in a pendulum type of straight arm arc

**DIAGRAM 1-1**
**Center Snap Action**

study of Figure 1-1 shows that the major portion of the quarterback's hands are to the left of the center finger of the top hands. Thus by skimming the ball off the left buttocks, the ball is placed directly into the center of the positioning of the hands. Figure 1-1 also shows that the inward rotation of the thumb of the right hand to position the hand under the center forces the hand positioning to have a slight downward tilt to the left. Thus by attempting to deliver the ball with a slight tilt so that the right end of the ball is slightly higher, the ball can best match the slight downward tilt of the quarterback's hand positioning. Diagram 1-2 shows the desired positioning of the ball off the left buttocks of the center with the right end of the ball slightly higher than the left end. The darkened area of the left buttocks is the point the center aims

**DIAGRAM 1-2**
**Center Snap Skidding Ball Off Left Buttocks (Darkened Area) with Right End of Ball Slightly Up**

for. The center will get the best results of breaking the quarterback's heels apart if he attempts to drive the ball beyond the point where the ball will hit the quarterback's hands so that the heels are actually wedged apart.

The center must be sure that he does not lift his buttocks (tail) up as he snaps the ball. He should be moving forward, keeping his back and tail level. He must avoid lifting upward.

The quarterback does little in the center-quarterback exchange. The center does all the work. The breaking apart of the heels (the "V") via the pumping action will naturally force his palms and fingers to envelop the ball. The quarterback must concentrate, however, on giving the center a fixed target. When he begins his moveout action away from the center, his hands must be left in place for the center to deliver the ball to. In addition, the quarterback must apply constant pressure to the seam of the center's pants all through the snapping action.

## COMMON CENTER-QUARTERBACK EXCHANGE PROBLEMS

A poor center-quarterback exchange does not just happen. A miscue is clearly the result of some type of technique error. More often than not the problem lies in a poor snap procedure by the center rather than an error by the quarterback. The most common error is the center's failure to pump the ball back to the target when attempting to wedge the quarterback's heels apart. Instead, the center lifts or swings the ball up.

Such a lifting or swinging of the ball upward in an arcing fashion will cause the ball to slap the top hand of the quarterback and then fall straight towards the ground. If the quarterback is lucky, he will be able to catch the ball by trapping it with his bottom hand in a reaching or grabbing motion. However, even if the ball is prevented from falling to the ground, the quarterback's timing and control of the ball will be off.

If the center fails to skid the ball off the left buttocks and instead skids the ball directly on the seam of the pants, the quarterback will end up gripping the ball uncomfortably towards the point of the ball. Conversely, if the ball is skidded too far to the left, the quarterback will grip the ball uncomfortably towards the bottom of the ball. This is seen in Figure 1-2.

Improper skidding of the ball by the center and the resultant poor top or bottom grip of the ball by the quarterback is usually not as

| Ball skidded off pants seam resulting in poor top grip | Ball skidded too far to left resulting in poor bottom grip |

**FIGURE 1-2**
**Poor Grips of Ball by Quarterback Due to Incorrect Skidding of Ball by Center**

serious a problem as the lifting or arcing of the ball to the top hand. However, a poor grip of the football in any fashion by the quarterback can easily lead to a fumble, a breakdown of timing as the quarterback is forced to adjust the ball or a further ball exchange complication due to a poorer grip by the quarterback.

Other center-quarterback exchange problems that can upset the technique are too early a snap by the center with the quarterback being surprised by the snap, too late a snap, and/or a pulling away of the hands by the quarterback before the ball is received. Any and all of these errors can lead to putting the ball on the ground, a loss of down or a loss of possession.

## "GOOSING" FOR THE FOOTBALL

A commonly used technique by many teams is to "goose" the center by lifting up with the hands to signal the center to snap the ball for a surprise quarterback sneak when the defense leaves itself vulnerable to such action. Two important points should be kept in mind when such "goosing" action is utilized. First the quarterback must give pressure to the center by lifting up with both hands. This will keep the hand positioning unchanged and give the center a consistent target. A lifting of only the top hand can create an unnatural spacing between the top and bottom hand, resulting in a handling problem if the center follows through on his strong effort to break the heels of the quarterback's hands.

Second, and more often the greater problem on a "goose" play, the center must follow through on his normal pumping action of the snap. It is a common error for the center not to pump the ball, but, instead, to lift or arc the ball up to the quarterback's top hand.

## OFFSIDE SNAP

Snapping the ball quickly when a defender has jumped offsides, whether the result of long-count tactics or just an overanxious defender, takes on many of the characteristics of the "goose" snap problem for the center. The center must be careful to pump the ball back to the quarterback in an effort to wedge the ball between the quarterback's heels and break the "V." He must not lift or arc the ball up to the top hand. This is a common problem especially when the defender jumps across the line of scrimmage in a surprise movement.

The center must also be careful that the defender has actually positioned himself in the neutral area. A defender may jump forward and yet never be in the neutral area. Thus, a snap of the ball will do nothing but totally break down the timing of the play and not draw a 5 yard offside penalty.

## WET BALL SNAPS

The snapping of a football on wet turf necessitates a definite teaching technique. The proper technique enables the center to snap to the quarterback a dry portion of the football. This technique is started by having the referee place the ball on the ground so that the laces face directly out to the sideline, to the center's right. As the center addresses the ball, he reaches down for the ball, twists the ball to himself so that the laces are straight up and angles the ball on the maximum 45 degree axis angle allowed. As the ball is twisted and lifted to this position, the center attempts to allow as little of the ball as possible to

26  Developing Center-Quarterback Exchange Techniques

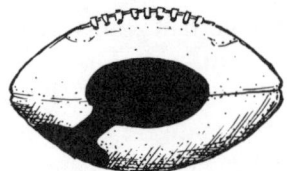

**DIAGRAM 1-3**
**Portions of the Ball That Are Wet
Via the Wet Ball Snap Technique**

Position of football on ground

Center twist and lift action to 45 degree axis
**FIGURE 1-3**
**Wet Ball Snap Technique**

come in contact with the ground and brush the ground's wet surface. In this fashion, only the portions of the ball darkened in Diagram 1-3 become wet. Neither of these wet spots is detrimental to the center's snapping action or the quarterback's reception of the snap. Figure 1-3 shows the proper positioning of the ball on the ground as the center addresses it and the proper twist and lifting action to place the ball on the desired 45 degree angle so that only the nonvital parts of the ball are the ones that become wet in relation to the center's snapping action and the quarterback's reception of the ball.

It is also important to occasionally practice the snap of a thoroughly wet ball to enable the center and quarterback to not feel uncomfortable when faced with such a situation. It is important to have a "Bucket Day" (wet the ball in a pail of water) in the practice routine prior to a predicted wet weather game day. The use of such a wet ball in practice will also greatly aid the backs and receivers in their practice of handling wet balls.

## CENTER-QUARTERBACK EXCHANGE PRACTICE AND DRILLS

The center-quarterback exchange is actually practiced every time there is a snap from center during practice. This is true whether it is a skeleton pass scrimmage, timing of backfield plays or a full tilt scrimmage, as long as there is a quarterback receiving a snap from a center. However, far too many coaches feel that such practice is all that is needed. Unfortunately, such practice concentrates on the scrimmage, the timing, or whatever the major focus of the drill is, and not on the center-quarterback exchange. Therefore, such practice of the technique can end up harmfully if incorrect performance of the skill is taking place. It must be kept in mind that practice can be practice of correct and incorrect performances. Whether proper psychomotor activity patterns are developed or not is dependent on the type of habits being established through the practice.

Practice of the center-quarterback exchange must, therefore, receive proper practice attention and coaching. This need not be extensive. A good time is during the prepractice warm up. If the period is well organized and the drill series efficiently run, a five to seven minute daily period will do nicely. The following drills are actually a series of the center-quarterback exchange fundamentals that need to be developed. Some need to be practiced daily and some only occasionally.

### Drill #1: Center Pump-Skid Action (Daily)

As soon as the centers arrive at the drill location, they begin practicing the pumping snap action with a football. The emphasis is placed on the pumping action and the skidding of the ball off the left buttock. The quarterbacks can stand behind the centers and hold their hand just off the left buttock to see if the ball slaps the hand backwards to signify proper pumping action that will break the heels of the quarterback's hands on a normal snap. Thirty seconds of rapid fire pumping and skidding is all that is needed. As a change of pace, the quarterback can place his top hand in normal snap position to see if the ball skids off the heel of the top hand.

*Coaching Points:* A proper pumping snap will cause the ball to skid off the left buttocks. The coach must be sure the ball is not being wrapped around the buttocks rather than skidded. A wrapping-around action is the result of a lifting or swinging action of the snap rather than the desired pumping action.

### Drill #2: Proper Fit (Daily)

The quarterbacks step behind the centers and place their hands in proper snap reception position. Initially, the center slowly brings the ball up to the quarterback's hands and places it in his hands until there is a proper fit of the ball. The center can actually drop his head to look the ball into the fit. The quarterbacks adjust the ball position to the way they want it delivered. The purpose of the drill is to help develop the kinesthetic feel of the proper positioning of the ball (fit) into the quarterback's hands as a result of the snap. After the initial fit, the center takes one or two more half-speed snaps to secure this proper fit.

*Coaching Points:* The quarterback is the coach in this drill. He tells the center how he wants the ball and/or what is wrong with the way the ball is being brought up to his hands.

### Drill #3: Closed Eye Ball Pump (Daily)

The quarterback places his hand in proper reception position, closes his eyes and receives pumping snaps from the center. No cadence is used as all snaps are surprises for the quarterback. Thirty seconds of rapid fire pumping snaps will do. Both the center and the quarterback must be sure to simulate initial movement action as they would on any play (the center firing out forward and the quarterback moving away from the center) to create a normal game-like practice situation.

*Coaching Points:* All of the desired pumping snap aspects are coached. The ball must wedge the heels of the quarterback's hands to break the "V." The ball must skid off the left buttock of the center. The laces must be where the quarterback wants them, etc.

## Drill #4: Cadence Snaps (Daily)

Both the drill and the coaching points take on all the aspects of the Closed Eye Ball Pump Drill except that the quarterback keeps his eyes open and the normal snapping off the cadence is practiced. One minute is a good allotment of time for this drill.

## Drill #5: Miscellaneous Cadence and Problem Snaps (Daily)

This drill is practiced daily. However, the specific miscellaneous cadences and problem snaps practiced are varied each day. Some are practiced often and some only occasionally. A checklist, however, should be kept to make sure that all types of cadences and problems are worked on. The miscellaneous cadences and problem snaps to be practiced are:

1. the "goose" snap,
2. snapping on the first sound,
3. audible cadence snapping,
4. long count snapping,
5. quick count snapping,
6. wet ball snaps,
7. late snaps.
8. early snaps,
9. offside snapping (coach simulates a defensive lineman),
10. center firing hard away from quarterback's movement on the snap, and
11. no snap.

The remainder of the allotted time for the period can be used for this drill.

*Coaching Points:* The practicing of many of these situations is self-explanatory. The coach must be sure, as in the case of the "goose" or late snap, to tell only the quarterback or center so that the opposite player is surprised, thus creating a problem for him. Late snaps refer to a slight delay of the snap by the center, which creates a timing problem. Early snaps refer to just the opposite. The center firing out hard down the line of scrimmage as the quarterback moves out hard in the opposite direction helps to create the most extreme movement problem for the exchange. An occasional no snap helps to test the quarterback to see if he is releasing pressure of his hands before the ball comes up.

**Drill #6: The Guess-Who Drill?**

This is a fun type of drill used for a change of pace. Have a center no count snap the ball to a quarterback with his eyes closed. See if he can guess who the quarterback is. Have the quarterback close his eyes. Place a center in front of him. See if he can guess who the center is. As a change of pace for this drill, you can put successive centers in front of the same closed eye quarterback, or vice versa. Have the quarterback or center rate the centers who have snapped the ball to him or the quarterback who has received the snap.

*Coaching Point:* Make sure the individual points out why he knew it was Joe or John (something done poorly, something done well). The same technique can be used for the rating of the quarterbacks or centers.

In all of this drilling, the center can fire out into a bag to work on specific types of blocks. It must be kept in mind, however, that rapid fire action is the key to getting a lot of concentrated center-quarterback exchange work practiced in a short period of time. It is also important that each quarterback work with a different center every day or even switch centers during the course of the drills once or twice. In addition, the quarterback must act as a coach in all of the drills. The coach can only watch one pair of centers and quarterbacks at a time. If the ball hits the top hand, the center must be told so. The same is true if the snap is slow, off to one side or the other, etc. Also, there must always be some type of forward movement by the center and a pulling away action by the quarterback (with the exception of Center Pump-Skid Action Drill and the Proper Fit Drill) since a standing-still action of the center and quarterback creates an ungame-like practice drill.

# two

# Developing Adept Ball Handling Skills

### SPECIFICITY

A major trend in football has been the concept of specificity in practice and practice drills. By specificity, it is meant the development of a psychomotor skill by actually practicing the skill as it will be performed in a game-like situation. Instead of the development of hand-eye coordination for a wide receiver in off-season via handball or racquetball, the receiver is given a set or series of ball catching drills that he can work on by himself or with a partner. Thus, the type of hand-eye coordination that will be needed to catch the football in a game is developed—not the hand-eye coordination of handball and racquetball.

On the practice field this has been taken one step further. Rather than use pure football skill drills which may not directly apply to the skills necessary to execute the offense's or defense's particular pattern of play, coaches have, instead, gone to their playbooks, examined what skills are being performed and then set up drills which are nothing more than game-like reenactments of these skills. This is what is meant by game-like drills—the performance and practice of the skills actually needed to execute the offense and defense. Artificial drills which practice skills that do not directly apply to the skills being performed in a game have been eliminated.

## "THE BALL HANDLING TRICKS"

This chapter does keep in mind the concept of specificity as regards ball handling. Ball handling refers to the ability of the back, whether a quarterback, halfback, fullback, tailback or wingback, to control the ball with his hands no matter how unsettled the situation or how out of control the ball is. It is difficult to create such situations in a practice purposely and it may even be undesirable to do so. The answer is a series of ball handling drills, or tricks, which can be practiced often and yet not take up any actual practice time. They are fun type drills that a player can practice sitting in a chair, during idle, leisure time, while waiting for the practice bus to take the team to the practice field, in or outside the locker room before a game or on the field just before practice. They are even an excellent means of warming up before a game since they have a tendency to work off nervous energy, pass the time and yet warm up the ball handling skills. They could even be put into a 5 to 7 minute drill routine in a practice period. However, if encouraged as a fun concept to be worked on continually during idle moments in the off-season as well as during the in-season, you will be amazed at just how much the backs will work on these ball tricks and how adept they will become at handling the ball.

Since these ball tricks are encouraged on more of a self-induced and motivated basis, the coach must be more concerned with what tricks the players will perform and how well they can execute them. As in any other type of skill, the players will have a tendency to practice and perform those ball tricks which they can execute most efficiently. Thus, the coach should constantly be aware of what the players can or cannot perform well and encourage the players to work on the skills they are least proficient at performing. "Let's see the one hand juggle. . . . the three ball juggle. Let's see if you can get them down by fall camp." These are the typical types of comments, criticisms and encouragements that bring the emphasis of the ball tricks into focus. They really are fun and it is amazing how hard the players will work on them if kept within such a framework.

## BALL HANDLING PRACTICE
## AND DRILLS (THE BALL TRICKS)

### Drill #1: Iso Grip

This is actually an exercise more than a ball trick. The back simply grips the football in one hand and squeezes it as hard as possible

*Developing Adept Ball Handling Skills*

for ten seconds in an isometric exercise type of concept to help develop grip strength. Three sets for each hand or three sets with a ball in each hand are desired.

*Coaching Points:* The coach should be sure that the back varies his grip constantly. The back should grip the ball toward the end of the ball, on the fat of the ball, with and without a grip on the laces.

### Drill #2: Two Man Tug-o-War

This is also more of a drill than a ball trick. Two backs each grip the end of a football and through steady pressure try to pull the ball away from the other back. It is best to pit right hand against right hand and vice versa helping to develop grip strength. The drill is seen in Diagram 2-1.

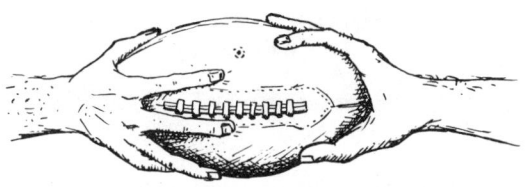

**DIAGRAM 2-1**
**Two Man Tug-o-War**

*Coaching Points:* This drill can also be utilized as a one man isometric type exercise. The back grips the ball at each end and holds it in front of his chest. He now pulls both hands away from each other as if he were having his own tug-o-war. Three sets of ten second periods are a proper allotment.

### Drill #3: Air Dribble

The back holds the ball out in front of his body, drops the ball, reaches down to catch it, pulls it back up to its original position and repeats the skill in rapid fire succession. The drill is shown in Diagram 2-2.

*Coaching Point:* Two balls can be used at the same time.

### Drill #4: Ground Dribble

The Ground Dribble Drill is the same as the Air Dribble Drill except that the back gets on a knee and bounces, or dribbles, the ball off the ground.

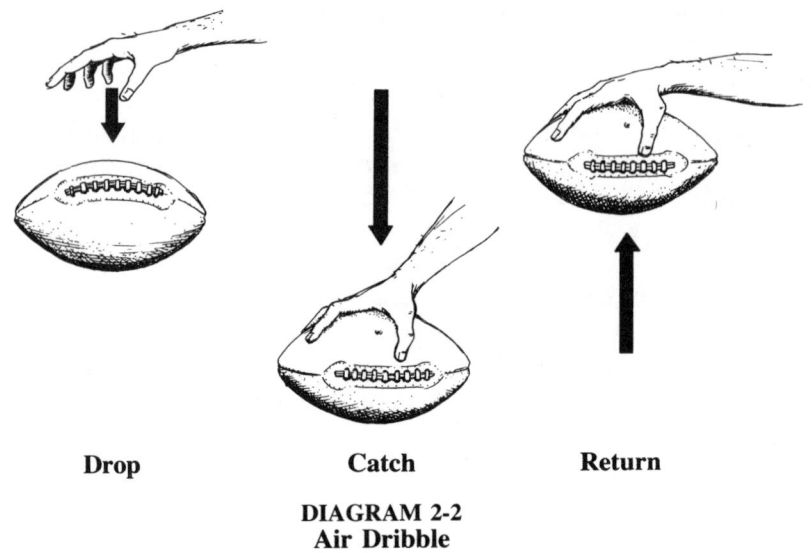

DIAGRAM 2-2
Air Dribble

*Coaching Point:* As in the Air Dribble Drill, two balls can be used at the same time.

### Drill #5: Forward Hand Roll

The back holds the ball at one end with the palm down. The back now rolls the ball over the finger tips to the back of the hand while the palm is still facing down. The back then reverses the action to return it to its original position. The drill is shown in Diagram 2-3.

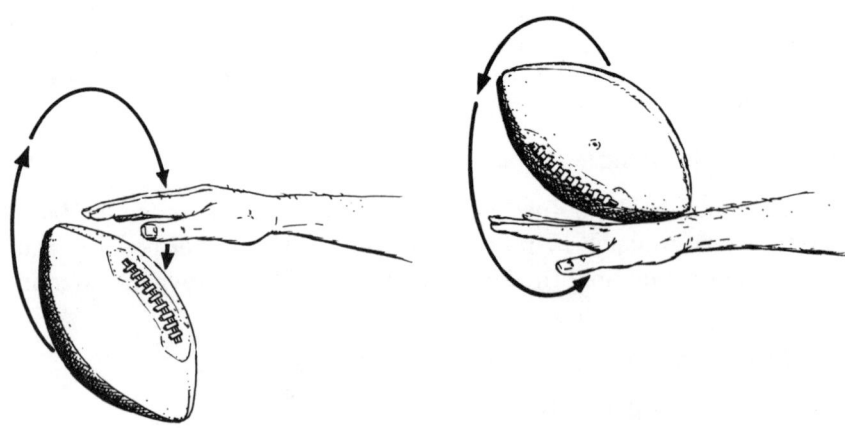

DIAGRAM 2-3
Forward Hand Roll

*Developing Adept Ball Handling Skills*

*Coaching Points:* The Forward Hand Roll Drill can also be executed with two balls at the same time.

### Drill #6: Forward Finger Flip

This drill is similar to the Forward Hand Roll Drill except that the ball is flipped into the air by the fingers to give it a full back flip so the ball comes down on the back of the hand. The back of the hand now hits it upwards to give it a full forward flip so that it returns to its original position. The drill is shown in Diagram 2-4.

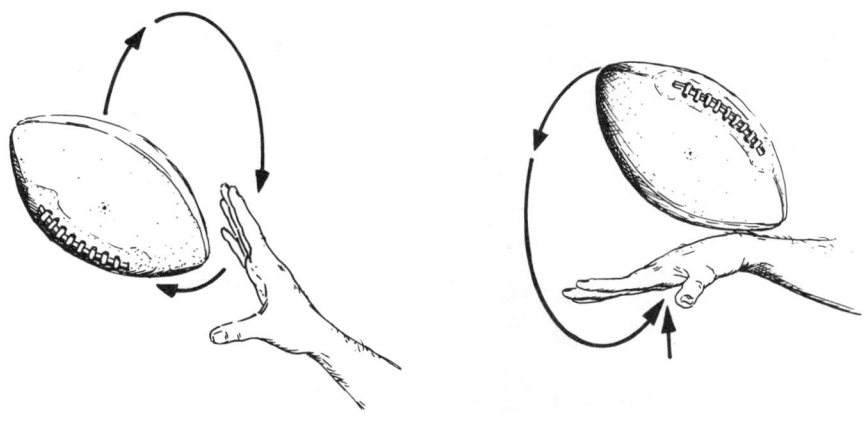

**DIAGRAM 2-4**
**Forward Finger Flip**

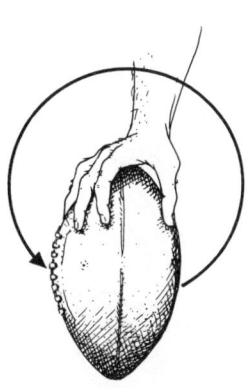
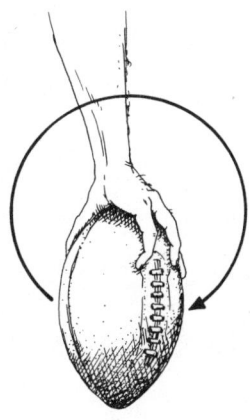

**Roll laterally**  **Return to original position**

**DIAGRAM 2-5**
**Lateral Hand Roll**

### Drill #7: Lateral Hand Roll

The back holds the ball by gripping it at one end with the ball perpendicular to the ground. The back now rolls the ball laterally over the back of his hand so that he grabs it at the opposite end. He now repeats the action in the opposite direction to return it to its original position. The drill is shown in Diagram 2-5.

*Coaching Points:* Two balls can be used in the drill simultaneously.

### Drill #8: Hand Circle

This drill is the same as the Air Dribble Drill except that as the ball is dropped, the back attempts to circle the ball with his hand before he catches it. The drill is shown in Diagram 2-6.

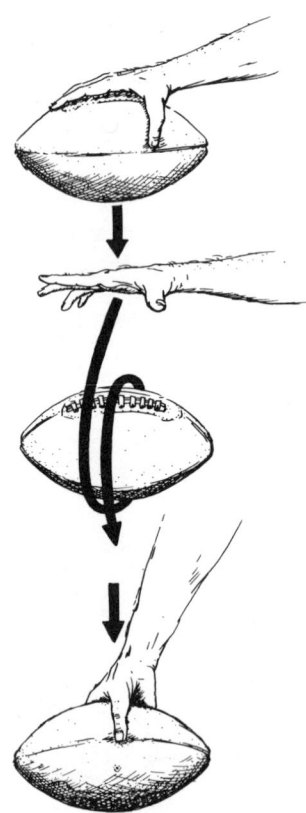

**DIAGRAM 2-6**
**Hand Circle**

*Developing Adept Ball Handling Skills*

*Coaching Points:* This drill can also be executed with two footballs at the same time.

### Drill #9: Globe Trotter

The Globe Trotter Drill has the back take a football and pass the ball from one hand to another behind his back, around his head, over his shoulder, through his legs, etc., Globe Trotter style. The back should continually change direction.

### Drill #10: One Hand Juggle

The back juggles two balls with one hand at a time.

### Drill #11: Two Hand Juggle

The back juggles three balls with two hands in a normal juggling fashion.

### Drill #12: One Hand Finger Passing

While walking to the field or standing apart from one another, two backs toss a ball back and forth to one another at a distance of 6 or 7 feet. All catching and tossing action is executed by the finger tips. The backs must be sure to switch sides so they work both hands.

The coach should stress both the working on the skills that the back performs least proficiently and the extra emphasis on the weaker hand. Working on the weaker hand on a 2 to 1 ratio is a proper allocation of practice time.

Added motivation can be created by continually pitting the backs against one another. Who is the best juggler? Pitting the halfbacks against the quarterbacks or the fullbacks helps to stir competition and challenge in a fun learning environment. Such techniques help to further motivate the backs to increase their ball handling skills.

# three

# Coaching Explosive Backfield Stances and Take-Offs

There are many coaches who feel that ballcarrying, or the skill of running with the football, is a natural skill. Either a player has it or he does not. In many instances, this may be quite true. Certainly there are many football players who are gifted runners and there are those who are better than others. Whether you have great runners or not, your role as a coach is to help each player to reach his level of self-actualization as a football player—the level of becoming all he is capable of being. In this manner, you will help your team be all that it is capable of being. Whether your backs are great ones or not, there are three aspects of running with the football that can be developed to each individual's fullest potential. The three aspects of ballcarrying are an explosive take-off, acceleration through the open hole or daylight and north-south open field running. Acceleration through the daylight and north-south open field running will be discussed in Chapter 5—"Coaching Your Backs to Run for Touchdowns."

## BACKFIELD STANCES

The quarterback's stance was already discussed in Chapter 1—"Developing Secure Center-Quarterback Exchange Techniques." Coaching an explosive backfield stance actually attempts to coach the best stance from which all backfield actions can be executed. Such a stance may not be the best stance from which to execute a particular action (for example a dive take-off). However, it must be kept in mind that a back cannot vary his stance for different actions or he might tip-off the play action and create a defensive key. A back who is leaning forward heavily to execute a dive on one play and is sitting back heavily on his heels to execute a pass play or some type of perimeter play the next, can easily be detected. A back can alter his stance slightly. However, he must be careful to disguise any such alterations. A back can ease the pressure off his front hand to help facilitate a lateral sweep-type take-off by placing more weight on his heels and yet still make the stance look as it would for a straight-ahead dive action.

An explosive two point stance is executed by taking a slightly uncomfortable or unnatural stance. The stance attempts to avoid any flat-footedness or hunching-over action. Either, or both, of these improper actions will slow down the back's take-off. The back places his hands flatly on the top of the thighs. The back is arched in an attempt to stick the chest out. The head is held up. Such head postitioning will allow him to look straight ahead and still use peripheral vision to study the defense and ready himself for taking advantage of possible alternate blocking schemes. A concentrated effort is made to face all body parts straight ahead. There is no lean or twist of the upper torso in one direction or the other. Most importantly, the feet and knees are pointed straight ahead. The toes should be perpendicular to the line of scrimmage. Some coaches even prefer a slight turning inward of the toes for a better grip of the turf with the inner portion of the foot, so as to insure an explosive take-off due to the better grip of the turf. Having the knees pointed straight ahead is more a concern for three and four point stances where a back may have a tendency to turn the knee of the back foot inward and, therefore, detract from the desired evenly balanced stance which can best facilitate all types of take-offs. The two point stance is shown in Figure 3-1.

The three point stance attempts a fairly even distribution of body weight on the down hand and two legs. The down hand rests on a bridge of the finger tips. The use of a five-fingered bridge helps to place more weight on the down hand. A three-fingered bridge of the middle three fingers helps to create a more balanced distribution of the body weight. Actually, which technique is taught is determined by coaching preference. It is important, however, that the back does not vary the finger-bridge techniques, creating a possible defensive key. The bridge of down hand is placed just inside the down hand's shoulder.

**FIGURE 3-1
Two Point Stance**

The top of the back should be parallel to the ground or at most at a slight downward angle to the ground with the butt slightly higher than the shoulders. It is extremely important, as previously mentioned, that the feet (toes) and knees are all pointed straight ahead in the three point stance. There must be no inner collapse of a knee off the perpendicular plane of the body to the line of scrimmage. Also, the feet should not vary from the 90 degree relationship with the line of scrimmage. Again, such turning of the feet and/or knees will detract from a balanced stance as well as slow down the back's take-off. The heels are slightly off the ground.

Foot stagger should never be more than heel to toe. Which foot is staggered is a coaching preference. Some coaches allow their backs to stagger whichever foot they want. Some utilize a left foot stagger on the left, and right foot stagger on the right so that both outside feet are back. Others will stagger both inside feet. Having backs stagger the same foot (inside or outside) from a split-back offense does have the advantage of consistent meshes for the quarterback both left and right since the back's steps will be mirrored to each side.

The back's should be up but not necessarily bulled. A bulling of the neck is uncomfortable and has a tendency to detract from the concentration on the take-off techniques. The back should keep his head up, however, and peer through the legs of the guard to be aware of any possible defensive alignment change. The back may not be able to see much of such an alignment change. However, sudden defensive alignment movement change in which a defensive tackle slides to a head-up position on the guard when he was previously covered by a linebacker helps to indicate the type of blocking scheme adjustment that may result. At the least, it will help the back to be aware of the possibility of some type of blocking adjustment.

The free hand in the three point stance has an extremely important function. It should be in a ready position to slide up to the bottom of the stomach to form a hand-off pouch. By ready position it is meant that the hand is in the supine position (palm up, facing the back's face) with the thumb pointing downward toward the line of scrimmage. The fingers are spread, taut and hyperextended backward as if they were trying to point to the ground. The top of the forearm, therefore, rests just above the knee. This is an unorthodox positioning of the free hand. However, it is again in a ready position to form the hand-off pouch. All that need be done is slide the hand up to the bottom of the stomach area. The purpose of such an exaggerated holding of the hand is to ensure the supine position of the hand when the hand-off pouch is made so that the fingers are hyperextended downward with the thumb facing downward and away from the body. Thus, there will never be an interference with the football by the fingers as the hand-off is being made. Far too often a fumble is the result of a back whose resting hand had its fingers curled inward, or even in a fist, and could not open the fingers in time to create a proper pouch, causing a fumble as the ball hits the fingers before they can be properly positioned. It is important that the backs utilize this ready positioning of the hand all the time and not just when they are to receive the ball on a hand-off or they will help create a possible defensive key. The ready position of the free hand in the three point stance is shown in Figure 3-2.

The four point stance is usually used for a fullback type of position at upback depth. The stance is intended to add an explosive thrust to a forward or slanting take-off. The four point action helps to put more weight forward to facilitate such a forward thrust. This thrust ability is gained at the expense of lateral movement or the ability to pass block. Such lateral or pass block movement can be performed. However, the four point stance does hinder such movement unless the back sits back on his heels. Such an alteration of the four point stance can be dangerous as it can provide the defense with an easily visible key.

**FIGURE 3-2
Ready Position of Free Hand
in Three Point Stance**

The four point stance also uses the finger tip bridge. Both hands are placed in the proximity of directly in front of the shoulders. The fingers are, however, placed out an extra 3 to 6 inches closer to the line of scrimmage. The four point stance usually has a more downward pitch of the back with the butt up higher than the shoulders, stressing the forward body weight positioning. The heels are, of course, off the ground a great deal more than they would be in a three point stance. The fullback's feet are kept fairly even with little, if any, foot stagger. Such foot positioning allows for efficient take-off to both the left and the right.

Although specific stance guidelines have been given, it is important to note that stance is an individualized concept. No two players will utilize a stance that is identical. There is no such thing as one perfect stance. A perfect stance is one which will best help a back perform all of the required types of take-offs he must execute in the offense. There are times when a coach must even deviate from the desired concept so as to best help accommodate a player's physiological make up. Actually, this is true of any skill. The purpose of coaching is to help the individual fulfill his potential. To change a skill that is being done successfully, for the sake of style, or to "do it by the book" can be a grave coaching error.

## EXPLOSIVE TAKE-OFFS
## VIA THE STEP TECHNIQUE

The step technique method for executing an explosive take-off is a sprinter's type of take-off which places all concentration on the ripping out of the step foot (the foot that the back initially steps out with) rather than on the planted, or power, foot. The only concentration that is made on the power foot is that it is firmly dug in. In the step technique, two goals are to be accomplished. The back is trying to get maximum thrust, or power, from the dug in power foot while getting maximum stepping distance from the step foot. If the back concentrates on a pushing off action from the power foot, he will get maximum thrust. However, he will not get maximum stepping distance to the line of scrimmage with the step foot. In addition, concentration on pushing off the power foot will cause the back to stand up slightly and thus slow his speed towards his running landmark. Speed is, in this sense, thought of in terms of distance per step. If the back concentrates on pushing off the power foot, raises up slightly and takes a six inch shorter initial step, he will, then, be six inches slower to the line of scrimmage. Six inches may not seem like much. However, at linebacker depth, it might mean the difference of breaking into the secondary or being tripped up by a linebacker who was just able to grab an ankle.

Conversely, if the back concentrates on a ripping out of the step foot as fast and as explosively as possible, such action can only be accomplished by maximum thrust off the power foot. Concentration on a ripping out of the step foot will accomplish both goals—maximum thrust off the power foot and yet maximum stepping distance with the step foot. An extra six inches in the initial step will mean that the back will be six inches quicker through the hole. In addition, the concentration on a ripping out of the step will result in a lower, more powerfully gathered carry of the body as the back approaches the line of scrimmage since he will not have straightened up as he would if he had concentrated on pushing off of the power foot.

Another important concept of the step technique in regard to executing an explosive take-off is keeping the elbows close to the body. If the elbows break away from the body, there will be a natural raising tendency of the upper torso. Raising up will, of course, result in a loss of speed and power. By keeping the elbows in tight to the body, the back will aid his own efforts for a low, hard, speedy drive to the line of scrimmage. By whipping the elbow opposite the step foot backwards, the back will actually help whip his step foot and upper torso forward more quickly and powerfully.

## THE DIVE TAKE-OFF

The dive take-off utilizes the step technique to the utmost in its effort to create an explosive take-off. All concentration is made on ripping out the step foot. This would be the rear foot, if the feet are staggered. As mentioned earlier in this chapter, by using the inside foot as the constant rear foot in a split backfield alignment, this would mean a constant mesh coordination to each side for the backs and quarterback for the same play. Some coaches prefer using the near foot as the step foot whether it is the up foot or rear foot. Using the up foot as the step foot does not produce as explosive a step foot ripping action. However, since the up foot is closer to the dive landmark, there is little difference in the end result. Whether the near foot or the rear foot is constantly used as the step foot becomes a coaching preference.

A great aid to an explosive take-off when the rear foot is being used as the step foot is to anticipate the snap count so that the back can shift his weight to his front, or power foot, just as the snap count is about to be barked out. This enables the back to roll off the front foot as he rips out the step foot. The back must be careful that he is not in motion on such shifting of weight or rolling off the front foot. Again, as was previously mentioned in the discussion of the step technique, the back must be careful to keep his elbows in tight to the body to ensure a low, powerfully gathered approach to the line of scrimmage. Any opening action of the elbows away from the body will result in a standing-up action with loss of speed and power.

## THE OFF-TACKLE TAKE-OFF

The off-tackle take-off utilized for such actions as the kick-out block, the off-tackle carry and the cut block, also utilizes the step technique. If the outside foot is the foot that is the back foot, the step technique is simply executed by ripping out the back foot at the intended landmark as quickly and explosively as possible. This will produce the desired maximum thrust off the front power foot and maximum stepping distance with the rear step foot.

If the inside foot is the rear foot, it should be used as the step foot in an explosive crossing over action. Coaches argue the pros and cons of the crossover step for such off-tackle and end run action. However, careful film study shows that there is a clear advantage to the utilization of a crossover step technique with the rear foot as compared to a lead step with the outside foot if it is the up foot. Lead stepping, even via the step technique with the outside foot when it is the up foot, will almost always result in a picking up of the lead foot and an almost exact replacement of the lead foot in the spot where it originally was positioned. At best the foot gains 3 to 4 inches of distance. Thus, the step is wasted. No distance is gained although time was taken to execute it. The crossover step, in comparison, will gain steady ground as it is ripped out via the step technique. Thus, if you were to measure the distance to the desired landmark on the back's first two steps on both techniques, you would consistently find that the back is closer to the line of scrimmage, and therefore faster, using the crossover technique.

The crossover step with the inside foot if it is the rear foot helps to ensure the desired excellent inside angle for the kick-out block. However, it does hinder the desired outside-in course of the cut block. Many coaches will sacrifice the more explosive take-off of crossover stepping with the inside foot if it is the rear foot for the better outside-in course that the outside foot lead step will give. Others feel that the outside-in angle can still be maintained when utilizing the crossover technique and therefore get the better, more explosive take-off.

It is again important to emphasize the need for keeping the elbows in close to the body to ensure a low, powerfully gathered stance and prevent loss of speed and power by standing up.

### THE END RUN TAKE-OFF

When taking-off for the corner, whether to block or carry the ball, the crossover technique provides the best stepping action. This is true no matter what foot is staggered. As already discussed, lead stepping with the outside foot will do little more than cause the outside foot to be picked up and put down near the spot of its original positioning. The crossover technique will allow for a positive gain of yardage in comparison.

The whip of the outside elbow can be a great aid on the crossover technique. Since the crossover action is actually a bit unnatural, the concentrated effort to whip back the elbow to the side of the intended movement can greatly help facilitate the overall action and help to propel a healthy crossover step by the inside foot. It is extremely important that both elbows are kept in tight to the body on the crossover action so that the back does not stand up to slow himself down and lose power. Opening up (elbows away from the body) and raising up are natural tendencies on such an outside lateral take-off action.

When aligned in some form of a split-back backfield set, a sweeping ballcarrier must make a slight adjustment on his initial crossover step technique so as to help provide a good mesh relationship with the quarterback. A direct crossover step creates a tough mesh for the quarterback to securely execute a hand-off due to the distance the quarterback has to maneuver to the deepened alignment. Thus, the sweeping split-back ballcarrier must step up slightly towards the line of scrimmage on an approximate 60 degree angle crossover step to accommodate the quarterback by providing a good mesh point. The ballcarrier must be sure that he steps up with his body so that his hand-off pouch is over the initial step foot. After the initial crossover step up towards the line of scrimmage and subsequent hand-off, the ballcarrier bellies back to get into his normal sweep run course. This action is seen in Diagram 3-1.

**DIAGRAM 3-1**
**60 Degree Initial Up-into-the-Line-of-Scrimmage Crossover Step for Split-Back Halfback on Sweep Play**

## THE COUNTER STEP TAKE-OFF

The use of the counter step to create a misdirection fake has come under increasing use. The same step technique action can be utilized after the initial counter step plant. The step foot is ripped out in the desired direction after the counter step is planted. The tight elbow concentration is again necessary as counter stepping, and, like end-run action, has a tendency to open up the body (elbows away from the body) and cause a raising up action.

The counter step, however, has some definite coaching points.

Coaching Backfield Stances and Take-Offs

The counter step should only be made to approximately a 45 degree angle. Overstepping to 90 degrees is unnecessary and slows the back down on the take-off action. This action is seen in Diagram 3-2.

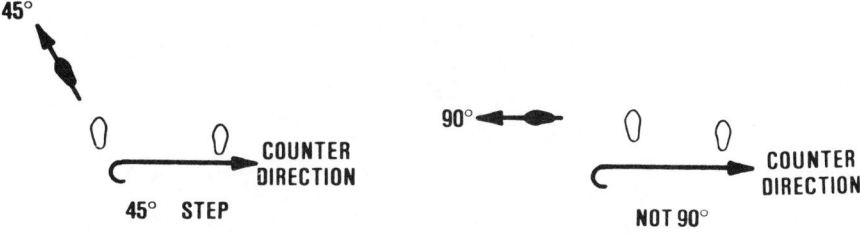

**DIAGRAM 3-2**
**45 Degree Initial Step of Counter Action**

The 45 degree step allows for a good plant of the foot from which to drive off when the step technique of the opposite foot is executed as the cleats will be allowed to be firmly dug in.

Secondly, the body turn on the counter action need not be more than a 45 degree turn which would place the body weight over the planted counter step foot. Any more of a body turn does nothing more than slow the take-off action. It should be kept in mind that the purpose of the counter step is to influence false flow by the linebacker. Overstepping with the counter foot will create a false influence for the linebacker. However, it will also give him plenty of time to recover and pursue since the back will slow down his own step technique take-off.

Again, elbow whip action is extremely important for both the propelling of the body in the desired direction and the creation of a low, tightly gathered approach to the line of scrimmage.

### THE COUNTER DIVE TAKE-OFF

The counter diveback executes his normal step technique take-off to the line of scrimmage with one major exception. The diveback's first step is both lateral and forward. The step rips out in a forward direction and the foot is placed down on the ground perpendicular to the line of scrimmage. The step puts the ballcarrier on a path directly into the center guard gap. Such action gives a slight lateral, counter type action while allowing for a quick-hitting explosive start towards the line of scrimmage. This action is seen in Diagram 3-3.

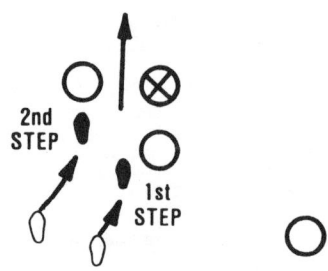

**DIAGRAM 3-3**
**Lateral, Ball Forward, Counter Drive Step**

Some coaches prefer to utilize a heavy counter step faking action as discussed under the counter step take-off. However, the general trend has been to sacrifice the better fake to get the more explosive hitting of the landmark via the lateral, but forward, counter step.

## THE QUICK-PITCH/SWING PATTERN TAKE-OFF

The quick-pitch and swing pass pattern take-off in which the purpose of the action is to get the back out flatly and immediately calls for a slightly different foot action. Initially, the back takes a slight position, or set, step with the inside foot of approximately 6 inches. The step actually crosses over slightly to help facilitate the second step to the sideline. The back now executes the step technique by ripping out the step, or outside foot, towards the sideline on a 90 degree angle. Such action will help get the quick, flat action desired for such plays as the quick-pitch or a swing type pass play. This action is seen in Diagram 3-4.

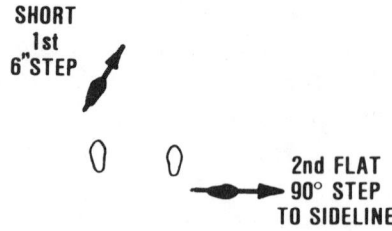

**DIAGRAM 3-4**
**Quick-Pitch/Swing Pattern Take-Off**

## TAILBACK "I" FORMATION TAKE-OFFS

The action of the tailback must often be altered to accommodate different actions. Since both feet are usually kept even, or close to it, there are few problems in attacking straight ahead or off-tackle. The tailback will often feel the need for a slight drop step to get good footing so he can explode forward on, say, an isolation play. Some coaches feel that this step should be eliminated since it is false movement and instead have the tailback concentrate on a direct step via the step technique. Other coaches feel it is not a problem since the delay often blends well with the running to daylight concept of the "I" run game. Either technique is correct and it is more of a coaching preference than an argument of which technique is correct.

The end run take-off again utilizes the crossover technique. The counter step, however, plays an important role for the tailback. This is especially true when tied to the option game. The "I" formation tailback is usually deeper in alignment than a normal fullback or halfback. Thus to maintain a constant pitch ratio of halfback or fullback depth with the quarterback, whatever that distance might be, the tailback is forced to step up initially to get into the proper quarterback-pitchback position ratio. The design of "I" offense plays will often tie together the counter step with the stepping up action to help facilitate the tailback's coordination with the fullback (up back) and the quarterback. Such counter stepping action varies very little from normal counter stepping action other than a deeper step towards the line of scrimmage and usually a little less sharp than the normal 45 degree angle—at approximately 30 degrees. In coordination with less of a counter step is less body lean into the counter action. Thus, there is actually a heavy forward motion in the counter step action which is increased on the second step to help get the proper relationship that the play requires. Such counter stepping action from the "I" is by no means limited to option plays. The counter stepping action from the "I" is shown in Diagram 3-5.

It must be noted that a tailback need not step up on an option play whether using the counter step or not to produce a pitch ratio of halfback or fullback depth with the quarterback. A tailback could go directly into his pitchback course from his approximate 6½ or 7 yard depth and maintain such a deeper ratio with the quarterback. Many "I" formation teams prefer the deepened ratio especially when they possess a speedy tailback. From the deepened ratio, it is thought that the tailback will have better cutting angles as in the design of the "I" isolation and sprint draw plays.

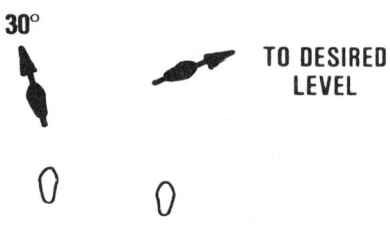

**DIAGRAM 3-5**
**Tailback Counter Stepping Action**

The tailback's sprint draw take-off to the exchange point is quite different than any other ballcarrier take-off to an exchange point. Ironically, the tailback's action takes on the same coaching points as that of the quarterback (as will be discussed in Chapter 4), lead step, crossover step and adjustment step. Actually, the third step is really a square up step to the line of scrimmage to better facilitate the wide variety of cutting angles the ballcarrier can execute. The first step is an open hip lateral step towards the sideline to help create corner flow by the defense. Such a step also helps to delay the draw action long enough for the blocking scheme to develop as well as help create a deep hand-off point to enable the ballcarrier to make the best cut off the blocking scheme. The second step is a crossover step on approximately a 45 degree angle to the line of scrimmage. The third step is the rip, or explosion step which attempts to square the ballcarrier up to the line of scrimmage although for the sake of balance it is still usually less than a true 90 degree perpendicular step to the line of scrimmage. The third explosive, yet adjustment type step will, again, help facilitate needed sprint draw cutting ability as well as open the inside hip to the quarterback to facilitate a proper hand-off pouch. The sprint draw take-off action for the tailback is seen in Diagram 3-6.

Proper coaching emphasis must be placed on not gaining too much ground towards the line of scrimmage on the three step movement to the exchange point. In addition, the third step must be squared up to help facilitate the hand-off. The tailback must *not* continue out laterally as shown by the dotted line step in Diagram 3-6 as this will only make across-the-grain cutting much more difficult (if that is where the daylight is). In addition, the inside hip of the ballcarrier will be closed to the quarterback necessitating a tougher reaching around the hip to execute the hand-off.

# Coaching Backfield Stances and Take-Offs

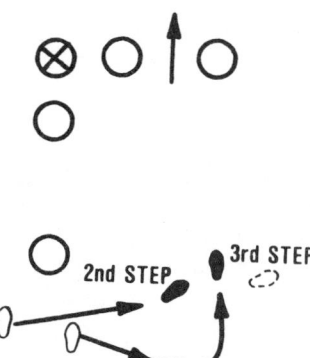

**DIAGRAM 3-6**
**Tailback Sprint Draw Steps**

It has become increasingly popular for some teams to utilize a sprint draw tailback take-off technique that is identical to the tailback isolation take-off action. The tailback takes his slight drop step for good footing from which to explode forward and executes the same isolation play take-off action. Of course, the design, blocking scheme and subsequent running action then take on the true sprint draw play design. Such a concept is premised with being able to run two plays (the sprint draw and the isolation) off the same backfield action. The practice of one action takes care of two plays. The limiting factor in the use of the isolation play design for the sprint draw is that the mesh of the quarterback and the sprint draw tailback is closer to center area. The quarterback, therefore, cannot threaten the perimeter as well since he will take more time to attack the corner on his sprint draw sprint out action. Since such a perimeter sprint out threat by the quarterback is so important in the sprint draw/sprint draw play action sprint out pass series, the effects of a lessened perimeter attack threat of the quarterback via the isolation type take-off must be considered.

## STANCE AND TAKE-OFF PRACTICE AND DRILLS

The practicing of stances and take-offs is usually not set apart in specific drills and practice time due to the need for compact practice planning and time utilization. The only exception for this might be early in the season when fundamentals are being taught or reviewed in their most basic forms. This does not mean that stances and take-offs are not practiced during the course of a season. They are practiced every day all through practice. Every drill, every minute allotted to individual, unit or take-off practice, requires the back to start from a stance and utilize a take-off technique. Each one of these situations offers the coach an opportunity to coach stance and take-off since without proper stance and take-off, the ability to execute an assignment properly is severely limited. If a player is having a particular problem with his stance or his take-off, the coach can pull him aside for individual correction, can have the individual stay after practice or can work with him on it the next day in prepractice. The running of sprints, form-running drills or warm up running also offers an excellent opportunity to coach stances and take-offs.

The following two drills help coach stances and take-offs. The Chute Drill is an excellent early season drill to help the backs develop a low, hard driving take-off, utilizing the step technique after a proper stance has been checked. The Stance, Take-Off and Landmark Drill is an excellent early season as well as in-season drill which helps to polish exact and precise stances, take-offs and the precise hitting of assigned landmarks. It is an excellent in-season drill because of the need for such execution coupled with the fact that in-season concentration on game preparation versus an opponent often leads to a slackening on the time spent on such fundamentals as compared to preseason fundamental work. The Stance, Take-Off and Landmark Drill allows for a maximum repetition of these important skills in a short period of time. (By landmark, we mean the point the back aims toward to receive the football before he cuts off the blocking so as to ensure a consistent mesh point with the quarterback—e.g., the guard-tackle gap.)

**Drill #1: Chute**

The backs, off a quarterback's or coach's cadence, explode from their stance through a normal lineman's chute. Quarterbacks can be added to couple the drill with hand-off work. The back must practice firing straight ahead as well as taking a stance on a 45 degree angle to the chute opening both left and right to practice slanting take-offs in each direction. This is shown in Diagram 3-7.

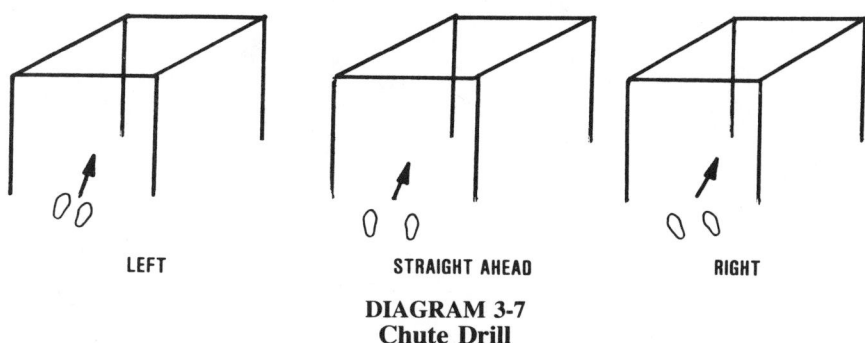

**DIAGRAM 3-7
Chute Drill**

*Coaching Points:* When working on the angled take-off the back's stance should be facing the opposite back post of the chute. The coach must be sure to check all points of stance and take-off (step technique). Crossover stepping for off-tackle and end-run action is impossible to practice through a chute due to the higher carry of the body on such action.

### Drill #2: Stance, Take-Off and Landmark

The backs take their proper alignment off a line spacing tape and run the play assignment call given by the coach. Two backs can usually go at the same time to execute, say, two dives to allow for more repetitions. A quarterback or the coach gives the proper cadence call. The drill is shown in Diagram 3-8.

*Coaching Points:* The coach must be sure to check all points of stance, take-off and landmarks. He must also be sure to carefully plan that all actions are covered, or at least the ones he wants covered, in the drill (e.g.—quick-pitch, sweep, counter dive, etc.).

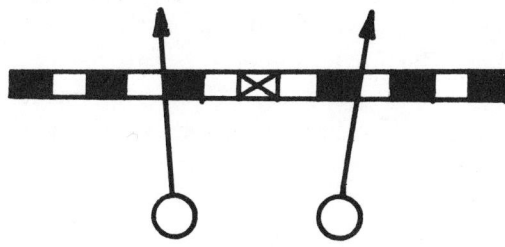

**DIAGRAM 3-8
Stance, Take-Off and Landmark Drill
(Two HB's Shown Running Two Dives)**

# four

# Developing Secure Quarterback-Ballcarrier Exchange Techniques

As mentioned in Chapter 1, unless the quarterback keeps the ball himself, there is always some type of ball exchange between the quarterback and a back or receiver. The exchange might be in the form of a hand-off, a toss, a quick pitch, an option pitch or a pass. Whatever technique is used, the exchange of the ball creates one of the most critical situations that the offense faces. A poor hand-off or pitch can easily result in a fumble and loss of ball possession. A strong scoring threat for a most needed touchdown can quickly turn into demoralization as the opposition takes over first and ten going the other way.

As a result of the quarterback-ballcarrier exchange being such a critical skill, it must receive careful practice and coaching attention. The quarterback-ballcarrier exchange must become as fail-safe as the center-quarterback exchange. All chance of error must be minimized to the fullest degree. The focus, therefore, must be on precise and demanding execution of the quarterback-ballcarrier exchange skills. The smallest variation can not be tolerated for "slightly off" may result in the disastrous fumble and the ball on the ground.

## QUARTERBACK MOVEMENT TO THE EXCHANGE POINT

Upon reception of the snap, the quarterback must immediately bring the ball to his third hand—his stomach. Such positioning of the ball helps to secure and protect the ball from any immediate defensive pressure that may tackle, or interfere with, the quarterback whether the quarterback is able to see such pressure or not. The hands are positioned so that the fingers run parallel to the long axis of the ball. The fingers are comfortably spread so that they securely envelop the ball. As the quarterback makes his movement to the exchange point (of course the technique used will vary greatly as to the action of the play's development and the type of exchange used), he must be sure to keep his shoulders parallel to the initial shoulder level of his stance all throughout the movement. Such parallel positioning of the shoulders throughout the movement to the exchange point is of *extreme* importance if there is to be a consistent mesh with the ballcarrier or a consistent delivery of the pitch or toss. Some prime examples of the necessity for parallel positioning of the shoulders throughout the movement to the exchange point can be seen on such actions as a dive hand-off or a reverse pivot toss. If the quarterback, especially a tall quarterback, raises up as he fronts out to mesh for a dive hand-off, he will have to hand-off on a downward direction. Since the diveback is in a low, powerfully gathered stance, this may result in the ball hitting the upper arm of the diveback as the quarterback attempts to put the ball in the diveback's pouch. Any such hitting of the upper arm could easily disturb the hand-off action enough to cause a miscue and possibly a fumble.

The reverse pivot toss is another prime example of the need for parallel positioning of the shoulders throughout the movement to the exchange point. Since the flight of the pitch is directly related to the follow-through action of the quarterback's arms and hands, a raising up of the shoulders in the reverse pivoting action will normally result in a higher release of the ball and, therefore, a higher toss. Consistent ball exchanging between the quarterback and a back demands an initial movement by the quarterback in which the shoulders are kept parallel to the level of the shoulders in the snap reception stance. The actual movement techniques of the quarterback to the exchange point will be discussed separately under each of the various types of quarterback-ballcarrier exchanges.

## THE QUARTERBACK HAND-OFF TECHNIQUE

The ball is secured against the quarterback's stomach (the third hand) until the ball is to be delivered to the pouch of the ballcarrier. The quarterback must immediately find a spot on the stomach of the ballcarrier which is dead center of the pouch. The quarterback must concentrate so intently on this spot through the hand-off action that he attempts to see the ball actually make contact with the hand-off spot of the ballcarrier's pouch (henceforth to be called the spot). Such concentration would be the same as a baseball hitter concentrating on the ball so intently that he attempts to see the bat make contact with the ball.

Anything less than hitting the spot is incorrect. Anything slightly off can produce disastrous results. A 6 to 8 inch difference can result in the ball hitting the pelvis bone or the bottom of the shoulder pads and cause a fumble.

The best hand-off is a firm two-handed hand-off. Two hands on the ball enables better security while holding the ball and helps the quarterback maintain better control of the ball as it enters the ballcarrier's pouch. Thus, the ball is held firmly and can be firmly placed in the ballcarrier's pouch in a constant parallel to the ground position. A one-handed hand-off does not allow such security and control and will often result in the ball being placed on the ballcarrier's pouch at varying spots with varying tilts, resulting in an uncomfortable exchange of the football to the ballcarrier.

The hand-off actually is made in two stages. First, the quarterback firmly places the ball on the spot with two hands on the ball with the back of the inside hand actually placed firmly on the spot. A firm placement is what helps signal the ballcarrier to fold his arms over the ball. Anything less than such a firm placement of the ball leads to unwanted movement of the ball in the ballcarrier's pouch.

The second stage of the hand-off is the push of the ball up against the spot with the outside hand as the inside hand slides out from behind the ball. The inside hand is actually held in position just off the ball so that it can be brought back simultaneously to the quarterback's body with the outside hand for the best quarterback hand fake action. The type of faking movement by the quarterback depends on the action of the play's design.

On whatever type of play action is being utilized on the hand-off action, the quarterback must be sure that his stepping action and subsequent foot and leg positioning do not interfere with the ballcarrier's running action. Such action may mean that the quarterback might have to take an abnormal adjustment step or take a drag or hesitation type of step in which the step leg is limply delayed to allow the ballcarrier to pass by before the step foot is laid on the ground. The quarterback must realize that all concentration and effort is placed on a perfect hand-off. All faking action comes *after* such a perfect hand-off.

*Developing Quarterback-Ballcarrier Exchange Techniques* 57

Another important idea to be kept in mind is that all hand-offs, if possible, should be made to the ballcarrier as deeply behind the line as is possible. This is especially true on dive plays due to the desire for explosive hitting of the line of scrimmage by the ballcarrier. A deeper hand-off also assures better cutting angles for the ballcarrier in his efforts to run to daylight.

## BALLCARRIER RECEPTION OF HAND-OFF

The ballcarrier hand-off pouch is made by creating a lateral "V" type of positioning of the arms so that the ball can be naturally placed on the spot. The bottom, or outside hand is simply lifted to the belt buckle area from the ready position of the bottom hand in the back's stance as discussed in Chapter 4. The pinky of the bottom hand should be in close proximity to the belt buckle. The ballcarrier must be sure that the fingers are hyperextended downwards so that they do not interfere with the hand-off. The fingers of both hands are well spread apart and held taut so as to give maximum breadth to the pouch.

The top, or inside arm is whipped upward in an attempt to raise the inside elbow as high as possible so that it also does not interfere with the quarterback's hand-off action. An inward pronation, or turning inward and downward, of the thumb of the top hand will help to raise the inside elbow in the proper manner. Figure 4-1 shows a proper pouch by ballcarrier.

It is extremely important for the ballcarrier to not look at the quarterback's hand-off action and attempt to watch the ball. The backs must understand that the hand-off action is the responsibility of the quarterback. The ballcarrier's job is to fix his eyes straight ahead to study the blocking scheme so that he can break to daylight after the reception of the ball is made.

An important concept for the ballcarrier, and actually for the quarterback as well, is that of explosively taking-off for the prescribed *landmark* as designated by the design of the play. The landmark is the initial aiming point of the ballcarrier (i.e., outside hip of the guard on a dive play) which provides a constant mesh point for the quarterback. The ballcarrier must never veer or vary from this course until the hand-off has been made. Such action will ensure a consistent mesh point for the hand-off each and every time a specific play is run. All breaking to daylight is, therefore, performed after the hand-off is made. Such an action may make breaking to daylight difficult. However, a poor approach angle is far less of a problem than a fumble as the result of a poor quarterback-ballcarrier exchange.

**FIGURE 4-1
Ballcarrier Pouch**

The back must be careful not to hunch, or bend over as he forms his pouch to receive the hand-off. Such action only causes the upper arm and elbow to become an obstacle to the quarterback's hand-off action.

The running action of the back and the formation of the pouch via the aforementioned arm positionings must exist as two separate entities. The back must create a steady pouch target for the quarterback that does not bounce or jiggle with the running action of the legs. The actual reception of the ball is made by a folding, or closing action of the arms over the ball. The back does not harshly clamp the arms down on the ball. Instead, the folding action attempts to envelop the ball to securely place the ball in the armpit of the bottom arm. A one-armed carry is essential. A two-handed carry in front of the body must not be attempted as the ball will not be securely tucked under an armpit. A proper two-handed carry is actually a one-handed carry with the ball tucked away securely under the armpit with the other arm and hand over the top of the ball to shield and protect it.

## QUARTERBACK REVERSE PIVOT ACTION

The reverse pivot, in an effort to produce false defensive keys, is commonly used in many types of offenses. There is, however, no one set reverse pivot technique, as the quarterback's steps are determined by the hand-off point of the play's design. The reverse pivot action is, however, basically a two step action. The first step, or drop step, is made with the foot to the side of the play action. Its depth into the backfield and width towards the sidelines is determined by the hand-off point of the play.

An explanation of the reverse pivot techniques for an "I" isolation play, a pro set kick-out play and a split-back sweep play, will help to show how the actual reverse pivot steps taken are a result of the quarterback's need to adjust his movement to the actual hand-off point. An isolation hand-off to an "I" set tailback requires a deep drop step with little, if any, lateral displacement away from center. Such action enables the quarterback to deliver the ball deeply (as desired) and yet keeps the quarterback out of the tailback's tight run path. This action is shown in Diagram 4-1.

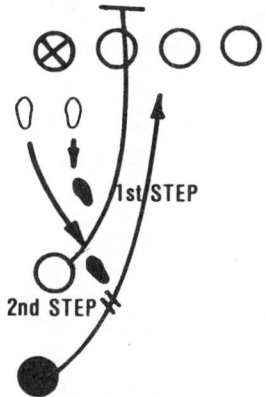

**DIAGRAM 4-1**
**QB Reverse Pivot Steps for "I" Isolation Play**

A reverse pivot action to hand-off to the fullback for an off-tackle run requires a drop step that is wide and, therefore, with less depth than the "I" isolation drop, so as to help the quarterback accommodate his movement to the off-tackle hand-off point. This action is shown in Diagram 4-2.

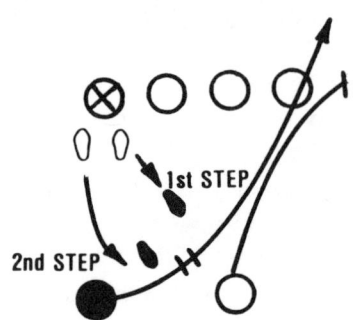

**DIAGRAM 4-2**
**QB Reverse Pivot Steps for Pro-Set Off-Tackle Run**

The reverse pivot action to a split-back halfback on a sweep play also requires a deep initial drop step to enable the quarterback to quickly get in front of the halfback's pouch and yet get to the deep hand-off point. The initial deep drop step is followed by either a short adjustment step or a possible drag/hesitation step so as to not interfere with the ballcarrier's sweep action. Such a drag/hesitation step, however, is usually only needed by a taller, long-legged quarterback to help accommodate his movement to the sweep hand-off point. This action is shown in Diagram 4-3.

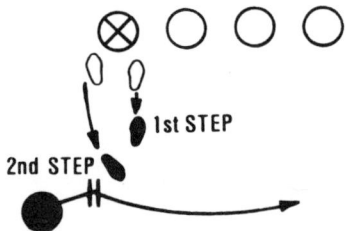

**DIAGRAM 4-3**
**QB Reverse Pivot Steps for Split-Back Sweep Run**

In all of these actions, therefore, the initial drop step is the pivot foot.

A special reverse pivot action to accommodate a tight slicing off-side back to the on-side for, say, an isolation play is needed. The technique is designed to get the quarterback out of the ballcarrier's tight path. This "Matador" reverse pivot action is executed by initially drop stepping with the off-side foot and pivoting off of it. The drop step is not a deep drop step as is the previous isolation type drop step since the quarterback must, again, stay out of the ballcarrier's path. The "Matador" reverse pivot action is shown in Diagram 4-4.

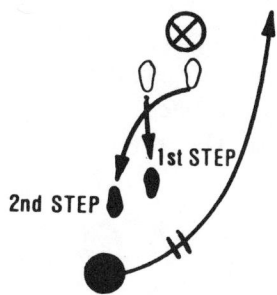

DIAGRAM 4-4
QB "Matador" Reverse Pivot Steps for Tight Run Path
to On-Side by Off-Side Back

An important concept to be kept in mind on all quarterback stepping actions to get to the exchange point (whether off reverse pivot action or not) is that no two quarterbacks will take step patterns that are exactly alike. It would be hard to expect a 6'5" quarterback to take the same stepping action as a 5'10" quarterback. The coach must help each individual quarterback to develop the stepping patterns which will best help him accomplish the quarterback-ballcarrier exchange.

## QUARTERBACK SPRINT-DRAW ACTION

The quarterback's movement to a sprint-draw hand-off point takes on its own distinct coaching points. Actually it is quite an easy skill. The emphasis of the quarterback's steps must be to get the ball to the sprint-draw back as deeply as possible to best facilitate his breaking to daylight action off of the blocking scheme. The quarterback's steps are lead step, crossover step and adjustment step. The first step is a front-out step at approximately 150 degrees off the line of scrimmage. Some coaches feel the quarterback should be "looking off" the linebackers on the first step. Others have their quarterback looking for the hand-off spot in the ballcarrier's pouch immediately.

The second step is a crossover step on a similar 150 degree angle path. However, it is most important that the quarterback begin adjusting to the mesh point with the ballcarrier. The third step simply carries out this adjustment to facilitate a perfect positioning for the hand-off. Some coaches have their quarterbacks execute an exaggerated two-handed hand-off in which the quarterback is well in front of the ballcarrier at the expense of a good play action fake. Other coaches have their quarterbacks execute a one-handed hand-off in which the quarterback's and ballcarrier's shoulders are almost parallel to create a better play action pass fake. The one-handed hand-off is, however, not as secure as a two-handed hand-off. The sprint-draw quarterback action is shown in Diagram 4-5.

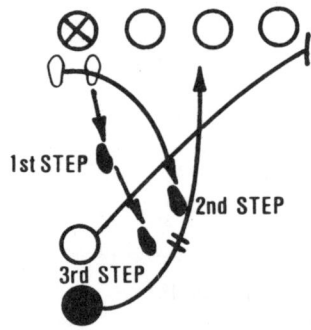

DIAGRAM 4-5
QB Sprint-Draw Steps

## QUARTERBACK COUNTER DIVE ACTION

The quarterback utilizes a four step counter action for the counter dive hand-off. The key coaching point is that the emphasis is on the delivery of the ball to the counter dive back as deeply as possible, not on the initial counter fake. The initial movement to the dive fake (or simply the reverse pivot counter fake action, depending on the play action) concentrates on the setup of the actual reverse pivot action. The quarterback's first step is slightly deeper than a normal dive action step. The second step is a slight crossover step to help set up the reverse step back to the diveback. The third step is the key step. The quarterback steps back to the counter diveback as deeply as possible to execute as deep a hand-off as he can. The fourth step is simply a sliding type step as a sort of adjustment step to help the quarterback keep his balance as he finishes executing the hand-off. The counter dive quarterback stepping action is seen in Diagram 4-6.

Again, the emphasis is on the deep third step to the diveback to execute the deep hand-off. On the initial step, the quarterback waves

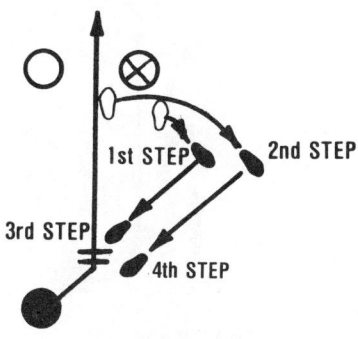

**DIAGRAM 4-6**
**QB Counter Dive Steps**

the ball in the direction of the dive fake. However, an overfake of the ball will only detract from the important third deep step back to the diveback.

## THE QUARTERBACK AND BALLCARRIER TECHNIQUES ON DRAW ACTIONS

The quarterback draw action can vary greatly depending on the type of drop back set up used by the quarterback. It is important that the draw action develops directly from whatever drop back action is used; back pedal, crossover, or a combination of the two. Whatever technique is used, there are three important concepts to be coached. First, the quarterback must "look off" the linebackers for at least the first drop step by staring out straight ahead. Second, no matter what drop back technique is being used, the quarterback must fully open his hip to the drawback by taking a deep open step 180 degrees from the line of scrimmage so that the quarterback has a good base from which to execute the hand-off. Third, the quarterback must keep in mind that his drop back pass action will cause him to carry his body higher than he would on any other hand-off action. He must take this into account so that he can be sure to get the ball in the pouch of the drawback underneath the drawback's top arm. Thus, the quarterback must be sure to have the ball low enough prior to delivery so that no such interference will occur.

Diagram 4-7 shows the 180 degree opening step of the quarterback off of crossover drop back action on the third step. Whatever step is used as the open step, it must be an adjustment type of step in which the distance is determined by the distance to the hand-off point.

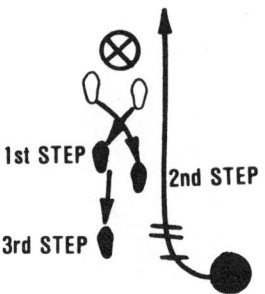

**DIAGRAM 4-7**
**QB Draw Steps**

The ballcarrier has two major concerns. First, he must realize that the critical situation is the quarterback's higher than usual carry of his body on his drop back action and, thus, the more difficult hand-off mesh. The back must, therefore, be sure to whip the elbow of the top

Hip open to line of scrimmage    Elbow whipped up to form pouch

**FIGURE 4-2**
**Drawback Set-Up Faking End Rush Pass-Pro Block**

arm up a little more quickly than usual and be sure that the elbow is exaggeratedly high to help facilitate the hand-off mesh.

Second, if the ballcarrier is faking pass protection towards the end of the line of scrimmage, he must do so with the upper torso of his body only. He must keep his inside hip square to the line of scrimmage so that the quarterback has the pouch open to him once the ballcarrier whips up his inside elbow. In this fashion, the quarterback will not have to reach around the ballcarrier's hip to hand the ball off. This action is seen in Figure 4-2.

## THE QUARTERBACK TOSS/QUICK-PITCH

The toss or quick-pitch can come off either a direct front out action (Figure 4-3) or a reverse pivot action (Figure 4-4). Whatever action is used, it is important that the quarterback maintains a parallel shoulder position so as to assure a consistent delivery and follow-through on the toss or quick-pitch. All concentration is made on a follow-through type delivery. The quarterback executes a straight arm toss or quick-pitch and sights the ball to the delivery point by peering over the finger tips. The palms of the hands should be "taking a picture" of the exact spot that the ball should be delivered to. This spot is a yard-and-a-half in front of the ballcarrier, belt high.

A low or a high pitch is usually the result of a follow-through to those low or high spots. If the hands are high as the ball is released, the ball will usually go high on its flight course. The same is true if the hands are "taking a picture" of a low spot—the toss or quick-pitch will go low.

The quarterback must also be sure to not lower the ball from his stomach area after the reception of the snap before he delivers the toss or quick-pitch. Such a "hitch" in the delivery will usually cause the quarterback to overcompensate for the lowering of the ball ("hitch") by releasing the ball higher than desired with a resultant high trajectory to the toss or quick-pitch.

The difference between the execution of the quick-pitch and the toss is that the quick-pitch must quickly get the ball to a ballcarrier who is already well outside of the quarterback. Such a ball delivery requires a lower trajectory of the ball in its flight at a greater speed than the toss. The follow-through is, therefore, more pronounced.

**FIGURE 4-3**
Front Out Toss/Quick Pitch

**FIGURE 4-4**
Reverse Pivot Toss/Quick Pitch

*Developing Quarterback-Ballcarrier Exchange Techniques* 67

The toss, on the other hand, need not be as rushed since the ball can easily be "tossed" to a point that leads the ballcarrier so he can catch up to it on his run path. A soft, end-over-end tumble produces the easiest toss for the ballcarrier to receive.

## THE QUARTERBACK OPTION-PITCH

A soft, tumbling end-over-end pitch is the easiest option-type pitch to receive. It is therefore the best pitch technique for the quarterback to execute. A key factor in the success of the option pitch is the prepitch carry position of the ball by the quarterback. He must be sure to carry the ball directly in front of his sternum to assure a proper arcing type flight of the ball to the pitchback. A properly executed pitch should direct the ball drop to a point approximately a yard-and-a-half in front of the pitchback at belt high level. A pitch action which originates from the sternum enables the needed kinesiological movement of the wrist and hand to properly execute such an option pitch. If the ball is held in a low carry, say in the belt buckle area, the kinesiological ability of the wrist movement is hindered in its ability to deliver the desired arcing, soft tumbling, end-over-end pitch which will fall belt level high to pitchback. Instead, the kinesiological limitations of the wrist and hand action will cause the pitch of a ball carried low to have a low trajectory in its flight and, as a result, fall to an undesired level of, say, the knee area.

To produce the soft, tumbling, end-over-end pitch, the quarterback extends the arm and hand out towards the desired pitch point and rotates the wrist so that the thumb pronates downward so that the arm,

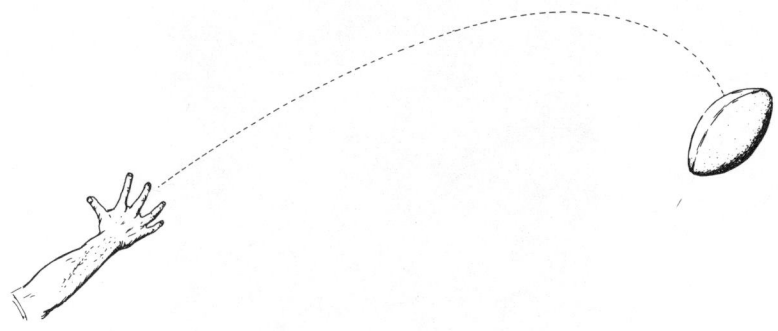

**DIAGRAM 4-8**
**Proper Trajectory of Option Pitch**

**FIGURE 4-5
Quarterback Option-Pitch Action**

wrist and hand produce a combined pushing and flipping action of the ball. The trajectory of the ball should look something like that shown in Diagram 4-8.

Such a trajectory, therefore, takes off sharply and quickly. However, it reaches its zenith approximately ⅔ of the way to the pitchback and falls more softly to the desired pitch point.

Follow-through is also a key to a successful pitch. The follow-through is accomplished by having the quarterback attempt to "take a picture" of the spot where he wants the pitch to go with the palm of his hand. A concentration on this technique will also aid the rotation of the wrist to pronate the thumb and hand. Figure 4-5 shows the proper sequence of an option pitch delivery by the quarterback.

## BALLCARRIER RECEIVING THE TOSS, QUICK-PITCH OR OPTION-PITCH

The technique used to receive either type of pitch or toss is basically the same. The only real difference comes in the positioning of the hands to receive the ball. However, since the approach of the pitches on each technique can vary greatly (high, low, too far ahead, too far behind, a pitch that dies and falls short, etc.), the reception of all pitches and tosses generally needs one overall technique.

Concentration by the pitchback is the key to the reception of the pitch. The pitchback must immediately focus his eyes on the ball in the quarterback's hands upon his first take-off step. He must concentrate on the ball as it is carried by the quarterback, as it leaves the quarterback's hand via the pitching action, as it progresses in flight to him and as it is received into his hands. Such concentration must be so great that the pitchback must see the ball hit his hands!

The pitchback forms a "basket" for the ball to fall into with his hands. The inside hand forms the bottom of the basket (thumb curled downward to prevent interference with the pitch) while the outside hand faces the ball to act as a "backstop" to prevent the pitch from going on by the pitchback. The fingers are open and spread as they are on a normal hand-off. The pitchback must be sure to look the ball into his hands. The pitchback *must not* attempt to read the blocking scheme until the ball is secured. A major problem resulting in pitch fumbles is that the pitchback will take his eyes off the ball a split second too soon in an eagerness to read the blocking scheme and will, as a result, end up bobbling the ball. Figure 4-6 shows the proper basket-type position of the hands to receive the pitch by the pitchback (or the ballcarrier receiving the toss).

**FIGURE 4-6**
**Ballcarrier Basket-Type Positioning of the Hands
to Receive a Pitch or a Toss**

## THE REVERSE HAND-OFF

The reverse hand-off confronts the problem of both backs going at one another at top speed making the exchange a tough one to execute. The back making the hand-off carries out all of the proper hand-off techniques (looking the ball into the pouch and placing it on the spot) with one exception—a one-handed hand-off technique is utilized.

The back receiving the reverse hand-off must, however, utilize an entirely different technique of forming a pouch to help handle the high speed single hand-off delivery. Instead of a normal "V" shaped pouch in which there is too much possibility of interference by the top arm, a basket-like pouch is formed with both hands at the bottom of the stomach area. The fingers are, as usual, spread and taut, ready to trap the ball into the stomach once it has been placed on the spot. The reverse hand-off pouch is shown in Figure 4-7.

*Developing Quarterback-Ballcarrier Exchange Techniques* 71

**FIGURE 4-7
Reverse Hand-Off Pouch**

## QUARTERBACK-BALLCARRIER EXCHANGE PRACTICE AND DRILLS

A coach has a tremendous opportunity to coach the quarterback-ballcarrier exchanges all throughout practice. Since so many of all practice drills start with some type of ball exchange, each situation presents the coach with a distinct coaching opportunity. For this reason, quarterback-ballcarrier exchange drills are often limited to early preseason fundamental work, brush-up type timing work or the practice of the more difficult exchanges such as the quick pitch and the option pitch. Only one option-pitch drill will be shown in this chapter, as the rest will be shown in Chapter 7—"Coaching the Backfield Option Game."

### Drill #1: Hand-Off Pouch and Reception

The Hand-Off Pouch and Reception Drill is an excellent preseason drill to utilize when basic fundamentals are being taught and/or refined. The drill is an odd looking drill. However, it is very useful in producing a maximum number of repetitions. The drill simply has a group of backs jog around aimlessly in an area 15 to 20 yards square. The backs practice forming a perfect hand-off pouch and then practice folding over a pretended hand-off action.

*Coaching Points:* The coach wants to make sure that the hand-off pouch is perfect—inside elbow up, fingers taut, spread and hyperextended backwards, etc. The carry of the upper body should be disengaged from the lower body run action for both the hand-off pouch and the folding over the ball reception action. The coach must be careful to check that the backs practice a left-handed and a right-handed pouch. In addition, the backs must smoothly fold over the ball without any jerking or clamping action. There should be no hunching over or head down action. The aimless direction of the drill enables the coach to check the backs' actions from all types of angles.

**Drill #2: Hand-Off Pouch and Reception Circle**

The Hand-Off Pouch and Reception Circle Drill takes on all of the characteristics of the Hand-Off Pouch and Reception Drill except that the backs are given a set circular course and the coach is specifically checking frontal pouch and reception action of one back at a time. The drill is shown in Diagram 4-9.

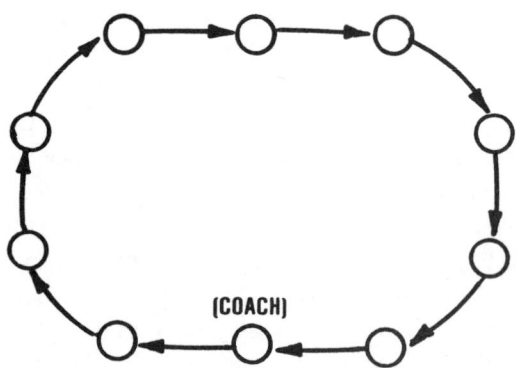

**DIAGRAM 4-9**
**Hand-Off Pouch and Reception Circle Drill**

**Drill #3: Timing**

The Timing Drill is perhaps the best overall drill for coaching the quarterback-ballcarrier exchanges. Actually, a center can be used to practice the center-quarterback exchange as well. Two tapes (or hoses) are laid on the ground parallel and even to one another. This will enable the coach to watch and coach two sets of backfields at the same time. The drill is executed by simply having the coach call out the desired play action and having the two sets of backs simultaneously carry out the proper ball exchange techniques. The drill is seen in Diagram 4-10.

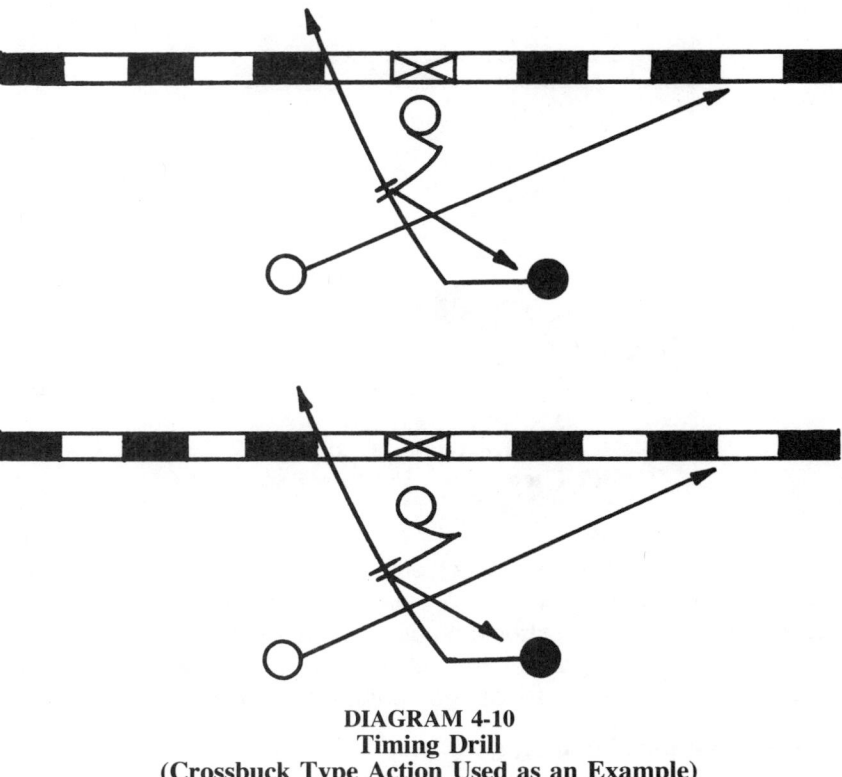

DIAGRAM 4-10
Timing Drill
(Crossbuck Type Action Used as an Example)

*Coaching Points:* One quarterback barks out the signals for both sets of backfields. The drill is actually a multi-purpose drill which enables the practice of such concepts as stance, alignment, take-off, landmark, center-quarterback exchange, quarterback-ballcarrier exchange and timing as well as the actual practice of specific run play executions. The coach must be sure to practice the quarterback-ballcarrier exchanges in relation to the desired time he wants to practice each skill. A dive hand-off may not necessitate the amount of practice a quick-pitch ball exchange might.

**Drill #4: Breakdown**

The Breakdown Drill is simply a breakdown of a specific aspect of the Timing Drill to get rapid fire action and maximum repetitions. Such a drill is premised with the practice of the more difficult exchanges such as the quick-pitch or, perhaps, the sprint-draw or a reverse-counter type action. Diagram 4-11 shows the Breakdown Drill practicing rapid fire quick-pitch action to a line of halfbacks as the example.

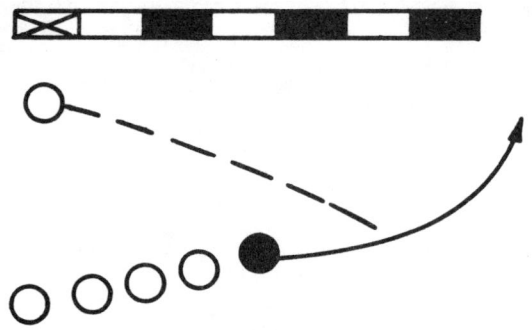

DIAGRAM 4-11
Breakdown Drill
(Quick Pitch Action Used for Example)

*Coaching Points:* The use of a center for a center-quarterback exchange is extremely important to create a game-like situation for the entire action. The coach should be sure to practice such action equally to both sides or even practice the action to the quarterback's weak side more than his strong side—i.e., going left on a quick-pitch.

**Drill #5: Option-Pitching on Knee**

The Option-Pitching on Knee Drill is a pure practice of the option-pitch action by the hands and arms while disengaging from the rest of the body. Two quarterbacks take a one knee (inside) kneeling position and face on a parallel plane to one another. Their positioning should create the desired pitch ratio (3½ yards by 3½ yards or 4 yards by 4 yards, etc.) on the desired 45 degree pitch angle. The two quarterbacks simply practice the execution of a proper option-pitch—a soft, tumbling, end-over-end pitch. The drill is shown in Figure 4-8.

*Developing Quarterback-Ballcarrier Exchange Techniques* 75

**FIGURE 4-8
Option Pitching on Knee Drill**

*Coaching Points:* The quarterbacks could take a standing position. The kneeling action does help separate the upper torso action from the leg action since this will often be the action on an option-pitch. The quarterbacks must switch their 45 degree angle relationship half way through the drill period so they can practice pitching with the opposite hand. The coach may even want to spend extra time on left-handed option-pitching.

## five

# Coaching the Backs to Run for Touchdowns

Running with the football, or ballcarrying, is a much overlooked coaching aspect. All coaches would love to have the natural, great runner who seems to take care of the ballcarrying problem all by himself. However, such a running back is more the exception than the rule. Far more often, the coach is faced with the sub-super back who must work as hard to develop his particular skills as any other player on the field.

As was previously discussed in Chapter 3, an explosive stance and an explosive take-off are paramount to effective ballcarrying. A back who hits a hole slowly may find such a hole close as he approaches it. A back who does not hit the hole in a low, powerfully gathered stance may find he does not have the drive and power to blast for the extra yard needed to get a first down. A slow take-off on a sweep may result in not being able to turn the corner because the defense is given the time to pursue to the corner and run the play down. There are, however, two other important factors besides an explosive stance and take-off that are essential to effective ballcarrying. They are an acceleration through the daylight, and open-field running. Acceleration through the daylight will be discussed separately under three distinct ideas; the dive concept, the "freeze" technique and end-run techniques.

## THE DIVE CONCEPT

The term dive refers to a ballcarrier's running with the ball directly off the blocking scheme without a lead or isolation blocker in front of him. The dive concept is, therefore, used on such run plays as a basic type of dive, the cutback dive, a draw, a sprint-draw or some type of counter dive or cross-buck type action. The dive concept is based on the ballcarrier's hitting of the landmark as quickly and as explosively as possible and breaking tightly north-south off the line's blocking scheme in an effort to accelerate through the daylight to burst into the secondary.

The ballcarrier attempts to hit the landmark, or point of attack of the play, as quickly and explosively as possible. By so doing the back will be able to burst through the opening caused by the blocking scheme as it unfolds. The ballcarrier is seeking a running head start to explode through the hole while it is there. Far too many backs try to ease to the line of scrimmage or wait until the daylight appears. Such delaying action usually results in the ballcarrier finding the opening closing as he approaches it. The ballcarrier must, instead, be at, or near, top speed as he approaches the line of scrimmage so that he has the speed to explode through the hole while it exists. In addition, it must be realized that linemen can only be expected to maintain the press of their blocks for so long. The slower a ballcarrier is in the approach to the opening caused by the blocking scheme, the greater will be the chance that the defenders can slip off the blocks to close the hole and pursue the ballcarrier.

Explosive running will aid the ballcarrier in another way. If no hole opens to accelerate through, the ballcarrier will be at maximum speed and power to lower his shoulder and blast out yardage on his own. Becoming one's own blocker is difficult to execute if a ballcarrier is approaching the line of scrimmage at less than full speed with less than full power.

It must be kept in mind that the term *landmark* signifies the point of attack of the play so the linemen may best develop their proper blocking scheme, as well as the point the ballcarrier explodes to on his take-off to provide a consistent mesh point for the ballcarrier and quarterback exchange. The ballcarrier can break from this landmark course to best adjust his course to accelerate through any daylight that may develop. However, such breaking to daylight can only be done *after* a perfect hand-off exchange of the ball by the quarterback and ballcarrier has been accomplished.

The design of the run play, and the resulting landmark, may produce as basic a dive concept as a diveback who explodes at one specific point (i.e.—hip of a guard, butt of a tackle) and breaks off one specific block. On the other hand, the run play may produce as complex a dive concept as breaking to daylight anywhere from inside a kick-out to all the way to the back side as on a sprint draw play. Such two extremes of the use of the dive concept are shown in Diagram 5-1 on a predetermined outside veer dive from a split backfield alignment and an "I" formation sprint draw.

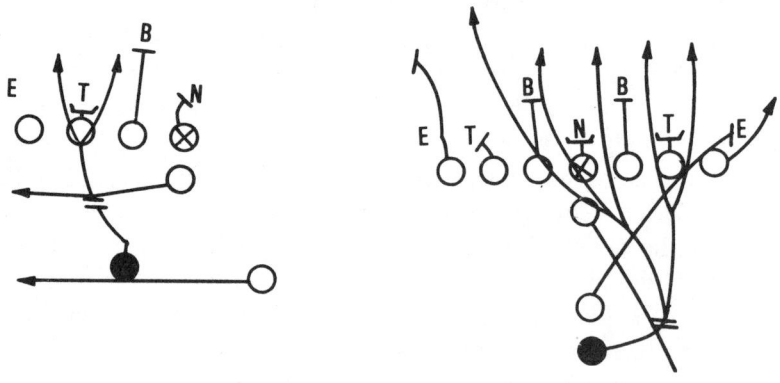

**Predetermined outside veer dive**             **Sprint draw**

DIAGRAM 5-1
**Extreme Examples of the Dive Concept Run Path Possibilities**

Some coaches believe that a deepened backfield alignment as in, say, an "I" formation is designed for a slow-hitting action of the ballcarrier to better read the blocking scheme and break to daylight. This concept is, in actuality, only partially correct. The deepened alignment of the ballcarrier is designed for a better sense of timing of the blocking scheme and the ballcarrier's approach to the line of scrimmage. In addition, the ballcarrier is better able to read the blocking scheme and the resulting daylight. However, the deepened alignment also permits the ballcarrier to get a running head start so that he can, again, hit the landmark as explosively and as quickly as is possible. Speed will best enable him to burst through the daylight to explode into the secondary.

Reading the daylight produced by the blocking scheme actually starts in the pre-set and set stance prior to the snap of the ball. By

Coaching the Backs to Run for Touchdowns

peering out straight ahead, and through the use of peripheral vision, the ballcarrier is often able to determine the defensive alignment, whose block to read, the possible pre-snap defensive adjustments and possibly how such blocking schemes will develop. Of course, such items as blocking calls and defensive movement after the snap of the ball can greatly alter such pre-snap reads.

An excellent example of how pre-snap reads of the defensive alignment can help determine the type of running action the ballcarrier might have to execute is seen in Diagram 5-2 versus four different defensive alignments.

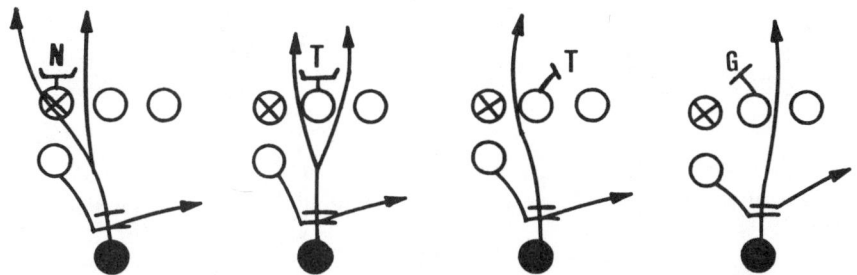

Cutback dive vs.  Cutback dive vs.  Cutback dive vs.  Cutback dive vs.
5-2 noseguard    4-3 defensive tackle  4-4 defensive tackle  wide-tackle 6
                                                             defensive guard

DIAGRAM 5-2
Pre-Set Reads to Help Determine Running Action

The cutback dive, depending on the design of the offense, is usually premised on the ballcarrier breaking off the block of the first covered lineman from the center to the playside in an attempt to slow pursuit by the middle interior defender(s). The cutback dive is especially effective when the defender(s) is overpursuing and getting to the perimeter quickly to help provide extra defenders versus perimeter types of run plays. Thus, determination of who the defender is and where he is aligned prior to the snap can help the ballcarrier to adjust his course properly to the block. Also, determination of how the defender is aligned can help to indicate how the ballcarrier may have to cut. A 5-2 noseguard or a 4-3 defensive tackle could result in a break to either side. A 4-4 defensive tackle *usually* means an inside cut as a Wide-Tackle Six defensive guard usually means an outside cut.

Again, these are only *general indications*. If the 4-4 tackle, in the aforementioned cutback dive example, happened to take an inside charge forcing the guard to block him inside, the ballcarrier would, of course, break to the outside of the block. The same would be true for a wide-tackle six defensive tackle taking an outside charge. If the offensive guard is forced to block him to the outside, the ballcarrier will have to break to daylight inside of the guard's block. This action is shown in Diagram 5-3.

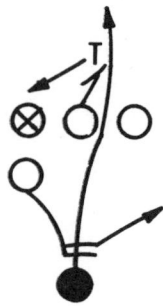 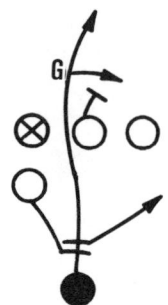

Cutting outside of 4-4 tackle's inside charge on cutback dive action     Cutting inside of wide-tackle 6 tackle's outside dive action

**DIAGRAM 5-3**
**Examples of How Defensive Alignment May Only Be an Indicator of Defensive Action**

Examples of how the line blocking calls and/or blocking schemes can affect the path of the ballcarrier is seen in Diagram 5-4. The split backfield halfback, upon hearing a call by the guard or tackle for a

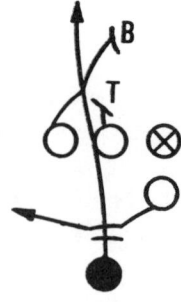 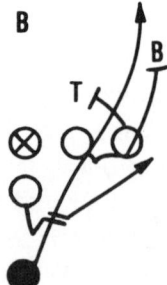

Dive with combo block vs. 4-4 look     Dive with fold block vs. 4-3 college look

**DIAGRAM 5-4**
**Ballcarrier Path Determined by Blocking Scheme**

combo block, knows that his course will definitely be to the outside of the scheme. The "I" or Wishbone formation fullback, hearing a fold block call, now knows he must break initially outside of the tackle's down block and then secondly off the fold block action of the guard on the linebacker.

Once the ballcarrier reads the blocking action of the blockers, he must break to daylight off the blocks, or block, as quickly and as tightly as possible. This is the best means of getting to the goal line as quickly as possible. Breaking upfield as tightly off a block as possible ensures north-south running. Any lateral distance left or right of a block means wasted time getting through the daylight in an effort to get to the goal line. In addition, wasted time getting to and through the daylight allows the defense needed pursuit time to get to the ballcarrier. An example of this concept is seen in Diagram 5-5 on an "I" formation fullback dive as the fullback breaks off the block of the guard on an even defense defensive tackle.

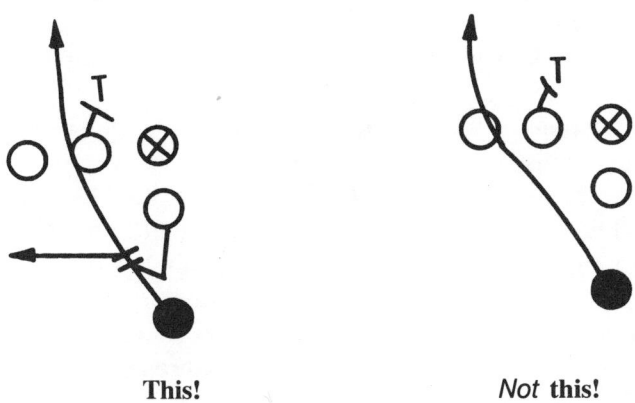

**This!**  *Not* **this!**

**DIAGRAM 5-5**
**Tight North-South Running off the Blocking Action**

All lateral movement detracts from the ballcarrier's north-south speed. It's the old story of the shortest distance between two points being a straight line. The more a ballcarrier has to vary from that straight line, the more he slows down his north-south effort. In Diagram 5-5, the ballcarrier may run the exact same distance in the two examples. However, one is further north-south than the other. Chapter 3 discussed how a poor take-off might mean a difference of 6 to 8 inches in north-south yardage—the possible difference of a linebacker being able to grab hold of a ballcarrier or not. The same concept can certainly be applied to a ballcarrier's variance off a north-south course as a result of not breaking tightly off a block.

The next important part of the dive concept, and actually an important part of *all* other running actions, is that of bursting through the hole to explode into the secondary. This is a slightly different emphasis than running to daylight. This concept stresses the more important "bursting through" the hole before the defense can close it. Every inch of quickness, again referring to speed in terms of distance, cuts down a defender's pursuit angle denying a greater ability to get to the ballcarrier.

The technique used by the ballcarrier in his effort to burst through the hole as quickly as possible is the opening up, or elongation of his strides as he goes through the daylight. This is the same concept as a basketball guard who takes long strides to the bucket after he beats his man on a drive. Such elongated strides help put greater distance between the driving guard and his defender on the same amount of steps in the same amount of time. The same is true for a back when he is carrying the ball. By opening up his strides as he goes through the opening, he will gain greater distance in the same number of steps in the same amount of time. In addition, he will cut down on the defensive front's ability to pursue and tackle him from behind. The ballcarrier who seems to "burst" into the secondary is the type of runner who has the ability to "pop" into the secondary before the defense has a chance to pursue due to such elongating of one's stride.

On all such dive concept running, it is important to emphasize that a good running back is able to utilize his speed and power to become his own blocker if there is no daylight to run through to grind out 2 or 3 yards. The ballcarrier must attempt to rip up under the shoulder pads of the defenders(s) much in the same fashion as he attempts to execute a drive block. The ballcarrier now attempts to rip upward and forward through continued leg drive. A good base is paramount to such drive. It is extremely important that the back bucks upward by arching his back, enabling him to keep his head up. A major fault of a ballcarrier blasting into defenders or blasting behind a wall of blockers is that he will often keep his head down. A tested adage that can be used as a coaching point is—"head down and you go down." This is often true whether there are defenders tackling the ballcarrier or not.

## THE FREEZE TECHNIQUE

The freeze technique is used to set up a defender for a block, whether it be a down block, isolation block or kick-out block. On the freeze technique, the ballcarrier runs directly at the defender being set up to be blocked to put him in a "freeze." By freeze, reference is made to the fact that the defender does not know where the ballcarrier is going to break and, therefore, must use a more passive, sitting and usually flat-footed method of play. For the defender to commit himself to one side or the other could be costly. This is especially true on a play such as an isolation play run at a linebacker, since the ballcarrier is given the ability to break opposite the attack of the linebacker and the block of the blocker via the design of the play. Plays such as an off-tackle kick-out play may not give the ballcarrier the flexibility to break inside or outside due to the emphasis of the play's design (double team down, kick-out). However, the end defender being kicked-out doesn't know this and if the ballcarrier is running directly at him, he will be put in a sweat as to the possible cut of the ballcarrier making him a more passive defender to be blocked.

The freeze technique is most effective on the isolation play. Since the ballcarrier has the ability to break opposite the action of the linebacker and the isolation blocker, both the ballcarrier and the isolation blocker can afford to be more aggressive since even a less than picture-perfect block will wall the linebacker off to one side or the other as the back explodes by in the opposite direction. If, on the other

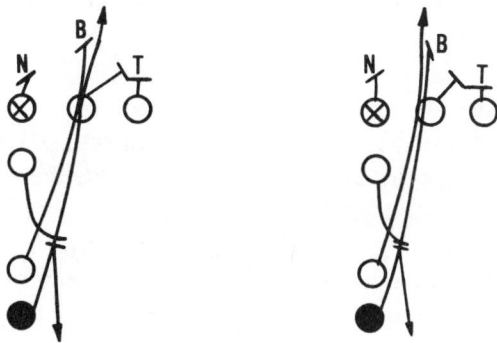

**DIAGRAM 5-6**
**Isolation Play Freeze Action**

hand, the linebacker tries to sit and fight the blocker off, he will have to contend with a blocking back exploding into him with maximum speed and power while in a catching position. Such isolation play freeze action is seen in Diagram 5-6.

Examples of the use of the freeze technique on trap and kick-out action are shown in Diagram 5-7. The illustration of the trap play shows the ballcarrier exploding directly at the linebacker to be downblocked. Such action will freeze the linebacker in place and prevent the unde-

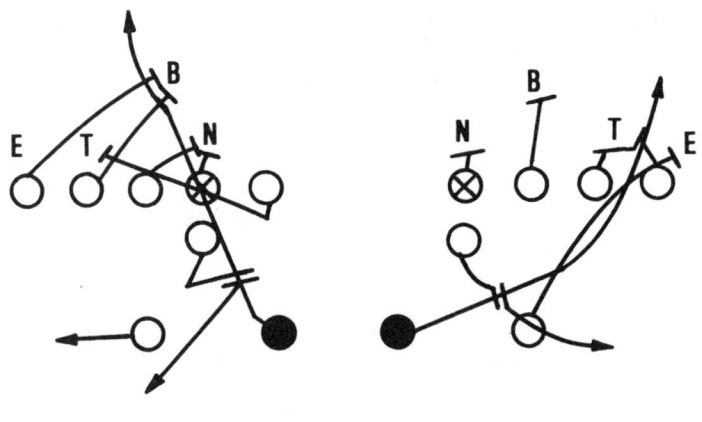

On trap action          On kick-out action

**DIAGRAM 5-7**
**Freeze Technique on Trap and Kick-Out Actions**

sired outside pursuit action that would result from the ballcarrier's breaking more widely off the trap action. Such action would result in a wider down block by the tight end and tackle and, therefore, a greater amount of east-west running by the ballcarrier to get around the block. Again, east-west running slows down the ballcarrier's north-south efforts to get to the end zone. Diagram 5-8 shows how failure to utilize freeze technique on the trap play results in this undesired east-west running action.

The ballcarrier's running action on the kick-out play, as shown in Diagram 5-7, has two focuses. Initially, the ballcarrier utilizes the freeze technique to help set up the kick-out block. Secondly, once the block is thrown, the ballcarrier cuts upfield sharply attempting to hug the double team blocking strength of the blocking scheme.

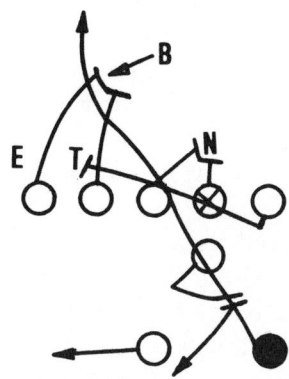 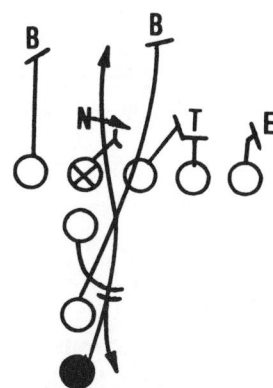

DIAGRAM 5-8
Failure to Use Freeze Technique on Trap Play and Resultant East-West Running

DIAGRAM 5-9
Defensive Action Causing Breakdown of the Freeze Technique

Again, the freeze technique helps set up a block. After the contact of the block is delivered, all of the techniques of the dive concept are now executed; the breaking tightly off the blocking scheme in a north-south direction, the opening up, or elongation of one's strides to burst through the hole and explode into the secondary and becoming your own blocker if there is no daylight.

An important concept to keep in mind is that although the design of a particular play may emphasize the freeze technique, defensive action may force the ballcarrier to revert to the dive concept. An example of this is seen in Diagram 5-9, an "I" formation isolation play with turn out blocking by the guard and tackle where the center is forced to drive block the nose guard to the onside due to his movement.

### END-RUN TECHNIQUES

End-run ballcarrying, whether it be off option action, sweep action, quick-pitch action, or any other type of end-run action also emphasizes the need for north-south running. The running action on all of these plays is premised on the outflanking of the defense with blockers to provide a run lane up the sideline or up inside of the perimeter support contain defender as he is kicked-out to the sideline by a blocker.

The take-off of the end run ballcarrier, discussed in Chapter 3, is of utmost concern since the ballcarrier's speed laterally must beat the pursuit of the inside defenders. There must be no wasted motion in the lateral stepping action by any standing up or loose carrying of the body.

Actual end-run techniques are determined by one of three end-run play designs: (1) following an arc blocker, (2) following a pulling lineman, or (3) sharply turning a hard blocked corner. Following an arc blocker is, perhaps, the most demanding end-run assignment since the combined action of the arc blocker and the ballcarrier relies so heavily on one another's actions. The arc block action will be more thoroughly discussed in Chapter 11. For now, it must be established that the arc block run action sets up the arc block for the actual arc blocker. The ballcarrier is kept on an arc course until the arc block is thrown. After the contact of the block is made, breaking upfield tightly north-south off the arc block becomes the new concern of the ballcarrier.

The ballcarrier must keep a constant 1 yard by 1 yard relationship with the arc blocker's outside hip. Since the arc blocker sets the arc shaped route, the ballcarrier is responsible for maintaining that relationship no matter how extreme the arc course established by the arc blocker. This relationship is shown in Diagram 5-10.

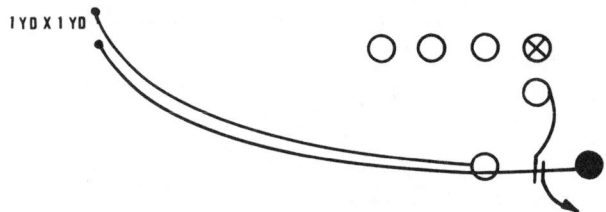

**DIAGRAM 5-10**
**Arc Relationship of Arc Blocker and Ballcarrier**

The design of the arc block action dictates that if the ballcarrier maintains this relationship, the defender will not be able to make the tackle. If the defender makes the mistake of attempting to go under the arc blocker, the arc blocker simply shapes his block up sharply into the defender as the ballcarrier breaks upfield sharply north-south around the block. If the defender tries to fight through the arc blocker's head, a perfect situation is created for the arc block delivery and the back is again able to accelerate upfield north-south around the arc block's execution. If the defender widens to the sideline so greatly that an outside run lane cannot be created via the arc blocking action, or if the defender comes upfield so far that the arc block cannot be executed without a dipping or bellying action, the arc blocker executes a reverse hip action as the ballcarrier breaks upfield sharply north-south up under the block. These actions are seen in Diagram 5-11.

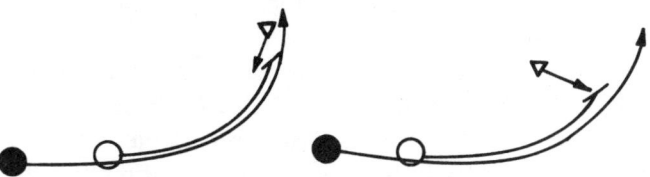

**Defender tries to go under block**   **Defender tries to fight through block**

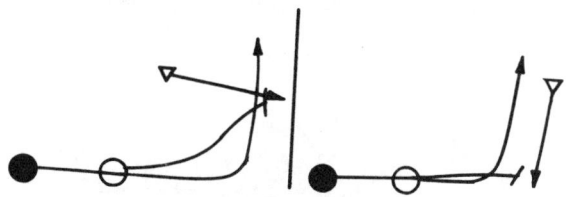

**Defender widens to sideline too far**   **Defender comes upfield too far**

**DIAGRAM 5-11**
**Ballcarrier and Arc Block Action vs. Various Defensive Reactions**

Again, the ballcarrier must maintain the arc relationship until the block is delivered. He must stay "on the hip and never dip." A failure to do so will break down the set-up of the block and enable the defender to play through the arc blocker to get to the ballcarrier.

Following a pulling lineman can actually utilize the arc block concept with the pulling lineman becoming the arc blocker. Such an action is common on a quick-pitch play as seen in Diagram 5-12. The

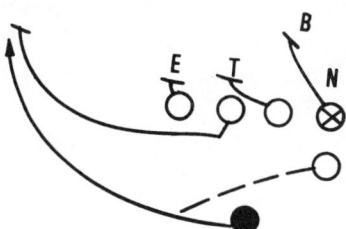

**DIAGRAM 5-12**
**Lineman Arc Block Concept**

tackle, in this case, and the ballcarrier carry out all the arc blocking reactions to the defender's play as shown in Diagram 5-11.

More often, pulling linemen are either given specific assignments such as a kick-out of the perimeter corner support defender or a lead block assignment. Both of these actions are seen in Diagram 5-13 on a split back pro sweep with two guards pulling and the blocking back load blocking on the defensive end. When the blocking scheme calls for a pulling lineman's kick-out action of the perimeter, corner support, defender, the ballcarrier can help set up the block by using the freeze technique. The ballcarrier attacks *upfield* directly at the defender to freeze him in his alignment. By utilizing the freeze technique, a defender is put into a bind and will have to play a more sitting, passive style of play helping to set up an easier block for the pulling lineman.

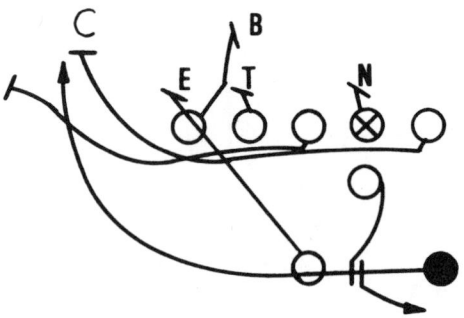

**DIAGRAM 5-13**
**Sweep Action with Pulling Guards**

If the pulling lineman is lead blocking upfield rather than having a specific kick-out assignment, the freeze technique can again be used. The ballcarrier helps put the defender in a bind by running directly at him to help set up the block for the pulling lineman. Although not actually within the scope of this book, it is worth mentioning that the pulling linemen must attempt more of a perimeter stalk block type blocking action than any more typical aggressive lineman run block action since the lineman would be trying to block a more nimble defender in the open field.

On both pulling types of action (kick-out or lead), an emphasis is placed on a north-south attack of the ballcarrier. A north-south end-run attack, whether on an option play, a sweep or a quick-pitch, attempts to get the ballcarrier around the corner and upfield as quickly as possible. What must be understood is that the more lateral the run action that has to be used, the more time the defenders have to pursue to the corner to support in the perimeter defense. The purpose of the offensive play is to outflank the defense with blockers and a ballcarrier. However, the more north-south the ballcarrier is as he turns the corner, the more he eliminates the pursuit angles of the interior defensive front defenders. This concept is easily illustrated in Diagram 5-14 where ballcarrier A has the defensive front outflanked and has all but eliminated their pursuit ability since he has passed them. Ballcarrier B has the defensive front outflanked. However, the defenders still have excellent pursuit angles due to the poor north-south progress of the ballcarrier.

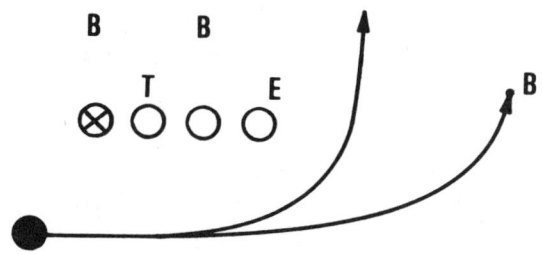

**DIAGRAM 5-14**
**North-South End Run Ballcarrying as Compared to Non-North-South End Run Ballcarrying**

North-south running is also a key on end-run ballcarrying versus a hard blocked corner. By hard blocked, we mean putting immediate blocking pressure on the corner, usually through the aid of a lead back cutdown type "H" or loadblock. Such action is shown in Diagram 5-15 versus an overshifted linebacker 5-2 defense to a split end side where the weak side defensive end is stacked behind the defensive tackle. The tackle is shown setting up the cutdown block for the lead blocker by slamming the defensive tackle before he releases for the stacked defensive end.

Such a hard-corner blocking attack emphasizes a total "burn" by the ballcarrier in an effort to tightly swing around the defensive front so as to outflank it and get upfield north-south before defenders have the ability to pursue.

The Green Bay (pro) sweep is another end-run action. However, the ballcarrier is given more of an option as to where to break in regard to the corner blocking scheme. Keyed on the block of the tight end, both the ballcarrier and the lead pulling guard read the tight end's

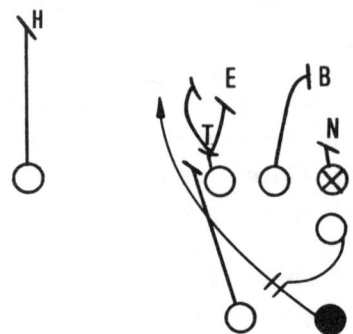

**DIAGRAM 5-15**
**Example of a Hard-Blocked Corner for End Run Action**

action to determine whether they cut up inside his block or continue out around it. The ballcarrier will, therefore, utilize the concept of explosively hitting and bursting through the open daylight as well as the emphasis of north-south running around the corner. Such action is shown versus a 4-3 pro defense in Diagram 5-16.

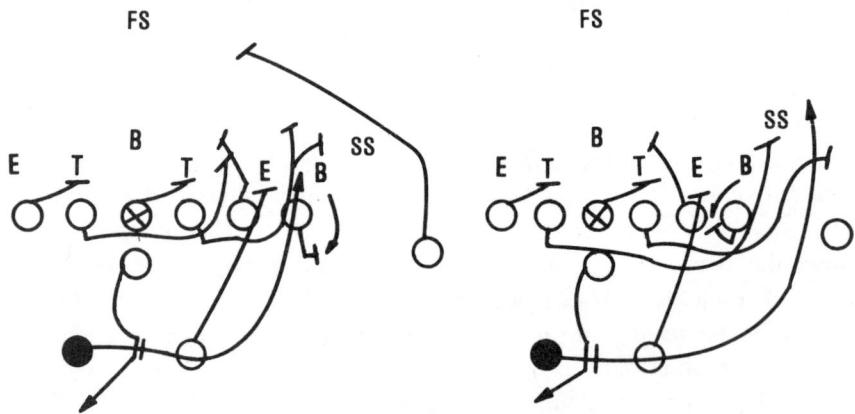

**DIAGRAM 5-16**
**Green Bay Sweep End Run Action**

As on the freeze technique, all of the aspects of breaking tightly north-south off the blocking schemes and opening up or elongating one's strides through the daylight are accomplished within the run action.

## OPEN FIELD RUNNING

There are many coaches who feel that there is not much you can teach a back once he breaks into the open on his way to the end zone. They feel a ballcarrier is pretty much on his own and that his natural running ability either will or will not get him into the end zone. It is true that the techniques that can be used to avoid a secondary defender are limited and that a back with great speed and good faking moves will have a definite advantage in such open field situations. However, there are some distinct techniques that can be taught to help the ballcarrier in the open field situation.

The first technique that is of great value in producing effective open field running is the concept of exploding north-south towards the goal line. Once in the open, the back must initially open up (elongate his strides) to get away from the linebacker pursuit and burst into and through the secondary towards the goal line. All cutting or veering action should come off "torrid" north-south acceleration. Such acceleration puts stress on the secondary to react quickly, helping to create better cutting angles for the runner based on the defender's reactions. In addition, such rapid acceleration helps to eliminate any possible pursuit by the front defenders who would otherwise have at least a possible chance to run the ballcarrier down if he were not running north-south. The north-south attack route thus helps to eliminate the number of possible defenders the ballcarrier will have to contend with.

The major fault that must be eliminated during open field running is the use of east-west running in an effort to avoid secondary defenders. Statistics have convincingly shown that although a ballcarrier will occasionally take the long route across field and outrun his pursuers up the opposite sideline, far more often he would have been more successful at gaining yardage towards the goal line had he knifed upfield and executed any cutting or veering action off such north-south action. More often than not, a heavy across field cutting action will only allow the defense more time to pursue, and better pursuit angles. As a result, the back not only has further to go, but will also have more defenders to contend with.

If a ballcarrier is knifing upfield north-south and finds a secondary defender directly in front of him, the freeze technique can again be applied. An early cut or veering action to avoid the defender will only give the defender a better pursuit angle, since the ballcarrier will have directed it for him, making any further cutting or veering action more difficult. Running directly at the defender will put him in a bind as to where the ballcarrier will break. Such action will force the defender to breakdown earlier and become slightly more passive and, possibly, flat-footed. The ballcarrier now breaks, or cuts, sharply just as he get on top of the defender accelerating at top speed by opening up or elongating his strides in an attempt to put distance between himself and the defender.

The back can aid his efforts via some type of head or upper body fake, stutter stepping, using a limp leg technique, change of pace running or any other type of faking action. Whatever faking action might be used, the back will find more success if he puts the defender in a bind first via a top speed, north-south attack directly at him.

Another important idea for successful open field running is that once the ballcarrier has broken into the open with no defender in front of him, he must run a 100 yard dash to the goal line. *Nothing* must detract from his speed, course and effort—especially turning around to look to see where his pursuers are. Turning around only accomplishes one thing: it slows the back down giving his pursuers a chance to catch him from behind.

A high step, or stride-out, type of action in which a ballcarrier kicks his feet out towards the goal line once a defender has dived to tackle him and is touching his back leg area, is of great value in helping the ballcarrier avoid such an effort to stop him. The ballcarrier simply strides out and reaches for the goal line with his feet as his upper torso has a slight backward lean.

Cutting back against the grain does at times have its merits. It must be executed, however, off of top speed north-south running with a tight north-south cutting or veering action. An excellent example of such use is shown in Diagram 5-17 where the defender has a good pursuit angle to hem the ballcarrier into the sideline.

Again, the success of the cutback action is the heavy initial north-south run threat up the sideline to force the defender to sell out on his pursuit effort. Thus, the defender's overcommitment, plus a tight north-south cut behind the defender to the goal line, helps such across the grain cutting action to be of tremendous value.

If the ballcarrier is hemmed into the sideline and sees there is no ability to cut back across the grain due to the defender's angle of pursuit, or due to too many defenders closing in on the ballcarrier, the ballcarrier should simply attempt to drive block himself up the sideline for as much yardage as he can get. By drive blocking, it is meant that

Coaching the Backs to Run for Touchdowns 93

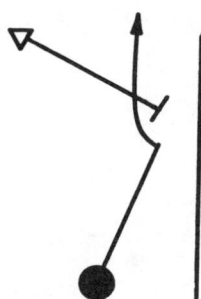

DIAGRAM 5-17
Open Field Cutting Across the Grain

the ballcarrier lowers his inside shoulder and attempts to drive up under the shoulder pads of his would-be tackler in an attempt to blast forward for positive yardage. Maximum follow-through via leg drive will help the ballcarrier get the maximum amount of extra yardage.

Spinning out is another widely used open field running technique. Since it can be used in a multitude of situations, however, spinning out will be discussed separately later in this chapter.

## DIVE JUMP TECHNIQUE

The technique of jumping over a pileup of blockers and defenders to gain needed short yardage for a touchdown or first down takes some definite techniques. Initially, the quarterback must make the hand-off as deep as possible to enable the ballcarrier time to pick his jump spot and gather his feet so that he can launch himself over the pileup.

The ballcarrier explodes to the line of scrimmage at top speed to get a running head start. At an approximate distance of a yard to a yard-and-a-half in front of the pileup, the ballcarrier gathers his feet closely together so that he can execute a two footed running broad jump at maximum speed and power. All effort is put into thrusting the upper torso (which is cradling the ball) forward to gain the necessary first down yardage or to cross the goal line. On the approach, the ballcarrier must locate the best spot to propel his body forward so that he can adjust both the launch point and forward propelling of his body towards an open area.

The ballcarrier must be careful, when striving for needed first

**Approach to launch point**     **Gathering of the feet**

**FIGURE 5-1**
**Dive Jump Technique**

down yardage, that he does not extend the ball out beyond his body risking poor ball security. The ball must be firmly tucked away so there is no risk of fumble upon contact with a defender or the ground, unless, of course, such an effort gets the ball across the goal line.

The dive jump technique, and actually the drill used for the dive jump technique, is shown in Figure 5-1.

## DIVE SQUEEZE TECHNIQUE

The dive squeeze technique is another technique that can be used to blast for needed first down yardage or to get over the goal line. The technique can be used going straight forward, slanting laterally or on a corner running action to get, say, inside the corner flag of the end zone yet over the goal line. Such situations are the only times that the ballcarrier lunges out to gain yardage rather than concentrating on a north-south leg drive follow-through.

The technique actually attempts to squeeze the ballcarrier between

FIGURE 5-1 (continued)

**Launch of the body**

defenders (or a defender and the end zone flag) by making the ballcarrier's tackling surface smaller. This is accomplished by having the ballcarrier drop a shoulder (usually the inside shoulder) in an attempt to turn his shoulders to a position that is almost perpendicular to the

**FIGURE 5-2**
**Dive Squeeze Technique Between Two Defenders**

ground. In this fashion, the ballcarrier presents less surface for the defenders to make contact with and the ballcarrier's lunging, forward thrust action is given a good chance of being wedged between two defenders.

The dive squeeze technique is shown in Figure 5-2.

### SPINNING OUT TECHNIQUE

There are many situations where a ballcarrier finds he cannot drive forward due to a pileup of blockers and/or defenders. However, he sees, feels or senses daylight to one side or another. A similar situation exists when a ballcarrier's forward progress is stopped by a single defender whose failure to wrap the ballcarrier up in his arms enables the ballcarrier to break away from the would-be tackler by spinning away from him.

The secret to successful spinning out action is a tight north-south spin in which the ballcarrier leans on the defender (arches his back to press against the defender) as he rolls off, or spins out, in an effort to thrust himself forward. Such action prevents any looping type action which puts distance between the ballcarrier and the defender allowing the defender time and a pursuit angle to reset himself to make the tackle. By rolling off the defender tightly, the ballcarrier will separate from the defender beyond the defender's alignment. The coach must be sure that the backs don't tangle their feet up on the spinning out action but, instead, maintain good foot balance and agility. Proper elongation

 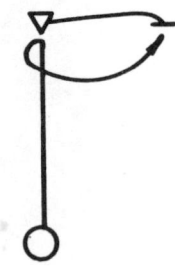

Tight north-south spin puts ballcarrier beyond defender     Looping spin enables defender pursuit angle to reset for ballcarrier

**DIAGRAM 5-18**
**Proper Execution of Spin Out Technique**

of the ballcarrier's strides, or opening up, will enable the ballcarrier to eliminate the defender's pursuit potential from behind. The difference of a proper tight spinning out action as compared to an improper looping action is shown in Diagram 5-18.

The proper north-south spin out action is also shown in Figure 5-3. Again, such north-south spin out action must not be overlooked as an extremely effective open field running technique.

**Forward motion stopped**

**Tight north-south spin arching of back on defender**

**Forward thrust north-south and an opening up of the stride**

**FIGURE 5-3**
**The Spin Out Technique**

## THE STUMBLE TECHNIQUE

The stumble technique helps the ballcarrier to regain his balance when he is stumbling rather than falling to the ground. The technique is a simple one. The ballcarrier uses his free hand to break his fall by

**Hand breaks fall**

**Head is bucked, back is arched, and chest is thrown out**

**Knees are pumped high to get feet under ballcarrier**

**FIGURE 5-4**
**The Stumble Technique**

placing it on the ground. From this stabilized position, the ballcarrier must buck his head up, arch his back and thrust his chest out. An effort is also made to pump the knees up high to help get his feet up under him. This action in itself will help the ballcarrier to regain his balance. Figure 5-4 shows the proper action for the stumble technique.

## DRAGGING OR CARRYING A DEFENDER

Dragging or carrying a defender is a skill that requires coaching attention and practice. Far too often a ballcarrier is pulled down too quickly by a defender when he could have driven for the extra yard or two that might have produced the first down or the touchdown.

Such dragging or carrying action takes on two major coaching points. First, the ballcarrier must maintain a good base as he takes short, choppy, but powerful steps forward. The body is kept in a low, powerfully gathered position as the ballcarrier churns for north-south yardage. Forward body lean and high knee pumping action are paramount to the success of this effort. Second, the ballcarrier must be sure to not swing the ball loosely during such churning action by taking it from the secure armpit position. This is a common fault of the ballcarrier during such action which leads to possible fumbles.

## BALLCARRYING PRACTICE AND DRILLS

Ballcarrying drills and practice are often the highlights of the drill sessions for the backs. They are fun type drills since they are associated with what most backs like to do most—run with the football. The coach is, however, often caught in a bit of a dilemma. Which drills are game-like and which are artificial? What the coach must keep in mind is the question of whether the drill helps practice a skill, or skills, which the backs need to execute assignments in the offense. If it does, it is a useful drill.

### Drill #1: Dive

The Dive Drill is an excellent means of helping to develop north-south running, tight veering or cutting off the blocking scheme and proper acceleration to burst through the hole and into the secondary. The drill is best executed by utilizing a quarterback for a quarterback-ballcarrier exchange and a proper play design so that the back can execute his dive or freeze technique type running in more of a game-like situation.

The drill puts an offensive lineman against a defensive lineman or linebacker. The back explodes behind the lineman and executes his proper running action off the lineman's block. Two cones are placed on the ground approximately 2 yards to each side of the blocker to act as hole markers so that the back does not cut unduly wide and too far away from the defender. Such a drill design will force the ballcarrier to utilize a shoulder drive technique if the defender is not properly blocked. The drill is shown in Diagram 5-19.

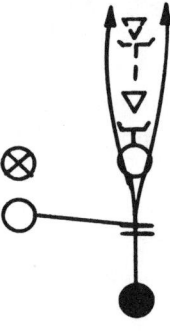

**DIAGRAM 5-19**
**Dive Drill**

*Coaching Points:* The drill can be executed off of any dive running action (i.e.—sprint draw, isolation, etc.). The drill is also an excellent drill for the offensive linemen and the defensive linemen and linebackers. The quarterback should be sure to alternate the side of his hand-off action so that the back cuts off left-handed and right-handed receptions of the ball.

**Drill #2: Nutcracker**

The Nutcracker Drill takes on the same characteristics of the Dive Drill except that three blockers and three defenders are used. Two, or three, backs can align behind the quarterback. However, only the back who is designated as the ballcarrier takes part in the execution of the drill.

The drill is run within a 5 yard square. The offense has three downs to get the ball over the far yard line. The coach designates the ballcarrier who dives straight ahead if aligned behind one of the outside linemen or to one side or other of the center as dictated by the coach if the ballcarrier is stacked behind the quarterback. The quarterback can also be designated as the ballcarrier. The ballcarrier simply executes all the aspects of the dive concept to get over the far yard line. The drill is shown in Diagram 5-20.

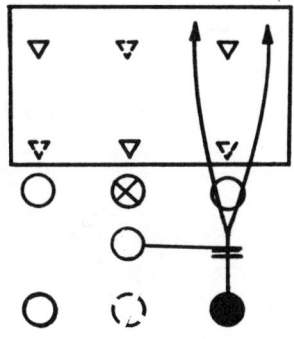

DIAGRAM 5-20
Nutcracker Drill

*Coaching Points:* The defenders can be aligned in a variety of defensive sets to give a particular defensive look. The drill is a great offense versus defense competition type drill. As in the Dive Drill, there are numerous benefits from the drill for the offensive linemen as well as the defenders.

### Drill #3: Sideline

The Sideline Drill helps develop the skill of explosively ripping up the sideline and using the inside forearm to ward off the blows of

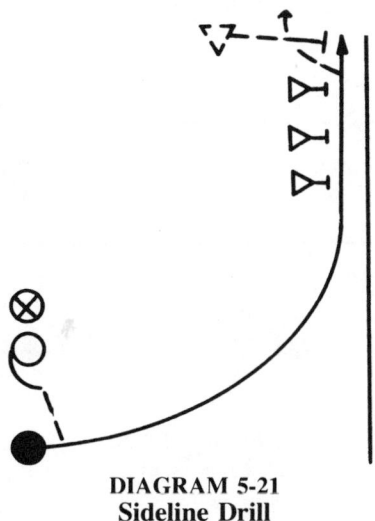

DIAGRAM 5-21
Sideline Drill

the simulated defenders. Three defenders position themselves with air bags 2 to 3 yards from the sideline and attempt to slam the ballcarrier out-of-bounds. The ballcarrier takes a toss, quick-pitch or option-pitch and breaks up the sideline simulating an end-run. The drill is shown in Diagram 5-21.

*Coaching Points:* The ballcarrier must secure the ball underneath his outside arm. He must drive up through the air bags by arching his back, slamming up through the bags with his free shoulder using a forearm lift to help shed the bags. Proper knee pump action and foot base are needed to help maintain his balance. An extra defender (as shown in Diagram 5-5 by the dotted triangle) can be used to occasionally attack the ballcarrier as he passes the initial three defenders from a sharp frontal angle to ensure the practice of an across-the-grain cutting action.

**Drill #4: Flag**

The Flag Drill helps develop the dive squeeze technique as well as the ability to get into the end zone inside the flag. Two large dummies are placed at the flag—one 2 yards straight out on a 45 degree angle and one about a half yard from the goal line. The dummies are held by extra ballcarriers approximately a yard apart. The dummies' holders jam the ballcarrier as hard as possible to prevent him from getting into the end zone. The ballcarrier takes some type of end run or off-tackle ball exchange from a quarterback and uses a low, powerful, lunging drive combined with the squeeze technique to get himself into the end zone in front of the flag. The drill is shown in Diagram 5-22.

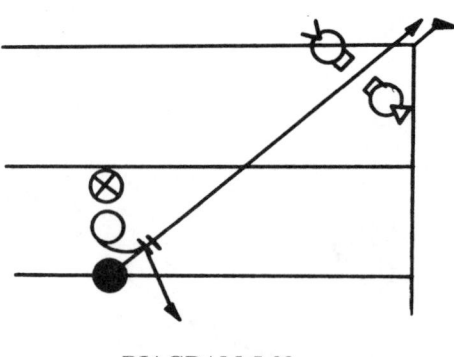

**DIAGRAM 5-22**
**Flag Drill**

*Coaching Points:* The coach must check to see that the ballcarrier covers the ball with his free hand and arm upon contact. The aiming point is slightly inside the flag to allow for the defender's lateral thrust. The ballcarrier attempts to blast out low as if ripping through the defender's legs rather than through the bulk of their upper torsos.

### Drill #5: Dive Squeeze

The Dive Squeeze Drill is a drill executed in a similar fashion to the Flag Drill except that the ballcarrier uses the dive squeeze technique to blast straight into the end zone. The bagholders hold the heavy dummies on the 1½ yard line and do everything possible on the jamming action to prevent the ballcarrier from getting into the end zone. The drill is shown in Diagram 5-23 as well as in Figure 5-2.

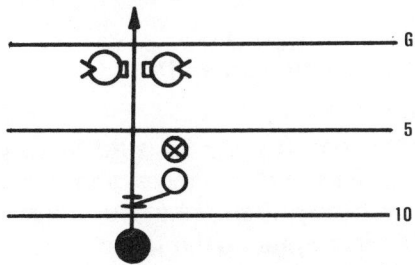

**DIAGRAM 5-23**
**Dive Squeeze Drill**

*Coaching Points:* Turning the shoulders so that they are perpendicular to the line of scrimmage is paramount to the ballcarrier's effort to get into the end zone. Such action lessens the surface area of the ballcarrier that can be made contact with by the defenders.

### Drill #6: Dive Jump

The Dive Jump Drill attempts to practice the skill of jumping over a pileup of blockers and defenders. The drill necessitates a quarterback to help the run properly develop off of a deep hand-off. All of the techniques of a running head start to the daylight opening, gathering the feet a yard to a yard-and-a-half in front of the pileup, a powerful two footed broad jump type action and a powerful thrusting of the upper torso with the ball securely tucked away are emphasized. The drill is set up by standing up four or five tall dummies in front of a high jump pit. The ballcarrier simply adjusts his approach to the pileup of bags and launches himself over the top. Placing the bags directly in front of the goal line gives the ballcarrier a target spot to cross over for the touchdown or first down. The drill is shown in Diagram 5-24 and Figure 5-1.

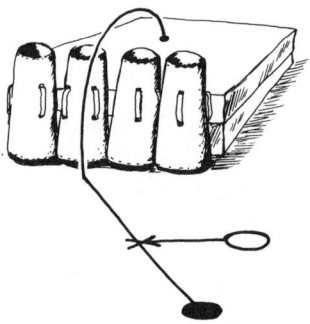

**DIAGRAM 5-24**
**Dive Jump Drill**

*Coaching Points:* The coach must be sure to vary all the types of hand-off actions used for the dive jump action and that the ballcarrier approaches the launch point from whatever angles the various play designs would have him approach the launch point.

### Drill #7: Seven Yard Line

The Seven Yard Line Drill is a drill that is set up in a similar fashion to the Flag Drill. The purpose of the drill is to check to see if the ballcarrier is maintaining proper follow-through drive after he makes explosive contact into the two bags rather than any lunging type action without a proper leg drive follow-through. The ballcarrier, after taking the hand-off from the quarterback, attempts to blast through the bags and yet retain enough balance to get into the end zone. The players holding the heavy bags attempt to jam the ballcarrier to prevent any forward motion. The drill is shown in Diagram 5-25.

*Coaching Points:* The ballcarrier must cover the ball with his free arm and hand to provide extra security just before contact is made. The ballcarrier must drive up through the dummies by arching his back and maintaining good knee pumping action to help maintain good foot balance. Occasionally, the coach signals the bag holders to fake the jamming action and, instead, offer no resistance at all to see if the ballcarrier is overextending himself, causing himself to fall down on his face rather than making it into the end zone.

Coaching the Backs to Run for Touchdowns

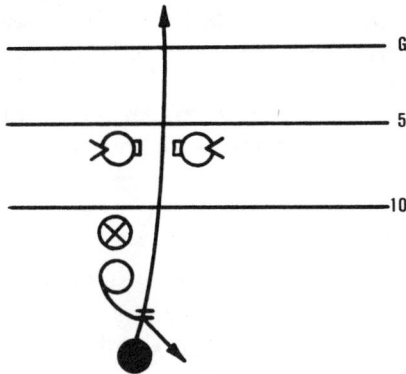

DIAGRAM 5-25
Seven Yard Line Drill

**Drill #8: Burma Road**

The Burma Road Drill helps the backs to develop the spinning out technique. Four bags are spaced 5 yards in width and 5 yards apart. They are held by other backs. The ballcarrier attacks the first bag, delivers a shoulder dive blow with his inside shoulder, and executes a spin out technique to the inside. The ballcarrier then repeats the action three more times on the remaining bags. The drill is shown in Diagram 5-26.

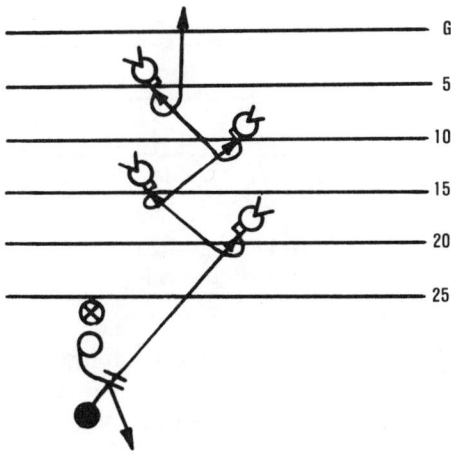

DIAGRAM 5-26
Burma Road Drill

*Coaching Points:* The coach must be sure the ballcarrier is using a proper shoulder drive action with an arching action of the back and good foot balance. The ballcarrier spins off the bag tightly by arching his back against the dummies to enable himself to spin off tightly north-south. Good foot balance and agility are important so his feet do not get tangled up.

### Drill #9: Stumble

The Stumble Drill helps develop the stumble technique of helping a ballcarrier to regain his balance when he is stumbling and falling to the ground. The drill helps create the stumble situation by having the ballcarriers place the palm of their hand on the first yard line from a 5 yard running start. This will cause the ballcarriers to stumble. The ballcarriers now execute the proper stumble technique actions (buck the head up, arch the back, stick the chest out and pump the knees to help get the feet under the ballcarrier) to help regain their balance. The ballcarriers now switch their balls to their opposite arms and repeat the action with the opposite hand on the next yard marker. In all, four repetitions are executed. The drill is shown in Diagram 5-27.

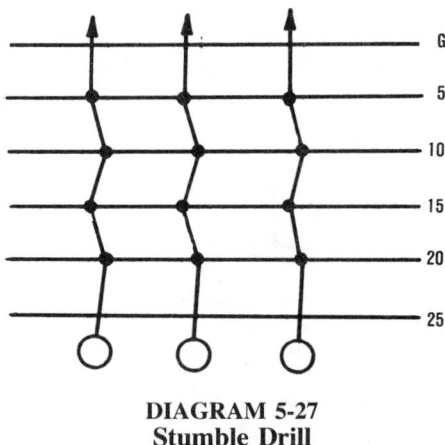

DIAGRAM 5-27
Stumble Drill

*Coaching Points:* The ballcarriers must touch the *palms* of their hands to the yard markers so that they stumble. The drill is useless if they touch the yard markers with their finger tips and do not stumble.

### Drill #10: Drag

The Drag Drill helps the ballcarriers develop the proper techniques for driving into the end zone while dragging a defender (proper

*Coaching the Backs to Run for Touchdowns* 107

body lean, high knee pumping action, proper foot base and good ball security). The ballcarriers, with other backs grasping around the waists of the ballcarriers to simulate tacklers, simply drive for 10 yards into the end zone. The drill is shown in Diagram 5-28.

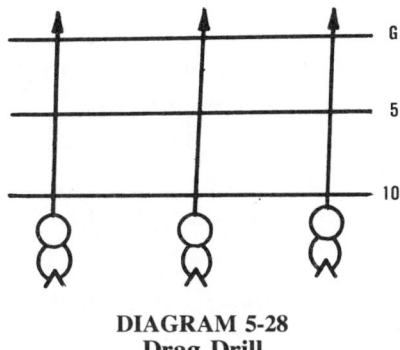

**DIAGRAM 5-28**
**Drag Drill**

*Coaching Points:* The backs simulating the tackle through the drag action must attempt to be as difficult an obstacle to the ballcarrier as possible on his attempt to get into the end zone.

### Drill #11: Carry

The Carry Drill is executed in exactly the same fashion as the Drag Drill except that the ballcarrier has the simulated tackler draped over his shoulder as if the tackler has jumped on his back.

*Coaching Points:* As in the Drag Drill, the simulated tackler attempts to make the ballcarrier's effort to get into the end zone as difficult as possible.

### Drill #12: Open Field Running

The Open Field Running Drill attempts to develop exactly what the drill title states—open field running skills. The drill is set up by creating a 25 yard by 25 yard square area with cones. A deepback type of defender is placed in position A, B or C. The ballcarrier is positioned in position I, II or III as shown in Diagram 5-29. Both the ballcarrier and defender's alignments are continually alternated to create all the various pursuit angles the ballcarrier may face. Upon the coach's signal, the ballcarrier attempts to use his open field running skills to cross the opposite line. The defender, of course, attempts to stop the ballcarrier. The drill can be run anywhere from live to two-hand touch depending on the purpose of the drill. The drill is shown in Diagram 5-29.

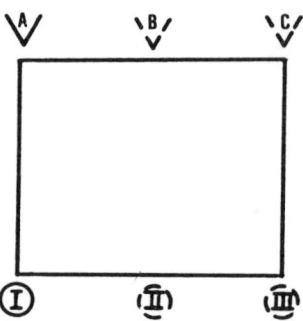

**DIAGRAM 5-29**
**Open Field Running Drill**

*Coaching Points:* The ballcarrier must attempt all open field running action off a north-south run threat. Such action, again, helps put the defender in a sweat while helping the ballcarrier to have the best opportunity to gain north-south yardage towards the end zone. All open field running techniques such as head and body faking, stutter stepping, limp leg action, change of pace running, high stepping, cutting across the grain, drive blocking up the sideline and spinning out should be emphasized.

# six

# Developing Total Ball Security

Ball security deals with the ability of the offense to control the handling of the football on all of its play executions. Many of the aspects of ball security have already been discussed (center-quarterback exchange, quarterback-ballcarrier exchanges) and others will be discussed in subsequent chapters (backfield pass receiving). This chapter will deal with actual ballcarrying security skills so that the ballcarrier does not "carry the ball like a loaf of bread," have the ball "pop-out" on him on a hard collision with a defender or fumble the ball as it hits the ground because he reached out with the ball in an effort to get an extra foot or so of yardage.

## PROPER CARRY OF THE FOOTBALL

A secure carry of the football has the ballcarrier attempting to envelop the ball with his hand, fingers, arm and armpit. The ballcarrier actually tries to cover as much of the ball as possible so that as little of the surface of the ball is exposed as possible. The more ball surface that is exposed, the greater is the chance of the ball being fumbled. Figure 6-1 shows the proper techniques of a secure carry of the ball.

The tip of the football is covered by the spread fingers. Actually, the fingers attempt to squeeze the football into the armpit in a vise-like locking action. The elbow plays a key role in the secure carry of the football. The elbow must be wrapped around and under the ball so that all parts of the ball are enveloped in the carry so that the hand and

**FIGURE 6-1**
**Secure Carry of the Football**

fingers can execute their proper vise-like squeezing action of the ball into the armpit. However, if the elbow is not wrapped around and under the ball with the elbow pointing down, and, instead, has the elbow pointing out away from the body, the bottom of the ball will be exposed. A blow to the top of the ball will result in no body part being able to prevent the ball from slipping out towards the ground, producing the fumble. This can be easily demonstrated to the backs by having a ballcarrier improperly position his elbow pointing out away from the body and having the coach forcefully punch down on the top of the ball to cause the ball to squirt out towards the ground.

A proper vise-like lock of the ball up into the armpit should secure the ball so tightly that there is no space seen between the top of the ball and the bottom of the armpit. A good coaching adage to use is that the coach should "see no air."

The proper and improper action of the ballcarrier's elbow is shown in Figure 6-2.

*Developing Total Ball Security* *111*

**Proper wrapping around action of elbow**

**Improper positioning of elbow out away from the body**

FIGURE 6-2
**Proper and Improper Elbow Action on Carry of Fooball**

### THE TWO-ARMED CARRY

Actually, a ballcarrier should *never* carry the ball in two arms. Such action takes the ball from under an armpit (the most secure place for it to be) and creates a less secure carry of the ball. A two-handed carry of the football in front of the ballcarrier will often result in the ball "popping out" upon a violent contact with a defender or the ground.

A proper two-handed carry is nothing more than a normal one-hand carry of the football with the free hand and arm placed over the football to provide extra protection. In essence, the free hand helps cover more of the ball surface while the extra arm helps to absorb more of the blow of the contact. Whenever a ballcarrier realizes he is going to have to lower his shoulder to attempt to blast over a defender, or defenders, he should try to execute a two-handed carry. A proper two-handed carry is shown in Figure 6-3.

**FIGURE 6-3**
**Two-Handed Carry of Football**

## CHANGING THE BALL FROM ONE HAND TO THE OTHER

Changing the ball from one hand to the other is not advisable. During such an exchange, the ball is in a very insecure position. A violent contact with a defender as the ball is being exchanged will often lead to a fumble. The question then arises—is switching the ball to the other hand worth the possibility of a fumble during the exchange? Whatever the answer, the backs must be coached to not attempt any such changing of the ball when surrounded by defenders. An example of this would be ballcarrier exchanging the football from one hand to the other on a dive as he is accelerating through a hole. Such an area has too many potential pursuers who could make such contact with the ballcarrier.

# Developing Total Ball Security

When such a changing of the ball from one hand to the other is attempted, the ballcarrier executes an exchange technique that is similar to a normal hand-off action. The exception is that the ball is already in the "bottom" hand and arm. The exchange is executed by taking the free hand and reaching over towards the armpit of the ball carry (almost as if to form the top arm and hand positioning of a normal hand-off pouch). The free hand reaches over and grips the end of the football from underneath the armpit. The ball is now carried (dragged) across the ballcarrier's body to the opposite armpit as the former hand that was carrying the football remains underneath the football to help guide it to the new armpit. Thus, the former hand carrying the ball helps to provide security to the changing action. The ballcarrier must be sure to firmly execute a proper one-arm carry of the ball under the new armpit.

## PROBLEM AREAS FOR BALL SECURITY

There are specific situations that lead to insecure ballcarrying actions. Such situations must be coached and emphasized in practice so that such improper ballcarrying actions can be eliminated.

As was mentioned in Chapter 5 in the discussion of the dive jump technique, extending the ball out away from the body to reach for extra yardage is extremely dangerous. Any action in which the ball is taken away from the security of one of the armpits leads to improper ball security. Such action exposes a tremendous amount of the football leading to an increased possibility of fumbling. There are only a few extreme situations when such reaching out with the football should be attempted. They are almost always desperation type situations; a last ditch effort for a touchdown on a fourth down, a desperate attempt to get first down yardage on a critical drive, etc.

Allowing the ball to open up away from the body on a hard cutting action by the ballcarrier is also a common ball security error. Again, any ballcarrying action which takes the ball from the desired vise-like grip into the armpit exposes more of the ball's surface leading to a greater chance of a fumble. The same problem is often seen when a ballcarrier attempts to drag or carry a defender to get extra yardage, and also on the dive jump technique. The coach must make his backs aware of these potential problems and be sure that proper practice attention is given to the elimination of these potential problem areas.

Two other critical situations that often lead to poor ball security are when a ballcarrier is rolling and when a ballcarrier is making an extra effort in general. Rolling, as a result of falling or contact with a defender, often results in a loosened carry of the football. The same is true when a ballcarrier is making a second, third or even fourth effort to struggle forward for extra yardage. The extra effort will often lead to a breakdown of ball security concentration.

## BALL SECURITY PRACTICE AND DRILLS

Ball security, like many other facets of backfield play, is afforded many situations for its practice all throughout the sessions. A ballcarrier who improperly carries the football under one arm in a drill, a ballcarrier who fails to cover up the ball with his free arm as he attempts to squeeze into the end zone in a goal line scrimmage, a ballcarrier who extends the ball as he dives over a pileup of players in a scrimmage, these types of situations offer the coach game-like practice of an extremely important facet of backfield play.

### Drill #1: Ball Iso

The Ball Iso Drill simply has the backs execute a proper one-hand carry of the football and squeeze the ball into the armpit as hard as possible for a ten second count in an isometric exercise type of action. Such a drill helps the backs develop the strength needed for the vise-like grip desired to keep the football secure in the armpit. The backs must be sure to iso the ball under both armpits.

*Coaching Points:* The backs must attempt to squeeze the ball so hard that they attempt to "pop the air out of the ball." The coach may emphasize extra ball iso action by the weaker arm and hand (i.e.—left hand and arm for a right-handed person).

### Drill #2: Arm Wrestle

The Arm Wrestle Drill pairs up two backs. One executes a proper one arm carry of the ball. The other back wrestles, grabs, rips, punches, etc., at the ball, arm and hand of the ballcarrier in an attempt to separate the ball from the ballcarrier. The action is carried out for a thirty second period. The ball is then switched (using the proper switching the ball technique) and carried out with the other hand and arm.

*Coaching Points:* Again, extra time can be allotted to the weaker arm and hand.

*Developing Total Ball Security*

**Drill #3: Ball Change**

The Ball Change Drill has the ballcarrier again teamed up with another back. The ballcarrier executes his proper ball changing technique from arm to arm as the second back executes the same action as the Arm Wrestle Drill with the emphasis on slapping, punching and grabbing rather than any actual latching on and wrestling action. The ballcarrier must get a maximum amount of repetitions of ball changes in the allotted time period.

*Coaching Points:* The Arm Wrestle Drill and the Ball Change Drill can actually be combined into one drill. The ballcarrier executes a proper one-armed carry as the other back executes the Arm Wrestle Drill. The ballcarrier then changes the ball to the other hand as the other back executes the Ball Change Drill. This action is repeated a maximum amount of times in the allotted time period.

**Drill #4: Two-Hand Carry**

The Two-Hand Carry Drill is executed as a rapid fire forearm shiver drill is executed. The ballcarrier executes a one-arm carry. Another back sets up slightly to the right front of the ballcarrier at an approximate distance of 2 yards. The coach stands behind the ballcarrier and signals the other back when to unload a blow into the ballcarrier. As the blow is unloaded, the ballcarrier must properly cover the ball with his free hand and arm to execute a proper two-handed carry and absorb the blow. During the delivery of the blow, the other back can add punches, slaps, ripping action, etc., to try to pry the ball loose. After four or five blows the ballcarrier switches the ball to the other hand as the other back switches to the left side of the ballcarrier and the drill action is repeated.

*Coaching Points:* The ballcarrier takes his free hand and arm off the ball after each blow is delivered so that he can execute the two-handed carry action for each blow.

**Drill #5: Rapid Fire Two-Hand Carry**

The Rapid Fire Two-Hand Carry Drill is executed in the same fashion as the Two-Hand Carry Drill except that two backs face the ballcarrier—one slightly off to the left and one to the right, again at a distance of about 2 yards. A blow is delivered by one of the two backs (coach signals). After the blow is delivered, the ballcarrier uses the proper switching the ball technique and then takes on a blow from the second back. The action is repeated a maximum amount of times in an allotted period of time. On each blow, the ballcarrier must properly cover up the ball with his free hand and arm via the two-hand carry technique. The drill is seen in Diagram 6-1.

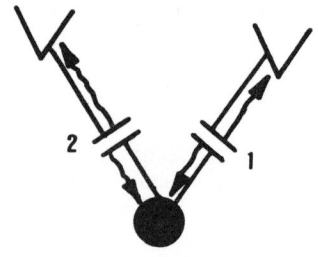

DIAGRAM 6-1
Rapid Fire Two-Hand Carry Drill

*Coaching Points:* The drill must not be so rapid fire that the ballcarrier does not have time to reset and be ready to properly execute the two-armed carry action.

### Drill #6: Rapid Fire Double Ball Carry

The Rapid Fire Double Ball Carry Drill is executed in a similar fashion to the Rapid Fire Two-Hand Carry Drill except that the ballcarrier has one ball secured in each armpit and takes on the blows of both backs at the same time. The back must attempt to drop his shoulders on each combined blow delivery so that he can rip up with his shoulders and absorb the blows with the shoulders rather than the arms, hands and balls. The drill is shown in Diagram 6-2.

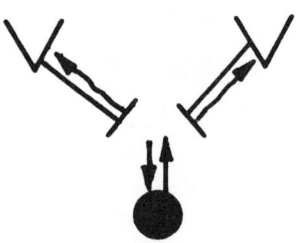

DIAGRAM 6-2
Rapid Fire Double Ball Carry Drill

*Developing Total Ball Security*

*Coaching Points:* The coach must allow the ballcarrier a proper amount of time to reset for each blow. Five to six blows per man is a good allotment per set.

### Drill #7: Monkey Roll

The Monkey Roll Drill is the typical three man monkey roll agility drill with the exception that all three backs have a football tucked under one arm.

*Coaching Points:* The ballcarriers have a tremendous tendency to loosen the desired vise-like grip of the one-armed carry. This, of course, must be checked. Only six or seven monkey roll repetitions should be carried out in one set, as the drill has a tendency to disintegrate beyond that number. Such a disintegration must be avoided to prevent anyone from falling on another's legs. The backs must be sure to alternate the ball under each arm.

### Drill #8: Gauntlet

The Gauntlet Drill is certainly not a new drill. Two lines of backs attempt to slap, rip, punch, etc., at the ballcarrying action to jar the ball loose. Taking a hand-off adds to the effectiveness of the drill since the ballcarrier must carry out proper ball security off proper hand-off action. The gauntlet is set up by forming two lines of backs a yard and a half from one another with a yard spacing between each back. Some of the backs can utilize hand-bags to slam the ballcarrier both high and low to help disturb his ball security efforts. The ballcarrier must attempt to rip through the gauntlet as fast and as powerfully as possible while executing proper ball security techniques. The drill is seen in Diagram 6-3.

*Coaching Points:* The ballcarrier must drive up and through the gauntlet by arching his back. He must also be sure to pump his knees high to help him maintain his balance. Such a drill also helps to practice other facets of ballcarrying.

Unit and team type drills and practice often finds that only one set of backs at a time is being utilized. The backs who are standing in line waiting their turn can put such extra time to good use by working on two of the ball security drills—the Ball Iso Drill and the Changing the Ball Drill. A simple rule is used. If you're not in the teamwork, scrimmage, etc., you must have a ball in your hand working on the ball iso action or the changing the ball technique. Extra emphasis can be added by utilizing the Arm Wrestle Drill concept during such action. A

DIAGRAM 6-3
Gauntlet Drill

coach can sneak up on a back in between the plays being run or just as the play is to be run and attempt to punch, rip or slap the ball out of the waiting back's arm. If the ball isn't secure and the ball pops out, a reinforcement such as ten push-ups or ten up-downs can be given to place extra emphasis on needed ball security.

Additional ball security practice emphasis can be made by demanding that proper ball security techniques be carried out all throughout practice. If a back carries a ball from one drill area to another, proper ball security techniques must be executed—"no air," elbow wrapped around and under the ball, fingers over the tip of the ball, etc. After a scrimmage, teamwork or timing period execution of a play, a back can be made to execute proper ball security techniques all the way back to the huddle. Such extra practice work helps to make full and efficient use of every available practice minute. In addition, a concentrated emphasis is embedded in the minds of those who most need to understand and know it—the players. Far too often a coach says he doesn't have the time to work on such drills or items. Careful examination of a practice shows that many coaches waste far more practice time than they realize.

# seven

# Coaching the Backfield Option Game

The coaching of the option game is certainly a broad topic. Of course, many teams base their entire offensive attack on a particular type of option. It is hard to discuss just one aspect of the option game such as backfield play without interrelating with some of the many other facets of offensive execution. It is, however, the purpose of this chapter to limit the discussion to actual backfield, option execution. Such discussion will be as broad in scope as possible so that the coach can apply the information to his particular style of option play.

## THE TRIPLE OPTION DIVE READ

The Triple Option Dive Read is the initial part, or foundation, of triple option football. By triple optioning, we refer to the quarterback's ability to execute a dive hand-off, keep the ball himself or pitch the ball to the pitchback according to the reactions of the defense. The reactions of the defense, or more specifically the isolated defenders whether blocked or unblocked, are the key to option football. In the case of the triple option, three offensive threats (dive, keep and pitch) attack two defenders who can only properly react to two of the threats. By reading the defensive reactions, the quarterback is aided in determining which is the proper option to execute.

The reading of the initial dive key (the defender designated as the defensive player who must stop the dive threat by the design of the play) starts for the quarterback before the ball is even snapped. Since the option game requires split second timing, the quarterback cannot wait till after the ball is snapped to locate the dive key defender to be read. By scanning the defense as he addresses the center, the quarterback can usually determine who the dive key defender is, and often how he is aligned. (Such information helps to indicate the types of action that could possibly ensue.)

The execution of the dive read takes on two design aspects; the dive read execution with a fullback such as in the "I" or Wishbone formations, and the dive read execution with a halfback such as in a split back veer formation. The fullback dive read relies on a mesh ride-and-decide action, and the halfback dive read relies more on a give or fake give action.

As was previously mentioned in Chapter 3, the "I" or Wishbone formation fullback takes a fairly evenly balanced four point stance. The dive read action is a major reason why. It is extremely important that the fullback's, or upback's, initial steps to the dive landmark are the same to both sides to ensure a consistent mesh for the quarterback. The landmark of the diveback can be anywhere from the outside hip of the guard to inside hip of the tackle depending on the design of the offense.

The quarterback steps back on a 45 degree angle and delivers the ball on a direct line to the fullback's pouch. The quarterback does not swing the ball out with a straight arm action. Instead, the quarterback reaches back with the ball to create the desired straight arm action of the ride. The quarterback must use his peripheral vision to locate the ballcarrier's pouch, since he must be reading the dive key all through such action. The quarterback must make his read by the time the ball is ridden to his belt buckle. Continued riding of the ball past the belt buckle towards the front leg will only create a disturbance of timing and mesh as the fullback's hip will begin to interfere with the quarterback-fullback coordination of the mesh, ride and decide action.

The read of the dive key is a simple one. If the dive key attacks the fullback by either closing down on the hole laterally or by taking a direct, penetrating angle charge at the fullback, the quarterback disconnects the ball from the fullback's pouch and options the keep-pitch key defender. If the dive key sits and reads, slants or loops to the outside or penetrates straight ahead into the backfield, the ball is given to the fullback. Such action is shown in Diagram 7-1 versus a 5-2 defensive tackle dive key.

Giving the ball to the fullback versus a sitting dive key defender is generally thought of as being the wiser decision for the quarterback to make. To pull the ball versus such a defender will often allow the dive

# Coaching the Backfield Option Game

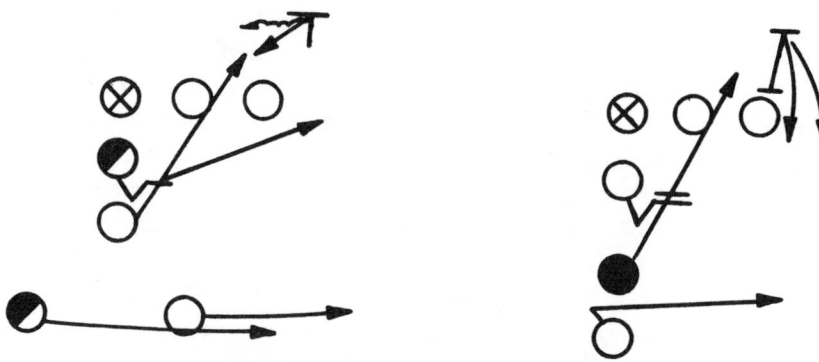

**DIAGRAM 7-1**
**Dive Key Read to Fullback**

key defender to react back to quarterback, especially if he has made little commitment to the fullback. Whether the dive key is able to get to the quarterback or not, his reaction back to the quarterback will often be enough to disturb the play. A give to the fullback versus a sitting dive key provides the safer option since the fullback's "head of steam" should produce positive yardage versus the more passive, sitting dive key defender. Whatever the philosophy, the decision to give the ball to the fullback will eventually force the dive key to "show his hand" earlier and make a more pronounced commitment one way or the other.

The emphasis on the dive read is to give the ball to the fullback unless the dive key reacts in a fashion that dictates pull. Such an emphasis helps create a firm ride of the ball in the fullback's pouch, a more precise hand-off if the read is give and a greater fake of the hand-off if the read is pull. The better fake is a result of the heavy sink of the ball into the fullback's pouch.

If the read is give, the quarterback carries out his normal hand-off technique. The ball, already on the hand-off spot, is simply pressed up firmly against the fullback's pouch by the outside hand as the inside hand is brought out from behind the ball. The inside hand is, again, held just off the ball to wait for the outside hand to come off the ball so that the two hands can execute a proper fake of the keep-pitch option action. If the read is pull, the quarterback disengages the ball from the fullback's pouch by snapping it forward as the quarterback draws the ball to his sternum to carry out the keep-pitch portion of the option.

The quarterback's ride, or second step is actually a feather type of action in which the front foot and leg are suspended in air as the ball is riden forward towards the quarterback's belt buckle. If the read is pull, the quarterback simply continues the midair suspension of the front foot and leg until the fullback passes him and then redirects the foot down the line of scrimmage towards the keep-pitch key. Some coaches feel the exact same action should be carried out if the read is give on the dive hand-off. Other coaches feel the front foot should follow the

**Initial mesh**

**Ride and decide action to QB's belt buckle**

**FIGURE 7-1**
**Quarterback-Fullback Dive Read Execution**

ride of the fullback and be planted on the ground to best accommodate the dive hand-off. Such action is executed at the expense of the keep-pitch option fake action.

It is important to note that the dive hand-off action or the disengagement of the ball to carry out the keep-pitch option should be as contrasting an action as possible. The ball must be firmly handed-off with a hard press of the ball against the fullback's pouch or there must be a heavy snapping action of the ball off the fullback's pouch. There must be little doubt in the fullback's mind as to whether the action is give or pull. The fullback dive mesh action is seen in Figure 7-1.

The halfback dive mesh is not able to utilize the fullback type mesh action due to the distance the quarterback has to go to get to the mesh point and the angle of approach the halfback has to take to hit his landmark. A comparison of these mesh courses is seen in Diagram 7-2.

The quarterback's initial two steps are straight down the line of scrimmage. (Some coaches teach a slight downhill approach to the mesh point to get the mesh point closer to the line of scrimmage.) The steps are controlled steps which sets the quarterback in the area behind the guard. (The actual positioning depends on the landmark of the diveback.) The quarterback attempts to make his dive key read on his first to second step. Actually, the read may be carried all the way to the third adjustment type step if a problem of reading exists.

The halfback dive key read execution, therefore, is not ride and decide. Instead, it is give or fake the give. The read of the dive key is the same as it is for the fullback dive key read execution as shown in Diagram 7-1. If the read is give, the quarterback executes a normal

**Fullback mesh course**   **Halfback mesh course**
**DIAGRAM 7-2**
**Comparison of Fullback and Halfback Dive Mesh Courses**

dive hand-off. The ball is firmly placed on the spot of the hand-off pouch. The hand-off must be made as deep as possible (the earlier the read, the greater the possibility of a deeper hand-off). As on the ride and decide action of the fullback, the quarterback must use peripheral vision to initially locate the halfback's hand-off pouch. However, once the dive read is determined as give, the quarterback switches all concentration to the ballcarrier's hand-off pouch.

The quarterback's third step is an adjustment type step to help facilitate the mesh with the halfback. A tall, long-legged quarterback may actually not need a third or even fourth step since his first two steps might position him properly for the mesh action. The fourth step takes on the same feather type action of the fullback dive mesh in which the front leg and foot are suspended during the give or fake action. Or, the front foot can step towards the line of scrimmage to help facilitate the give or fake give to the halfback. The feather technique, whether for the dive fake or for the dive, lets the halfback pass on his dive course until he clears the quarterback. At that time, the quarterback redirects his feather step down the line of scrimmage to the keep-pitch key.

If the read is keep, the quarterback fakes a dive hand-off by reaching back with the ball to place it on the front hip of the halfback, and rides the diveback to his belt buckle. Due to the timing of the mesh, this faking action may be little more than a jabbing, waving action. The quarterback must be sure, however, to execute such a faking action to delay his down-the-line action long enough to allow the pitchback to get into his proper pitch ratio. A quarterback who breaks out of the mesh too quickly breaks down the timing needed to allow for proper positioning of the pitchbacks in the option design.

## THE OUTSIDE VEER TRIPLE OPTION
## DIVE READ

The outside veer triple option dive read is executed in a similar fashion to the halfback dive mesh. The only major difference for the execution of the outside veer dive mesh is that the mesh point for the outside veer dive is one hole further down the line of scrimmage. The positioning of the quarterback is approximately behind the tackle. The stepping action of the quarterback is, again, a four step action. However, the third step is not an adjustment step but rather a healthy, full step to get the quarterback to the widened dive mesh point. The third step, however, is slightly back toward the diveback as on the third step of the normal inside veer mesh. The quarterback now carries out the give or fake give dive key read execution.

## THE COUNTER OPTION TRIPLE OPTION DIVE READ

Although not commonly used, there are some teams that execute triple option action on the counter option rather than predetermining the dive and option actions. The counter option triple option action takes on the mechanics of the fullback dive mesh execution on the inside veer. The quarterback, on his four step reverse pivot action, steps back deeply on his third step to place the ball in the diveback's pouch and then snaps his head to the dive key. The normal ride and decide action is carried out as the fourth adjustment type slide step is brought up to the third step to accommodate either the dive give or dive fake action. The fifth step is taken with the back foot (the same foot of the fourth adjustment type step) as it is redirected on the 30 degree angle downhill attack course to option the keep-pitch key defender.

## THE KEEP-PITCH READ DOWNHILL ATTACK

The key to the attack of the keep pitch key is a hard, downhill attack. By downhill, it is meant that the quarterback is taking an approximate 30 degree angle towards the line of scrimmage. Such an angle of attack is taken either immediately (lead option) or after some type of dive fake (inside veer, counter option, trap option). The downhill attack is not executed, however, on the outside veer option. Diagram 7-3 shows the downhill attack off the various option attacks.

The concept behind the downhill attack is that such an attack puts the pressure on the keep-pitch key, forces him to make a more pronounced commitment sooner and gives the option action a shorter corner to turn in attempting to gain north-south yardage.

By attacking downhill on a 30 degree angle the keep-pitch key is put into a bind or sweat. The upfield, positive yardage angle of the quarterback's attack forces the keep-pitch key defender to take a pronounced, sharper angle of attack to get to the quarterback—similar to a closing down type of action on an off-tackle play if he is the defender assigned to the quarterback. This action is seen in Diagram 7-4 from lead option action.

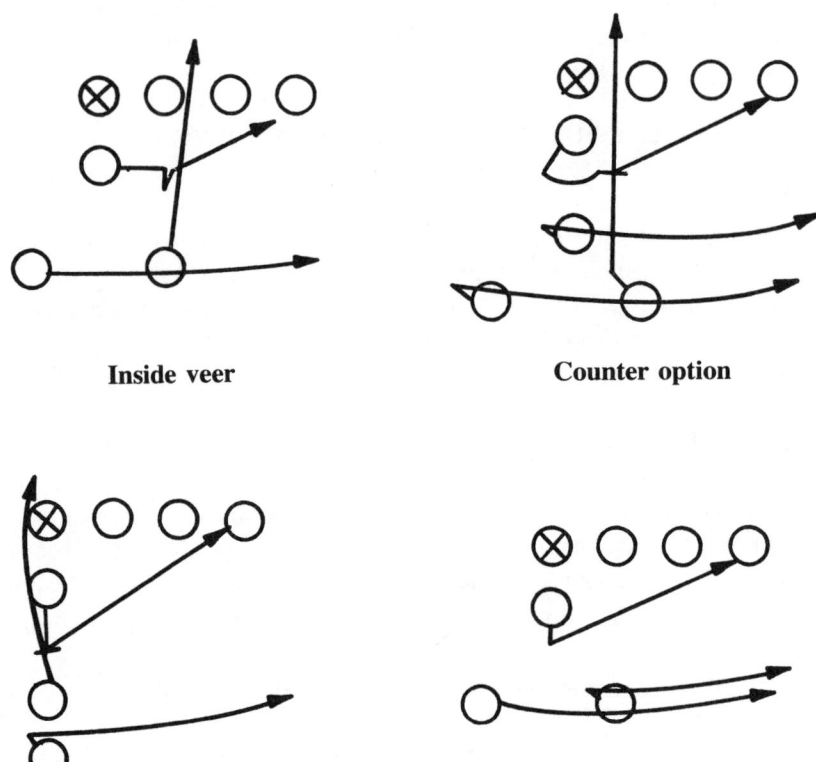

**DIAGRAM 7-3**
**Keep-Pitch Key Read Downhill Attack**

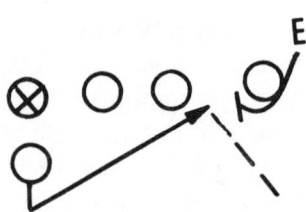

**DIAGRAM 7-4**
**Downhill Attack Forcing of Sharp Angle of Attack by Keep-Pitch Key Dictating Pitch**

*Coaching the Backfield Option Game*

Forcing such a pronounced, sharper attack angle by the keep-pitch key enables a sharper corner for the pitchback to turn in his attempt to gain north-south yardage. This is seen in Diagram 7-5 in which a downhill attack forces a sharp commitment by the keep-pitch key defender producing a sharper corner to turn as compared to a flat down the line attack which creates a more rounded course for the pitchback to take in his attempt to gain north-south yardage. The lead option is again used for example.

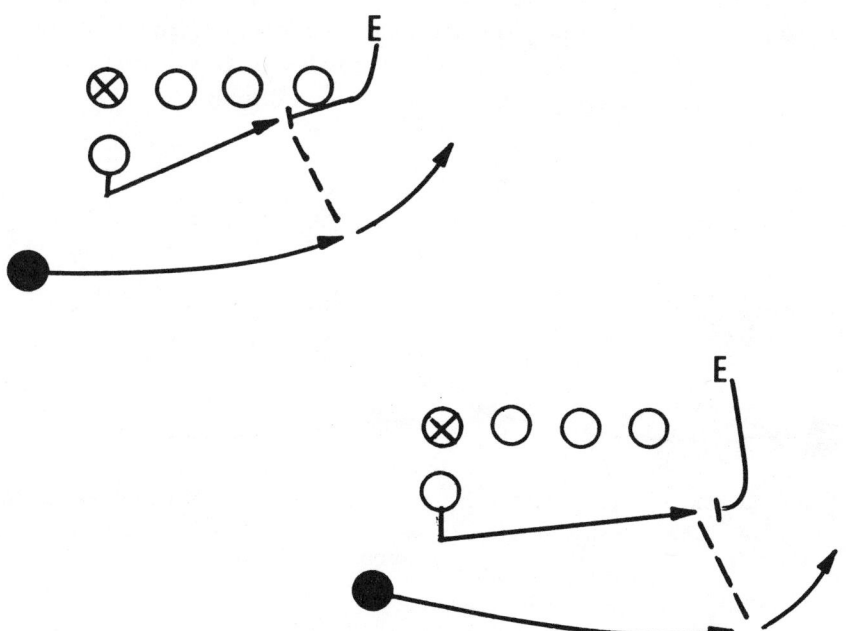

DIAGRAM 7-5
**Comparison of Effect of Downhill Attack to Non-Downhill Attack**

The difference of the pitchback courses seen in Diagram 7-4 is extremely significant. If the pitchback is able to turn it up sharply as a result of the downhill attack and get north-south more quickly by wasting less time on east-west yardage, he will have a greater opportunity to beat the pursuit of the interior defenders. As on any corner running action, the more a ballcarrier has to run east-west to turn the corner, the greater is the chance of such interior defenders being able to pursue and run the ballcarrier down before he can get upfield and turn the corner.

Once the keep-pitch defender commits to quarterback (actually, commitment refers to a positioning of the keep-pitch key defender in which he can no longer get to the pitchback), the quarterback attempts to flatten out at the keep-pitch key defender's downfield shoulder so that the defender is unable to interfere with the pitching action. This action would be in comparison to a continued line of attack which would position the quarterback directly in front of the keep-pitch key defender, or even worse, inside of him. A position directly in front of or inside of the keep-pitch key defender will often enable the defender to interfere with the pitch since the quarterback will often be attempting to pitch through the defender. Examples of this are shown in Diagram 7-6 again using the lead option for example.

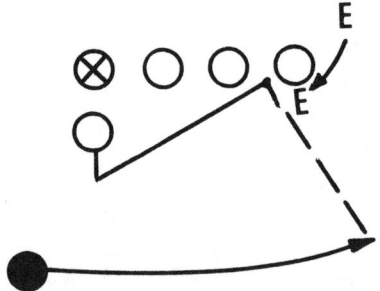
**Inside attack, giving defender an excellent chance to interfere with the pitch**

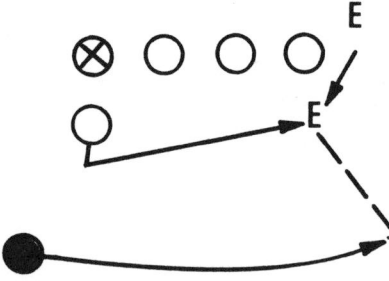
**Attacking directly at defender, giving a good chance to interfere with the pitch**

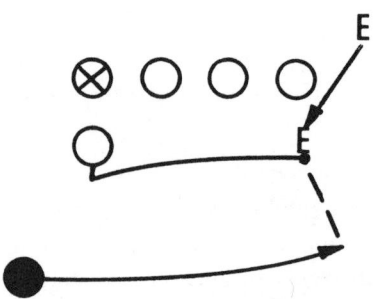
**Flattening out to downfield shoulder, eliminating defender's ability to interfere with the pitch**

**DIAGRAM 7-6**
**Flattened-Out and Non-Flattened-Out Attack of Keep-Pitch Defender**

## Coaching the Backfield Option Game

It must be understood that such a flattened out attack of the downfield shoulder of the keep-pitch key defender is not always possible. The optimal situation for the quarterback would be to attack the downfield shoulder via such a flattened out course, step out to the pitchback and look directly to the pitch spot. Varied attacks and styles of play by the keep-pitch key defender and two defender cross-charge actions will force such non-optimal pitch actions as coming out of a dive fake early to get off an immediate pitch, pitching in the midst of taking a step, pitching off an inside foot step, etc.

A crash type charge by the keep-pitch key defender is the most drastic action to be dealt with by the quarterback. This is especially true when the quarterback is executing a dive fake or coming out of a triple option read pull action. Two points are important. Initially, the quarterback must disengage from the fake action immediately upon the read of the crash charge to initiate the pitch action. Again, commitment by the keep-pitch key defender is a positioning where he can no longer react to the pitchback. A crash charge usually puts the defender in this position immediately. Such action eliminates the ability of the crashing keep-pitch key defender to interfere with the pitch. Secondly, the quarterback must be sure to get the ball back to his sternum area before pitching to allow for the proper pitching action as discussed in Chapter 5.

Another problem that the quarterback must be concerned about with a heavy crash type charge is how to absorb the blow of the defender once the pitch is made. The quarterback simply gives with the blow as much as possible to eliminate the hard contact.

Perhaps the most difficult keep-pitch key defender option is the lightly feathering defender who is playing the "cat-and-mouse" technique to the utmost. Such a defender shows neither a commitment to the pitch nor the keep action. The worst mistake, and the most common, that a quarterback makes in this situation is to slow down his downhill attack and/or flatten out the downhill attack at the defender before he commits to the quarterback. Such action only helps to give the interior defenders time to pursue the play as the quarterback directs the option action on the undesired east-west course. Such an east-west course plays right into the hands of the lightly feathering defender, helping to string the play out to the sidelines. This undesired action is seen in Diagram 7-7 using the lead option action for example.

The quarterback must handle the lightly feathering keep-pitch key defender in the same fashion as he would any other action. The quarterback must attack on his downhill 30 degree angle course at top speed to force the defender to react one way or the other. If the defender

DIAGRAM 7-7
Undesired Slow Down and/or Flattening Out Action of QB
vs. Lightly Feathering Keep-Pitch Key Defender

continues to feather, the quarterback will suddenly realize he is even with, or beyond, the defender thus dictating the keep. If the defender throttles down to react to the quarterback, the quarterback will flatten out to the defender's downhill shoulder and execute his normal pitch action.

If the keep-pitch key defender feathers heavily (flies out laterally), penetrates across the line of scrimmage or loops to the outside to take on a pitch support action, the quarterback's downhill 30 degree angle attack will help the quarterback's decision-making process by dictating keep according to the relationship of the quarterback and the keep-pitch key defender. The quarterback, by staying on his course, will see that he will eventually become even with or go past the keep-pitch key defender, telling the quarterback to plant his outside foot and head upfield. This action is seen in Diagram 7-8.

Two points need examination on such keep read actions. Initially, the quarterback must scan upfield as he cuts north-south to be sure that some type of cross-charge isn't taking place. If there is, the quarter-

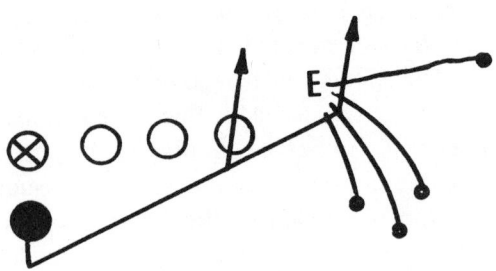

DIAGRAM 7-8
Downhill Attack Dictating QB Keep Due to Keep-Pitch Key Feather
or Penetration Action

back simply carries out his normal pitch action attacking the downfield shoulder of the new keep-pitch key defender. Such action is shown in Diagram 7-9.

Secondly, when the quarterback plants his outside foot to head upfield, his initial aiming point is upfield north-south to the end zone flag. Such action enables north-south yardage while getting away from

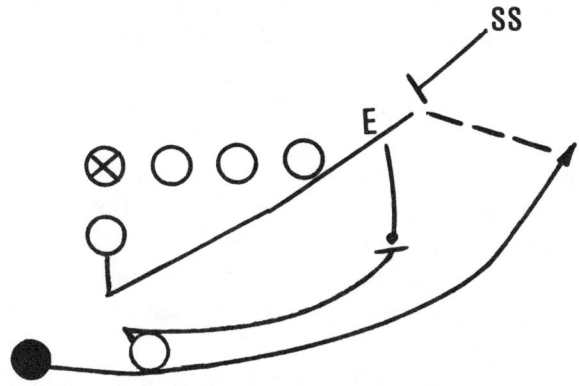

**DIAGRAM 7-9
Optioning Cross-Charge Action**

the inside pursuit. A sharp north-south cut might put the quarterback into the thick of such inside out pursuit. Of course, running to daylight is still a major consideration in such action.

It is important on all such downhill attack of the keep-pitch key defender that the quarterback thinks pitch first and keep second. The pitchback is the player you want to carry the ball just as the diveback was on the dive-keep option. The purpose of the keep-pitch option action is to attack downhill to force the keep-pitch key defender to commit to the quarterback so that the pitch can be executed. A keep by the quarterback is simply a reaction to the play of the keep-pitch key defender. Such an emphasis must be the concern of the option action.

## INSIDE VEER OPTION ACTION

The inside veer dive action, whether to a halfback or a fullback, has already been well discussed in this chapter. The only point that needs further mentioning is the initial redirection step of the quarterback down the line of scrimmage. If the fourth step of the dive mesh action is a feather step, the quarterback simply hangs the inside leg and foot in the air long enough for the diveback to pass him and whips the inside foot out on the desired 30 degree angle downhill course.

If the fourth step is a plant step into the line of scrimmage to help facilitate the dive action, the back foot initiates the 30 degree angle downhill course. In both cases, as soon as the quarterback begins to pull the ball from the dive fake action he must immediately switch his eyes to the keep-pitch key defender to pick up any possible crash charge. In addition, the quarterback must pull the ball up to his sternum immediately so that he is ready for immediate pitch situations.

## LEAD OPTION ACTION

The quarterback's initial action to get into the desired 30 degree angle downhill attack course is a three step action with the first two steps helping to get the quarterback away from the center to help create the downhill angle. In addition, the first two delay type steps help to freeze the linebackers while giving the pitchback time to get into a proper pitch relationship.

The quarterback's first two steps are straight back. The first step is taken with the foot to the side of the option action. The second step with the foot away from the option action is a plant type step from which the quarterback pivots and pushes off to take his 30 degree angle downhill third step with the foot to the side of the option action. The second step is slightly deeper than the first step.

The first two steps, again straight back, must not show any direction via turn of the body towards the option side. The premise of such an action is to attempt to freeze the linebackers in position by not giving any direction until the third step. The stepping action for the Lead Option is seen in Diagram 7-10.

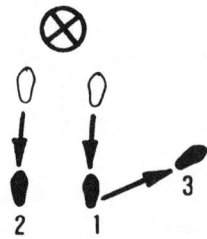

**DIAGRAM 7-10**
**Lead Option Quarterback Steps**

## COUNTER OPTION ACTION

The counter option stepping action by the quarterback was already discussed in both Chapter 4 and this chapter. The points that need further emphasis are that the quarterback must snap his head to the keep-pitch key on his third redirection step back to the counter dive back to read the possible crash type charge of the defender. (If there is triple option counter option action, this would, of course, take place after the dive read.) The fifth redirection step on the desired 30 degree angle downhill attack course with the back foot after the counter dive fake action is, again, a key coaching point. There must be no bellying action off the desired downhill course. It must be a sharp, 30 degree angle downhill attack step. As on all other option action, the quarterback must be sure to bring the ball to his sternum as soon as he comes out of his counter dive action stepping.

## TRAP OPTION ACTION

The quarterback's initial action to get into the desired 30 degree angle downhill attack course is a three step action with the first step facilitating the dive fake. The first step is taken with the foot away from the option action. It is a deep 135 degree plus step if the fake is to a halfback and a 180 degree plus step if the fake is to a fullback. The ball is extended out towards the diveback's pouch but it is never placed

Split backfield trap option steps     "I" formation trap option steps

**DIAGRAM 7-11**
**Trap Option QB Steps**

in the pouch. The second step is a crossover type step which continues on the same plane as the first step. However, it goes beyond the first step by approximately 18 inches. Actually, this plant step turns the toes slightly in the direction of the crossover to facilitate the pushing off action for the third 30 degree angle downhill step.

It is important that the quarterback snaps his head around fast as the second step is planted to enable the read of a possible crash charge by the keep-pitch key defender. Also, the ball must be immediately brought back to the sternum on the second step to help facilitate a possible immediate pitch action. Such action is shown in Diagram 7-11 from both split back and "I" formation alignments.

### OUTSIDE VEER OPTION ACTION

The outside veer option action takes on a different execution technique due to the wider mesh with the diveback (landmark being one hole wider) and the different angle of attack of the keep-pitch key defender. The outside veer, it must be remembered, double team blocks the normal dive key and forces the normal keep-pitch key to become the dive key and the normal contain defender to become the keep-pitch key. This is seen in Diagram 7-12 from a split-back alignment. The design of the play is actually premised on forcing defenders to take on option assignments they are not used to executing.

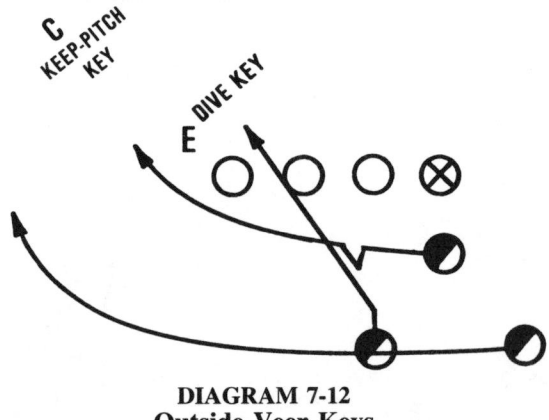

DIAGRAM 7-12
Outside-Veer Keys

Due to the wider mesh point with the diveback, most quarterbacks find it quite difficult to utilize the feather technique of the inside foot on the fourth step. Another reason it is difficult to use a feather type fourth step is that the keep-pitch key attack action is not the typical 30 degree angle downhill attack. Instead, it is a bouncing around type

## Coaching the Backfield Option Game

action in an effort to jump around the collision of the diveback and the dive key defender in an effort to attack upfield at the keep-pitch key defender.

The fourth step is, therefore, a slight adjustment type step into the line of scrimmage to accommodate the dive mesh action. The fifth step is a "jump-around" type step which attempts to put the quarterback on a course which actually "jumps around" the collision point of the diveback and dive key. The important execution point is that the quarterback tries to have the foot of the fifth jump-around step no more than parallel to the line of scrimmage to help facilitate a north-south pushing off action to attack the keep-pitch key defender. The key to the entire action is to get around the collision of the diveback and the dive key defender as quickly and as tightly as possible. The more the stepping action away from the line of scrimmage to get around the collision, the slower will be the north-south attack of the quarterback resulting in a greater chance for the interior defenders to pursue the quarterback. The stepping action is seen in Diagram 7-13.

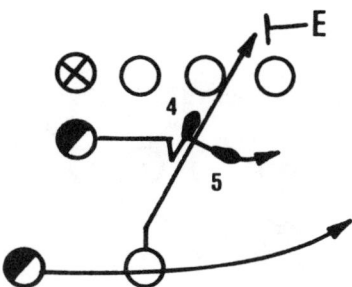

**DIAGRAM 7-13**
**Outside Veer QB Keep Steps**

Once the quarterback bounces around the collision point, he attacks north-south and options the keep-pitch key defender in the same fashion as he would option a perimeter-type defender who is attacking on a cross-charge type action versus an inside veer keep-pitch action by the quarterback.

### QUARTERBACK-PITCHBACK PITCH RATIO

The quarterback-pitchback ratio is always the responsibility of the pitchback. Whatever the ratio may be (3½ yards by 3½ yards, 4 yards by 4 yards, etc.) the pitchback must be sure that the relationship of him and the quarterback is identical for all option plays. The timings may be different, but the relationship of the quarterback and pitchback cannot be different.

What the pitchback must realize is that no matter what the quarterback does (or is forced to do), it is the pitchback's responsibility to maintain the pitch ratio. If the quarterback slows down, is forced to bounce around the block of a penetrating defender, elongates his attack of a feathering keep-pitch key defender, bounces off a collision of blockers and defenders, the pitchback must be in the exact spot of the desired pitch ratio. Even if the quarterback action is incorrect, the pitch ratio must be maintained so that a pitch can be executed.

Once the quarterback cuts upfield, the pitchback must continue to trail the quarterback wherever he goes for a possible upfield pitch. The ratio, however, changes. The same width distance is maintained; however, the pitchback trails the quarterback by a yard to a yard-and-a-half. This action is seen in Diagram 7-14 from inside veer option action.

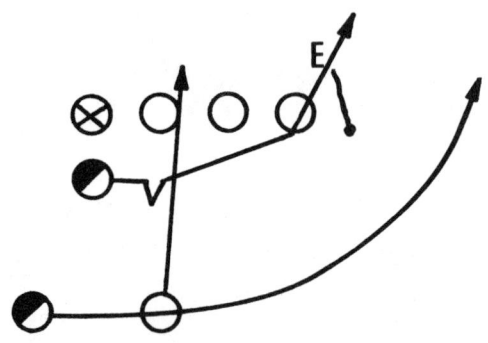

**DIAGRAM 7-14**
**Upfield Pitch Ratio**

An important point for all keep-pitch key option action is that the quarterback must come out of the dive fake (if there is one) and accelerate at top speed. A major fault of many quarterbacks is a slow acceleration either out of the dive fake or just down the line of scrimmage as on lead option action. A slow acceleration simply buys time for the defense to pursue to the option action and give support to defending both the keep and pitch possibilities.

## BACKFIELD OPTION PRACTICE AND DRILLS

It is the belief of the author that there is only one correct way to practice option skills—set up a game-like enactment of an option play or a part of an option play versus varied defenses and their varied styles of defensing options. Other than the practice of pure pitch skill work and the reception of the pitch skill work, such game-like drill work helps to develop the skills necessary to execute the option game on the field. Some pure pitch drills were already shown in Chapter 5, therefore, only one such drill will be shown here.

### Drill#1: Down-the-Line Pitch

The Down-the-Line Pitch Drill is a pure quarterback pitch skill drill which helps to develop proper pitching action. The drill is set up by having two quarterbacks work down two 5 yard lines (actually, their distance apart should coincide with the pitch ratio). One quarterback holds the ball on his sternum ready to pitch the ball, and jogs in place. The other quarterback runs out away from him down his yard line marker to create a proper pitch option ratio. Once the proper pitch-option ratio is created, the quarterback with the ball takes off down his yard marker and executes his normal pitch execution to the quarterback out in front of him.

Once the quarterback receives the pitch, he jogs in place till the other quarterback can run ahead to create a new pitch ratio for him to pitch to. This action is repeated all the way across the field. The drill is shown in Diagram 7-15.

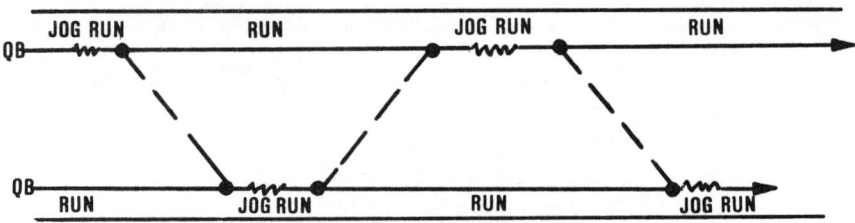

**DIAGRAM 7-15**
**Down-the-Line Pitch Drill**

*Coaching Points:* The quarterbacks must be sure to turn around and come back the way they came so that the quarterbacks practice pitching left-handed and right-handed.

## Drill #2: Rapid Fire Option Pitch

The Rapid Fire Option Pitch Drill allows for the practice of maximum amount of pitch-keep key reads and reactions and option pitches. Two quarterbacks work back and forth on a tape versus a simulated defensive end carry out normal option actions. After each repetition, the quarterbacks switch roles as quarterback and pitchback. After two repetitions, the quarterbacks retrace the first two repetitions to practice the option action both left and right. The drill is shown in Diagram 7-16.

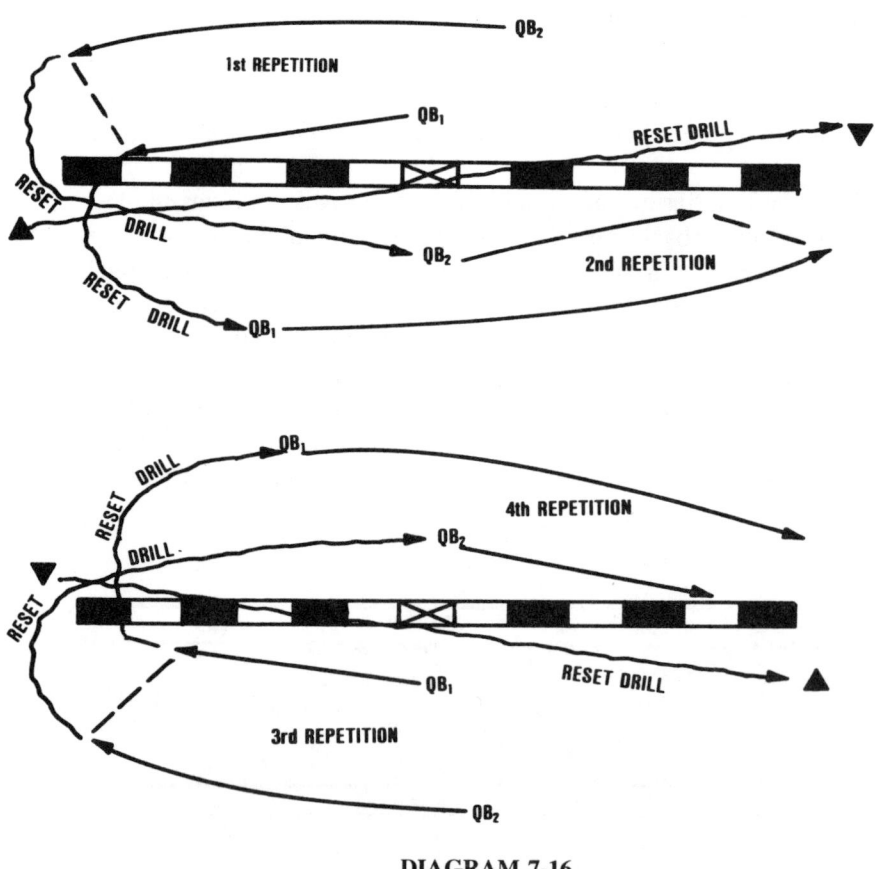

DIAGRAM 7-16
Rapid Fire Option Pitch Drill

*Coaching Points:* The player simulating the defensive end varies his defensive option play on each repetition. The defender can sit, penetrate, crash, feather lightly, feather heavily, etc. The coach can jump in occasionally (or a second defender can be used) to create cross-charge situations. Thus, the coach is checking all of the proper quarterback reactions to the defensive play (keep or pitch) plus proper pitching action.

### Drill #3: Dive Read

The Dive Read Drill is nothing more than a breakdown of triple option action to practice the dive read portion of it. The drill can be run anywhere from live to a thud type of action utilizing hand bags or shields. The defender is given signals as to what type of defensive reaction to make. Diagram 7-17 shows the Dive Read Drill practicing an inside veer dive read to a Wishbone or "I" formation fullback and an outside veer dive read to a split back formation halfback.

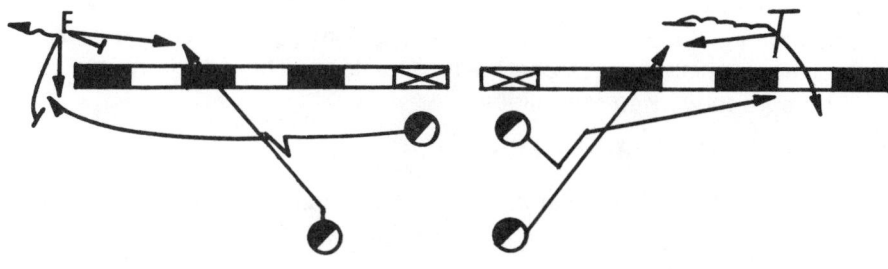

Outside veer dive read action      Inside veer dive read action

DIAGRAM 7-17
The Dive Read Drill

*Coaching Points:* The coach must be sure to vary the actions of the defender. All mesh skills, landmark running, reading action, hand-off skills, acceleration from the mesh by the quarterback, faking action, etc., is checked by the coach. The coach must be sure to work the reading action to both sides.

### Drill #4: Triple Option Read

The Triple Option Read Drill carries the Dive Read Drill one step further. A second and third defender are added to the drill. The quarterback and backs now carry out their normal triple option action versus the defensive alignment shown and the reactions given by the defenders after the snap of the ball. The inside veer triple option action from a split backfield set is used for example in Diagram 7-18.

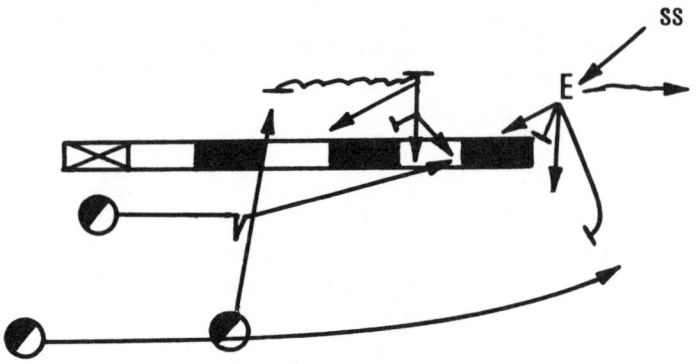

DIAGRAM 7-18
The Triple Option Drill

*Coaching Points:* The coach must be sure to vary the defensive alignments and the defensive reactions. The third defender can be utilized to give occasional cross-charge type actions. The coach must, again, be sure to work to both sides.

### Drill #5: Individual Option

The Individual Option Drill is a drill that is identical to the Triple Option Drill except that it practices the option plays that only have a double option potential (lead option, counter option, trap option or predetermined inside veer option and outside veer option). Thus, a dive key defender is not utilized since the quarterback is only optioning a keep-pitch key defender and a possible linebacker or strong safety/cornerback type on some type of cross-charge action. Diagram 7-19 shows the drill with trap option action used as the example.

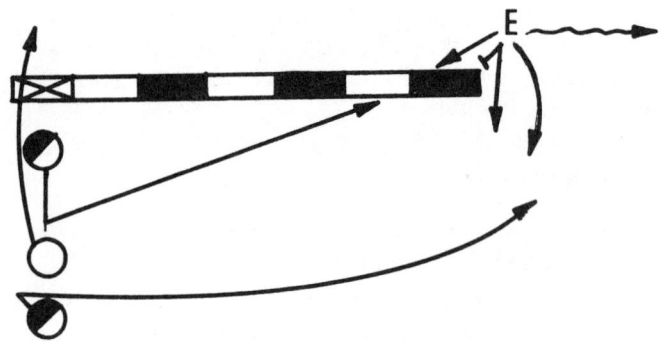

DIAGRAM 7-19
The Individual Option Drill

Coaching the Backfield Option Game  141

### Drill #6: Multi-Option

The Multi-Option Drill is an excellent option drill that helps to get maximum repetitions of the option plays. It actually combines all of the actions of the Dive Read Drill, the Triple Option Drill, and the Individual Option Drill into one game-like type drill. As in the other drills, it can be simply executed on defenders utilizing a noncontact action with, perhaps, hand bags or shields. Or, it can be run live or semi-live.

Two tapes, or hoses, are set up with the center's "X" on the hash mark. A skeleton defense is set up utilizing those defenders needed to make all the necessary reads. Two offensive backfields are used to get maximum repetitions so as not to waste any time. The first repetition is started on the left tape and is an option play run into the sideline. All of the desired backfield option skills are checked. As the first backfield is finishing the play's execution, the second backfield is ready to go, and repeats the same play. As the second backfield is finishing its execution, the first backfield sets up to execute an option play to the right into the open field. When they finish, they set upon the tape on the right hash mark as the second backfield repeats the same play. When the second backfield finishes, they hustle behind the first backfield as the first backfield readies to start the whole process over again. After the first four repetitions from the left hash mark, the defenders switch to the tape on the right hash mark. Thus, four option plays are run from the left hash mark—two into the sideline and two into the wide side of the field—and four option plays are run from the right hash mark—two into the sideline and two to the wide side of the field. The plays are run in rapid fire action to ensure maximum repetitions, one backfield beginning as soon as the other finishes.

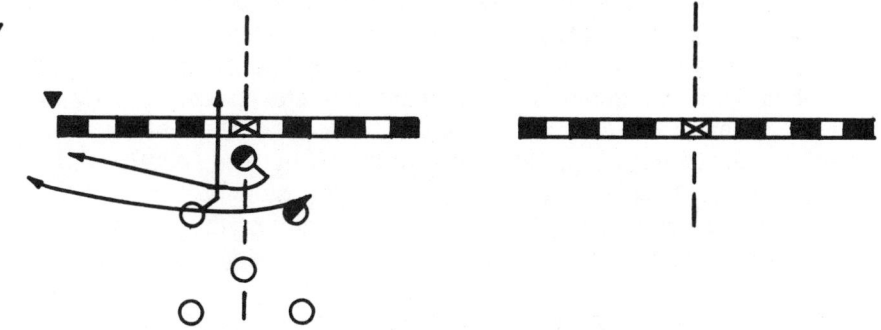

**DIAGRAM 7-20**
**The Multiple Option Drill in Its Simplest Form**

The drill can be set up simply with the practice of only double option plays against two service defenders as shown in Diagram 7-20. Or, the drill can be as complex as that shown in Diagram 7-21 in which the defense brings over all of their people who are involved in the optioning action as the offense adds its tight ends to stalk block or seal inside on linebackers. The counter option is used for example.

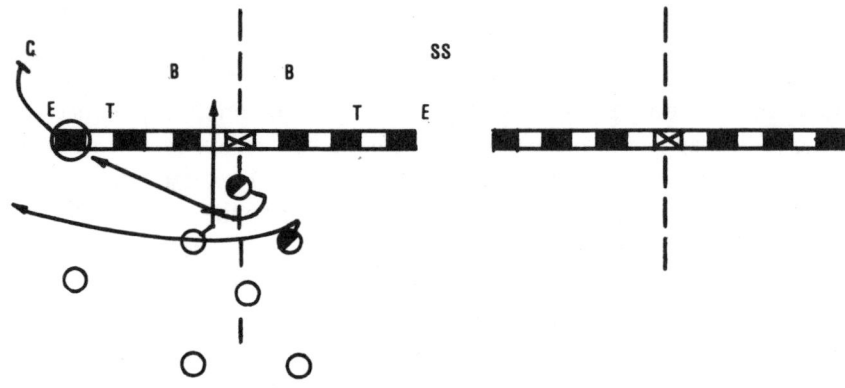

DIAGRAM 7-21
The Multiple Option Drill in Its Most Complex Form
vs. a Skeleton Defense and Utilizing Tight Ends

*Coaching Points:* It is important that if a defender is not blocked by the skeleton offensive unit, he does not interfere with the execution of the option action. In the Multi-Option Drill it is good to have a second coach to help expedite the action of the defense. In addition, the drill must also be practiced with the tapes placed halfway between the hash marks and the center of the field as well as from the center of the field using only one tape. In this fashion, the option plays are practiced in game-like situations from the various positions that the ball could be placed on the field. Thus, the important dimensions of lateral space, sidelines and field bevelment are added to the drill. The concern for field bevelment itself is an aspect of option play grossly overlooked. A pitchback is definitely faster going downhill towards the sideline just as he is markedly slower going uphill towards the center of the field when an option play starts from a hashmark. Such varied pitchback speed must definitely be taken into account due to the extreme need for split-second timing and exacting quarterback/pitchback ratios on all option plays. (This if course, does not apply to a flat, non-beveled field.)

**Drill #7: Perimeter Option**

The Perimeter Option Drill simply combines the backfield option action with the receiver blocking actions. The drill helps players practice the timing of the backfield option action with the perimeter blocks, and helps coordinate possible switching of blocking assignments of lead backs and wide receivers or inside receivers such as on cross-blocking assignments. All of the option plays used in the offense are practiced to both sides. Enough defenders are used to help create all the necessary option reads as well as to provide perimeter defenders for the perimeter blocking actions. The drill is shown in Diagram 7-22 using a lead option play with a cross-blocking scheme as the example.

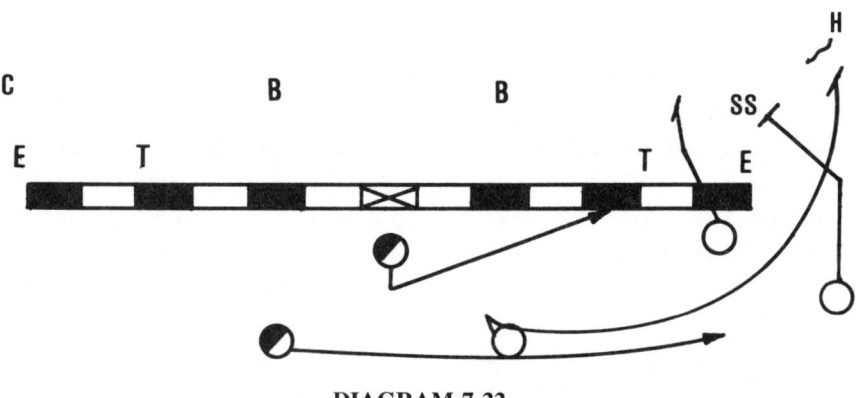

**DIAGRAM 7-22**
**The Perimeter Option Drill**

# eight

# Coaching the Quarterback Passing Techniques

Just as with the truly great runner, the truly great passer is more the exception than the rule. More often than not, the coach is faced with coaching the sub-super passer. Much of passing, however, is technique—and technique can be taught. Far too often a team does not pass because it does not have a good passer. Far too often the reason the team does not have a good passer is that he is not coached properly. Just because a quarterback is not a natural passer does not mean he cannot learn to become a good passer. Sound passing techniques can be taught, coached, practiced and drilled. As in the execution of the skills of any other position, sound passing skills can also be developed if given proper coaching attention.

An extremely important point to remember when coaching a passer is that no two individuals throw in exactly the same fashion. It is not the role of the coach to impose strict fundamental rules on how to pass on a quarterback. Instead, it is the role of the coach to help an individual perform to the best of his ability. Kinesiological differences cause some to throw differently than others. The coach must help the quarterbacks to get the most out of their particular styles. Just as there is a great variety of baseball pitching styles, there can be a similar variety of football passing styles. A quarterback may be an excellent sidearm passer. Sidearm passing is not the desired "textbook" style. However, if sidearm is the only way a particular quarterback can get the job done and via that technique he does it well—why change that style?

*Coaching the Quarterback Passing Techniques* 145

## GRIPPING THE FOOTBALL

The quarterback assumes a firm, comfortable grip in which the ball is gripped by the fingers, the thumb and the heel of the hand. The ball must not be palmed as this, as well as the index finger being too far from the end of the ball, is the major reason for a hard, nose-down ball which is hard to catch. Making sure that there is daylight between the palm and the ball, as well as making sure the index finger is extended towards the rear of the ball, helps to get the nose of the ball up producing a softer, easier-to-catch pass.

The actual grip of the ball may vary. A small-handed quarterback will usually grip the ball more towards the end. A bigger-handed quarterback will grip the ball more towards the middle. Wherever it is gripped, the fingers must be well spread as this will aid the control of the ball and help to produce a spiral-type pass. Generally, the bottom three fingers are placed across the laces as the index fingers extend up towards the end of the ball and the thumb naturally wraps around the ball in the opposite direction to produce the firm, comfortable grip. The proper gripping technique is shown in Figure 8-1.

**FIGURE 8-1**
**Proper Grip of Ball for Passing**

## SETTING-UP

Setting-up requires movement to the launch point, stopping such movement and assuming the cocked position so that a quick-release delivery can be executed. Setting-up in this discussion will refer to the movement of the quarterback away from the line of scrimmage to a fixed point which is usually inside the tackle-to-tackle area from which he will launch (throw) his pass. Thus, the quarterback will be in a fixed (set) position and not moving. Throwing on the move (i.e.—sprint pass action) will be discussed separately. Such drop back movement away from the line of scrimmage can take the form of straight drop back action (whether back pedal, sprint back, or a combination of back pedal and sprint back), quarter roll, half roll, throw back or one of the many play action type set-ups. Since there can be such a great variety in such drop back set-up actions and since such actions can vary greatly as to the philosophy of the set-up technique (i.e.—selling sprint action influence to set-up the throwback pass, dump passing to hot receivers, etc.), only the key points of the drop back movement to the launch point will be discussed—depth and speed of the drop back action, the throttling down and stopping of such movement and the assuming of the cocked throwing position.

Whether the drop back action is a seven step straight drop back set-up to throw to a curl pattern or a fake isolation play action pass, depth and speed at getting to the required depth are of extreme importance. Actually, depth of the set-up and speed in getting to the launch point go hand in hand. The faster a quarterback can set-up at his launch point, the less protection he will need from his blockers since he will allow himself more time to read the defense and/or the receiver and get the pass off. The same concept is seen in the depth of set-up in a given number of steps. If on a five step straight drop back pocket set-up one quarterback is a yard-and-a-half deeper than another, he will not need the amount of protection that the other will and, as a result, will have more time to view both the defense and the receivers.

Vision is a key on all set-up actions. Such viewing of the defense will help the quarterback to unload the ball if he is faced with an overloaded blitz problem from the linebackers or secondary defenders, or to move away from rushers if his protection breaks down. Certain types of drop back set-ups offer the quarterback greater vision than others. However, no matter what set-up technique is used, vision is aided by a quick and deep set-up which gives the quarterback more time for such viewing.

Whatever the drop back movement to set-up is, the last two steps take on the same techniques. The next to the last step is a throttle-down step and the last is a plant, or stop step. The throttle step shifts much of the backward momentum weight of the body back towards the line of scrimmage as the weight of the body begins shifting over the next to the last throttle step. Such throttle-down action helps to bring the body under enough control so that the last step can act as a break to stop the backward movement to set-up. The next to last step is also utilized heavily as the pivot step on certain actions to wheel around the plant step for the desired positioning of the body on the set-up.

The final plant, or stop step must put the quarterback in the cocked position ready to deliver the pass. The bulk of the body weight is on the back foot ready to be transferred to the front foot during the delivery action. Both knees are bent slightly to help accommodate the necessary delivery movement. Placing all the weight on the balls of the feet and not on the heels also helps the delivery movement as well as the balance of the body in the cocked position.

The ball is held in a gathered position in front of the rear breast so that the ball has a minimum distance to go backwards for the delivery motion. The term gathered in this sense refers to the gathering of all the body parts in a ready position to begin the transfer of body weight from the back to the front foot and begin the delivery of the ball action. The ball should, however, not be held so closely to the body that it restricts the delivery motion of the arm in any way. The free hand is placed on the ball during the set-up action to help provide ball security in case the quarterback is blind-side tackled. The back shoulder of the set-up must be cocked. By cocked, it is meant that the shoulder should have no further backwards to go to execute the delivery of the ball.

## THE DELIVERY OF THE BALL

The delivery of the ball is where most poor passers have their problems. Actually, it should be the part of passing which can aid good passing even if the quarterback does not have the strongest of arms. Many quarterbacks are deemed weak armed when actually the problem is lack of transferral of weight from the back to the front foot to help put body momentum and thrust behind the throwing action of the arm. Such quarterbacks sit back on their back foot and simply "wing" the ball with a whipping action of the arm only. Such action produces a passing action that is like "throwing a grenade"—too much trajectory and too little power. The transferring of weight is best seen in the action of a baseball pitcher. When a pitcher winds up, all weight is on the back foot, and the leg is kicked up in the air. It is then swung down and forward toward the delivery spot helping to propel the front hip in the same direction. All this action helps to whip the upper torso towards the delivery spot—trunk, chest, shoulder then arm. The weight of the body is transferred from the back foot to the front foot in a psychomotor pattern which helps to add thrust to the delivery of the ball.

Throwing a football takes on this same movement pattern in an effort to transfer the weight of the body from the back foot to the front foot to help propel the ball towards the intended target. The quarterback pushes off the back foot as he steps toward the intended delivery spot. Such a target is not necessarily at the receiver but to the point where the flight of the ball will intersect the path of the receiver's route. The quarterback must actually attempt to point his toes at delivery spot to help direct the total body motion to that spot. As the forward stepping action takes place, the hips swing around on the same plane and help to whip the upper torso and eventually the arm action in the same direction. Balance of the body is actually regained from the transferral of weight from the back foot to the front foot once the front foot is placed on the ground. The action of the hips (amount of opening towards the target spot) is actually determined by the forward step of the quarterback. A pointing of the toes beyond the target spot may be the result of an over-opening of the hips and probable causing of the ball to be thrown beyond the receiver. A pointing of the toes behind the target spot may be the result of an under-opening, or close hips and the probable result of the quarterback throwing behind the receiver.

The actual arm throwing action takes on the motion of a catcher's peg to second base or the throwing of darts. The optimal situation is a direct overhand throw. However, most quarterbacks find that they are more comfortable with a plane that is substantially less than directly overhead. Again, individual style must be accommodated to help the indiviual produce his most efficient means of throwing. Whatever the amount of angle off the direct overhand throw, the ball must be released as high as possible to aid in the fullest range of motion of the arm that is possible as well as being able to throw over the raised hands of the pass rushers.

The throwing action of the arm is actually one continuous coordinated motion made up of two parts. The heel of the free hand helps to push the ball up, back and away from the hold position so that the ball is cocked in the approximate area of off the back shoulder and yet still slightly in front of the front of the body. The elbow is drawn back so that the upper arm is approximately parallel to the ground. The bend or extension of the arm in the cock position depends on what is comfortable to the individual. The position of the ball, position of the upper arm in relation to the ground and the bend or extension of the elbow can only be spoken of in approximate terms due to the variation that occurs for the varied distances that the ball must be thrown, as well as the varying trajectories that must accommodate the ball's flights. The degree of push of the free hand is also in relation to both the distance and trajectory of the pass with a heavier push for a greater cock. In comparison to a baseball pitcher's throw, however, the elbow is slightly in front of the ball in the cock position.

The forward motion of the ball delivery begins with the free hand and arm. They are extended out towards the target spot to lead the chest. Such action also helps to maintain body balance. Sticking out, or leading with the chest helps put maximum upper torso thrust into the delivery. Of course, all of this upper body action is in a continuous movement coordinated with the stepping out action and whipping hip action. It is important that the wrist is kept firm and straight during the delivery to help avoid a wobbly pass. The wrist is never turned to attempt to produce a spin action on the ball. The natural action of a straight wrist delivery will help produce the desired spiral spin. The actual release of the ball is a screwball delivery type of action in which the thumb is pronated down to the ground so that the palm is facing down to the ground also. The ball is snapped off with a snapping action of the wrist and a full extension, or lock of the elbow to help put extra snap or zip into the release. The ball should leave the index finger last, not the ring finger.

The action to the cock position and the action of the forward release of the ball are, again, executed in one continuous motion—as if throwing a dart but in more of a circular or rounded fashion. Speed of delivery for the desired quick release is not just in relation to the quarterback's ability to move the ball forward from the cock position to the release. Far more often, a slow release is the result of a winding up action to get the ball to the cock position. Holding the ball too low, too close to the body or too close to the midline of the body instead of in front of the rear breast, not having the back shoulder fully cocked requiring further movement in drawing the shoulder backwards—all of these actions slow down the total delivery action of the ball, producing a slow release.

Another related value of the stepping forward action is that the quarterback steps up into the pocket of his protection. Most pass blocking effort is designed to ride the rushers out away from the launch point. Stepping up action helps the quarterback to move up inside of the pushing out and around action of the blockers.

There is quite often extra time that the quarterback has in his set-up before he executes the delivery of the ball. The time might well be spent in reading the coverage and receiver action. There are other situations when a timed deep pass just needs a slight delay to allow the receiver to get into the proper position to receive the pass. Watching of such a receiver by the quarterback as he works to get free might only tip off the action and provide the secondary with a key to read. Looking the defense off is a good technique to provide false influence for the defense. By looking with his eyes at a different target or receiver, the defense will often be forced to flow to, or at least honor, the look-off threat. The arm pump fake is also an excellent false influence action. The quarterback must be properly set when attempting such action. The free hand is used to stop the fake throw and help the quarterback regrip and recock the ball.

## FOLLOW-THROUGH

A key to effective passing is proper follow-through. The most common error in passing is a lack of follow-through. Pointing with the index finger as the ball releases it is the most influencing feature of follow-through. A good coaching point is that where the index finger points as the ball is released is where the ball will go. Of course, there are many other factors involved in proper passing action. However, such follow-through emphasis greatly helps to increase the degree of success of the passing action. The hand and index finger are not, however, suspended in air in a pointing fashion. The pointing action is combined with the release. The hand and arm must continue its follow-through action across the body and down to the ground as the hand is pronated palms down.

A full extension, or lock, of the elbow is another key to proper follow-through. Such full extension of the elbow or lock action helps to produce a full range of the arm movement. Opposite such full range of the arm is the arm action in which the ball is released before the arm is fully extended and the hand is frozen at the release point rather than following through naturally. Such action is quite common when the quarterback is required to throw a soft pass. Full follow-through action, as on any pass, must be carried out. Force can be taken off the upper body and arm thrust. However, proper arm and hand follow-through must be executed to insure the proper flight of the ball.

## PASSING TRAJECTORY

Varying the distance of a pass is not the difficult part of passing. Varying the trajectory of a pass, however, is. There are many quarterbacks who can hit a target all over the field with a direct line pass. Ask the same quarterbacks to hit the same target with greater loft on the ball and they are lost. Passing with varied trajectory is difficult. However, as with all passing, it is simply a matter of executing proper techniques and receiving a proper amount of coaching and practice emphasis.

To get greater trajectory on a pass is simply a matter of adjusting the horizontal plane of the shoulders, front arm and hand, and rear passing arm. The greater the height and/or distance that is needed, the greater the tilt of this horizontal plane so that the rear throwing shoulder is dropped as well as the throwing elbow and resulting cock of the ball. Conversely, the front shoulder is held higher, as the free arm and hand reach out higher as they are extended to begin the throwing motion. The key, however, is the throwing elbow since its position will directly correlate to the forward throwing motion of the ball. The release will be higher and earlier. As a result, the wrist action will be slightly more extreme in its bend as the ball is brought forward to the release point. A straight wrist release, index finger pointing, a thumbs down pronation of the hand, and proper follow-through of the throwing hand and arm are still carried out.

The greatest problem the passers have in trajectory passing is executing a floating type of ball with the nose up that seems to hang in the air at its zenith and then die (lose its forward thrust and fall quickly) with the nose of the ball remaining up as it descends. Such a pass throws the receiver off as it will usually be underthrown. The key to preventing such a "floater" is, again, proper follow-through. The key is making sure that the index finger is pointing at a fixed point in the air that the ball must pass through at its zenith to get the desired trajectory. By throwing through at such a fixed point with all the proper follow-through action, the ball will fall nose down with proper trajectory and distance.

## PASSING ON THE MOVE

Move-out passing in this text will refer to the action of passing on the run. Such passing action is typical on such passing actions as sprint-out, roll-out and bootleg passing. (Actually, on any of these actions, the quarterback could move to a fixed launch point, stop, set-up and execute the throwing action that has already been discussed. For this reason, move-out passing will be limited to passing while moving.)

The major concept of move-out passing is that the upper torso body action must be divorced from the run action of the legs. The action of the chest, shoulders, and arms should be the same on move-out passing as on any other passing action. Of course, this would be the optimal move-out passing execution which is often difficult to achieve under game conditions. However, it is what is strived for in execution and practice. The goal is that from the chest up, all throws should look and be the same.

Move-out action is usually premised with the threatening of the corner by the quarterback by getting outside of the defensive contain so that the defense is faced with an added threat in its efforts to defend the play—the run threat of the quarterback. Once the quarterback starts his move-out action (this may be right away on a sprint-out or roll-out action or delayed on some type of bootleg pass action), he must accelerate to the outside as fast as possible to break the containment, threaten the secondary with his run threat and get away from interior pursuit. A major fault of such move-out passing is that the quarterback starts cocking the ball too soon which, in turn, enables the defense to pressure him from the inside as the secondary can play more of a cat-and-mouse game since his corner pressure is not as great. Thus, the quarterback's first three to four steps (depending on the pattern used and, of course, more steps on bootleg action if the quarterback's initial movement is away from the launch point) are taken at top speed with the carry of the ball in front of the sternum held in a position that will best accommodate the run action.

On the third or fourth step the ball is cocked in a ready position for the throw. Such a cocking action is no different than the holding of the ball in the set-up position with the slight exception of the ball being held slightly higher and with the elbows out away from the body slightly to help accommodate the running action. The passing shoulder is, therefore, cocked—a position in which it will not have to be moved back any further once the throwing action begins. The strain of the cocking action is placed on the twisted stomach area as the chest is faced to the pass target. Sticking the chest out to the pass target helps to gather the entire upper throwing action as well as put proper upper body lean into the forward arm delivery of the ball.

The upper torso of the body must be ready to execute the move-out pass without the aid of the legs and feet. What is hoped for, however, is that the quarterback will be able to gather his feet to help adjust his body direction to at least open up his hips to the target. Opening (facing) the hips to the target point will all the more aid the upper torso throwing action.

Follow-through is, again, a definite key to move-out throwing.

There is a common tendency for the quarterback to not fully extend his elbow in a locking fashion since such action is awkward to execute in relation to run action of the legs. This is especially true when the move-out action is to the side of the throwing arm, and when the quarterback is moving opposite his throwing arm and has to pass towards the inside rather than out towards the flank where his run action is threatening. Such an inside throw when running away from the throwing arm side often requires a side-armed spinning type of throw in which the hand is supinated with the thumb turning outward as the palm turns upward. Whatever the technique used, proper follow-through by pointing the index finger and locking or fully extending the elbow is paramount to the success of move-out passing.

## HALFBACK OPTION PASSING

The throwing action for a running back on some type of run-pass option is no different than a quarterback's passing action in the move-out game. The back must learn to disengage the throwing action of his upper torso from the run action of the legs and execute the pass in the same fashion as a quarterback would if he were sprinting or rolling out. Since the halfback option pass is for the most part more of a supplemental play action pass rather than a bread and butter play of the offense, the coach usually finds it difficult to spend an extra amount of time for its practice. For this reason, the coach is probably far better off to find the one or two running backs who can throw effectively and concentrate on having them work on the halfback option pass techniques. Spending an inordinate amount of practice time on backs who throw poorly and will, as a result, probably not be used to execute the skill in a game is a definite waste of precious practice time. The coach must also be concerned with the back's ability to get the ball to the desired target spot rather than the technique used to get it there. Whatever the passing technique used (from directly overhead to sidearm), the coach must simply work to improve the back's effective delivery style. The greatest aid to such back passing is to concentrate on the back's follow-through techniques—usually the weakest area of the back's passing action. The key factors are making sure that the back points with the index finger at the target spot on the release of the ball and that the full extension of his elbow is in a locked position.

Threatening the corner with a run threat outside the defensive contain is also paramount to the success of the halfback option pass concept. Just like the sprint-out quarterback who shows pass too soon and does not effectively attack the corner, the back who throttles down too early to set up for the pass invites interior rush pressure as well as helps the secondary defenders to play a cat-and-mouse game by neither committing fully to the pass nor to the run threats. The running back must be sure to sprint to the corner to sell the run action and not show any pass action until the back has broken the defenses' contain. An effective technique that can be utilized is to have the back take his normal north-south end run course and then flatten out to create the run-pass option threat. Such action is shown in Diagram 8-1.

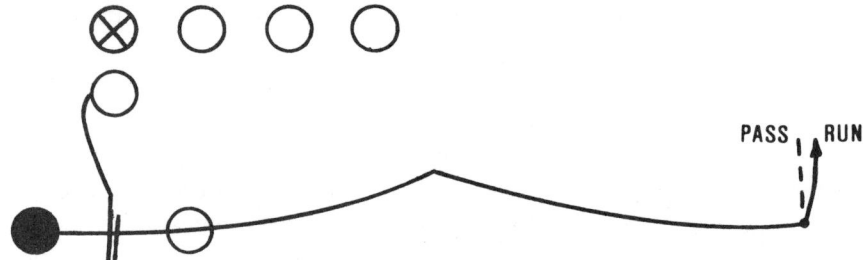

**DIAGRAM 8-1**
**North-South End Run Course with Flattening Action**
**to Accommodate Halfback Option Pass**

## QUARTERBACK PASSING TECHNIQUES PRACTICE AND DRILLS

The practicing of a quarterback's passing techniques is not a difficult task to work on and encourage. Encouraging a quarterback to work on his passing techniques is about as difficult as encouraging a baseball player to take extra turns in the batting cage. Passing is what quarterbacks like to do best (with the possible exception of optioning). What is so fascinating about working on passing skills is that a quarterback can work on these skills all year long with little need for practice facilities. A football and an indoor area during the cold weather is about it. A quarterback can actually even work by himself if he has a number of footballs and a target as simple as a suspended tire or some type of passing canvas. A minimal amount of area can allow all of a quarterback's drop back or move-out actions.

Finding a person to throw to is also easy. What receivers like to do more than anything else is catch the ball. Backs rarely balk at working on their route running and pass catching skills. The quarterback is, therefore, afforded year-round opportunities to develop his passing skills. Such work is much desired as passing practice must take on the characteristics of quantity as well as quality. Quantity of quality helps to develop the strength of the throwing arm, set-up techniques, ball delivery action, following through and trajectory passing as well as timing with the routes of the receivers.

Drills for the passing skills must, again, be as game-like as possible. The practice of the move-out passing game should have the quarterbacks throwing to their receivers as they execute the routes that are part of the offense. If the design of the pattern is to have the quarterback throw the ball on a timing coordinated with a flanker's ten step out cut, then that is the action that should be practiced when the quarterback practices his move-out passing action. If the design of the pattern involves the reading of the receiver's cut or the reading of the secondary's movements, then such defensive situations must confront the quarterback and the receivers in the drills used. It is senseless to simply throw twenty-five passes to a receiver breaking on a post pattern without any defenders if the actual play action of the pattern calls for a hook-up option by the receiver depending on the secondary movement and play. If the concept of the post pattern is a timed five step drop by the quarterback, step-up and throw as long as the defender does not have deep position on the receiver, then that is how the practice of throwing to a post route should be executed. Working with a center whenever possible also helps to coordinate the entire action associated with all the passing actions as well as helping provide further practice work on the important center-quarterback exchange.

### Drill #1: Warm-Up

The Warm-Up Drill is one of the most important drills to utilize each day. Actually warming up can take place by slowly throwing a ball back and forth between two quarterbacks for an extended period of time. Quarterbacks cannot warm their arm up enough. Usually, they are not provided enough time to do so. The quarterbacks must get to the practice field as early as possible so they are afforded extra warm-up time.

The Warm-Up Drill is executed by having two quarterbacks stand 15 yards apart and warm-up their arms throwing in their proper overhand fashion. The quarterbacks must be concerned with vertical accuracy by trying to bisect the opposite quarterback down the middle of his body. Initially, they should not worry about horizontal accuracy for total pinpoint accuracy. As the drill progresses, and as the arms begin to warm, such horizontal accuracy efforts are added. The drill is shown in Diagram 8-2.

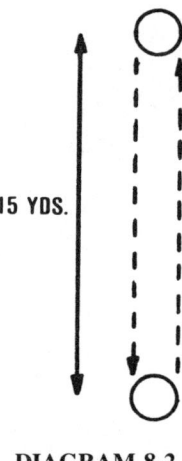

**DIAGRAM 8-2**
**Warm-Up Drill**

*Coaching Points:* An extended period of time should be allotted to this drill. Quarterbacks need plenty of time to warm-up their arms. Initially the emphasis is on vertical accuracy of bisecting the opposite quarterback. The effort for horizontal accuracy is added only when the arms feel well warmed-up. The emphasis must be a gradual working up from slow, soft throwing to hard throwing.

**Drill #2: Double Kneel Throw**

The Double Kneel Throw Drill helps to develop the concept of separating the upper torso throwing action from the lower body run action as in move-out pass action. Even if such move-out pass action is not utilized, the drill is of great value as it helps develop the importance of leading the forward throwing action of the arm with the chest to help develop the understanding of the importance of the upper torso in the delivery and follow-through action.

The drill is set up in the same fashion as the Warm-Up Drill shown in Diagram 8-2 with the exception that both quarterbacks kneel on two knees and space themselves approximately 12 yards apart.

*Coaching Points:* **The coach must be sure to stress the importance of**

*Coaching the Quarterback Passing Techniques* 157

the chest leading the throwing arm to help develop both the understanding of the importance of such upper torso action in the throwing motion, and the proper execution of the chest lead of the arm delivery so proper thrust is added to the passing action by the upper torso.

### Drill #3: Set-Up and Throw

The Set-Up and Throw Drill helps to develop all of the proper set-up actions utilized in the offense. The quarterbacks simply receive the snap from center, and execute a proper drop back and set-up action and a proper delivery of the ball to a target or receiver. The drill can be as simple as throwing to a fixed target, to timing a specific pass to the cut action of a receiver's route, to creating a one-on-one, two-on-one or two-on-two receiver-defender modified pass scrimmage. The drill helps to develop proper drop back action after a proper center-quarterback ball exchange, proper set-up techniques and proper delivery action of the pass. Such action is outlined in Diagram 8-3, which shows some of the various launch points from which the pass could be thrown.

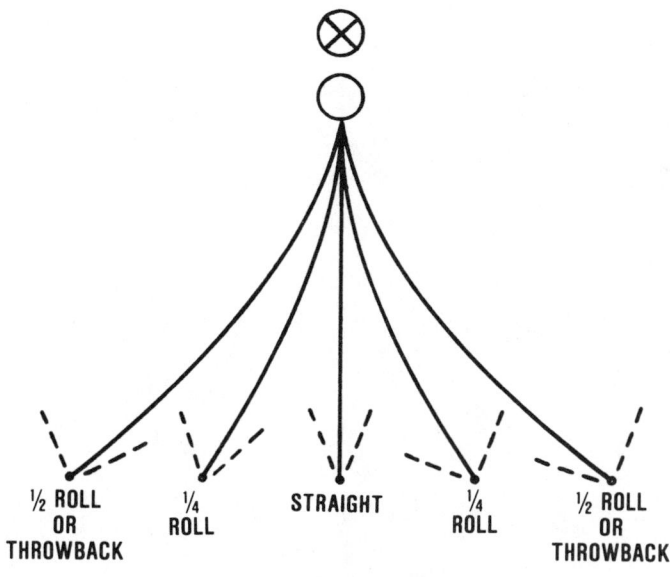

DIAGRAM 8-3
Set-Up and Throw Drill

*Coaching Points:* All of the various set-up actions utilized in the offense must be practiced—drop back, quarter-roll, half-roll, throw back and all play action set-ups. Such items as depth of the set-up, speed of the set-up, proper throttle-down action on the next-to-the last step, proper breaking, or stopping action on the last step, proper set-up and arm and shoulder cock action as well as proper throwing action are all checked. Again, the drill can be performed with any combination of receiver route action and defender play.

### Drill #4: Varying Foot Position

The Varying Foot Position Drill helps to develop proper upper body throwing action while separating such action from the run action of the legs. The drill is set up in the same fashion as the Warm-Up Drill with two quarterbacks facing one another at a distance of 15 yards. However, the throws are executed by placing the feet at varying angles away from a direct facing of the opposite quarterback. The quarterbacks practice throwing with their feet facing away on a 45 degree angle, a 90 degree angle and a 135 degree angle, both to the left and right as the upper body is turned to the opposite quarterback. The foot angles are shown in Diagram 8-4.

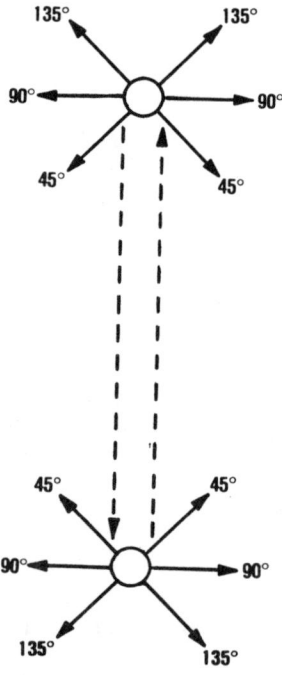

**DIAGRAM 8-4**
**Varying Foot Position Drill**

*Coaching the Quarterback Passing Techniques* *159*

*Coaching Points:* At the 135 degree angle, the trunk twist will be overly contorted. However, it will help the quarterback to practice the upper body throwing action at its most extreme divorce from the lower body leg action.

**Drill #5: Foot Adjustment**

The Foot Adjustment Drill aids the quarterback in developing quick fluid feet to help him adjust his set-up to the route of the receiver. From a set-up position, the quarterback readies himself for a throw with a proper hold of the ball and shoulder cock. A receiver runs a random zigzag, crossing pattern in front of the quarterback. All through the random run action, the quarterback must utilize quick, agile feet to adjust his set-up to a target spot which will permit a proper pass to the receiver. On a signal by the coach (''now''), the quarterback must have his feet properly set so he can execute a proper delivery of the pass. The drill is shown in Diagram 8-5 with a random route action of the receiver.

*Coaching Points:* The coach must vary the timing of the signal for the throw so that the quarterback executes proper foot positioning all through the drill's execution.

**Drill #6: Move-Out Pass Ready**

The Move-Out Pass Ready Drill helps to develop proper shoulder

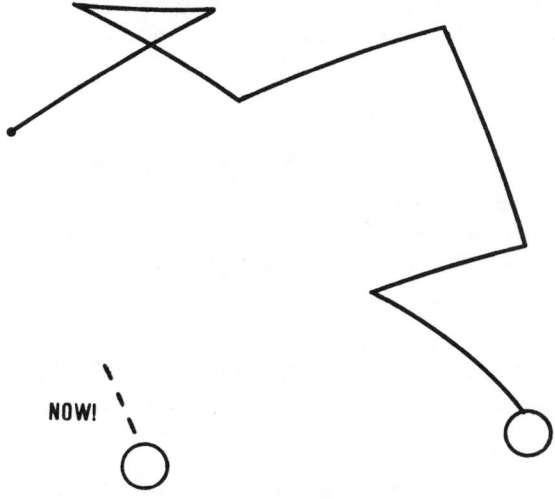

**DIAGRAM 8-5**
**Foot Adjustment Drill**

cock as the quarterback is running. A quarterback executes his normal move-out action (sprint, roll-out, bootleg) as a target (moving or stationary) is placed out in the flat. On the coach's signal, the quarterback must have his shoulder cocked properly so he is ready to execute a proper delivery of the pass on the move. The drill is shown in Diagram 8-6 using sprint-out action for the example.

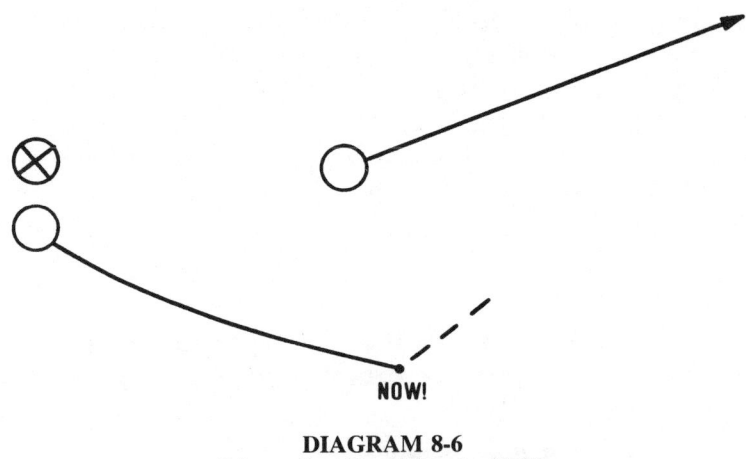

DIAGRAM 8-6
Move-Out Pass Ready Drill

*Coaching Points:* The coach must be sure to vary the "Now!" signal to ensure that the quarterback is cocked and ready to deliver the ball by the fourth step and on all subsequent steps.

### Drill #7: Move-Out and Throw

The Move-Out and Throw Drill is set up in exactly the same fashion as the Set-Up and Throw Drill except that the quarterbacks execute all of the move-out actions that are encompassed within the design of the offense. It can also be designed to be as simple as throwing to a fixed target, to timing a specific pass to the cut of a receiver's route, to some type of modified defender-receiver passing scrimmage. The drill helps to develop proper move-out passing action. Diagram 8-7 shows some of the various launch points from which the pass could be thrown.

*Coaching Points:* All of the various move-out actions must be practiced both right and left. The coach must check for proper threatening action of the corner by the quarterback as well as all the proper move-out passing techniques.

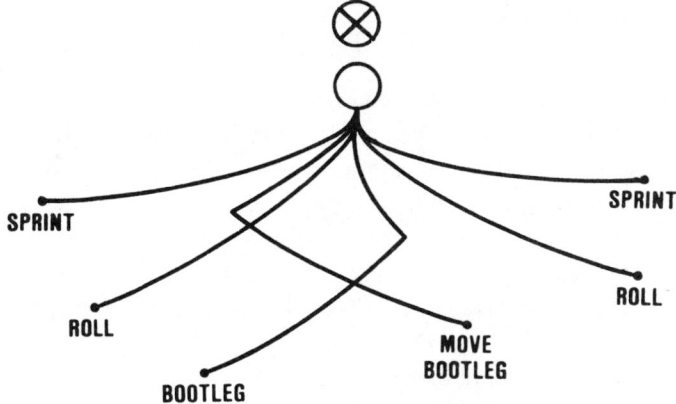

DIAGRAM 8-7
Move-Out and Throw Drill

### Drill #8: Trajectory Passing

The Trajectory Passing Drill enables the practice of varied trajectory passing skills. Two quarterbacks start out standing 15 yards apart and practice throwing straight line passes, high trajectory passes and passes in between the two levels of trajectory. The quarterbacks continue the drill by increasing their distance apart by 5 yards until they are a distance of 40 yards apart. The drill concept is shown in Diagram 8-8.

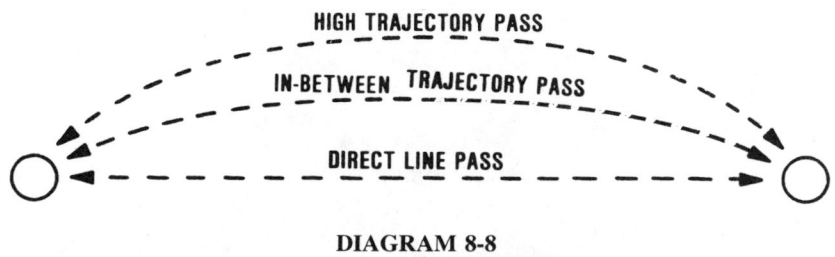

DIAGRAM 8-8
Trajectory Passing Drill

*Coaching Points:* The number of repetitions at each 5 yard interval can be predetermined by the coach. However, each throw should alternate a direct line throw, a high trajectory throw and an in-between trajectory throw. Such alternation will help to develop a sense of the need for different trajectories of a pass for different situations.

## Drill #9: Deep Passing

The Deep Passing Drill helps, simply, to develop a quarterback's deep passing skills. From whatever launch points utilized to throw the deep passes to whatever types of deep routes utilized in the passing offense, the quarterbacks set-up and throw. The drill can be set up as simply as a timed drill in which the quarterback throws to a particular deep route of the receiver, or as complex as a modified pass scrimmage against defenders. It is important that the method used to execute a deep pass in the offense (timing, reading of the coverage, reading of the receiver, etc.) be incorporated in the workings of the drill. Diagram 8-9 shows the drill being executed from drop back action in which the receiver is executing post, deep or flag routes.

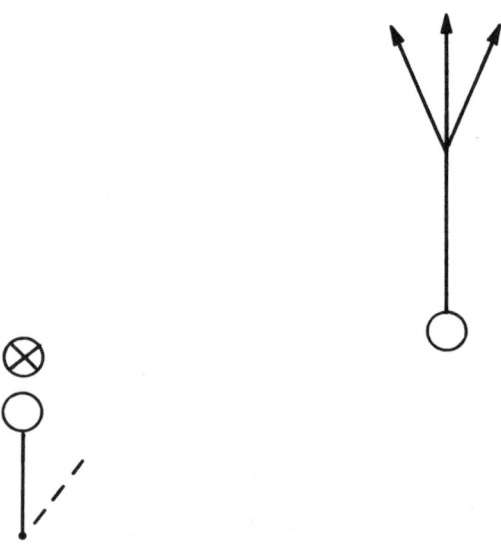

**DIAGRAM 8-9**
**Deep Passing Drill**

*Coaching Points:* The deep pass should initially be overthrown. Overthrowing makes such an on-target adjustment to the receiver's speed easy since all the quarterback has to do is take something off the throw. This is far easier to do than initially underthrowing and having to increase such thrust and delivery effort. The quarterbacks must be sure to vary the trajectories of their throws.

**Drill #10: Skeleton Pass Scrimmage**

The Skeleton Pass Scrimmage Drill simply pits the quarterback, set backs, wide receivers and tight ends against the secondary, linebackers and ends. The drill should be a competitive drill in which the offense executes all of its pass offense against the defense's pass coverage action. The defense must be sure to vary its coverages so the offense faces all the types of coverages it might see in a game. The drill is shown in Diagram 8-10 with the offense in a pro set skeleton formation and the defense in a 5-2 skeleton defense.

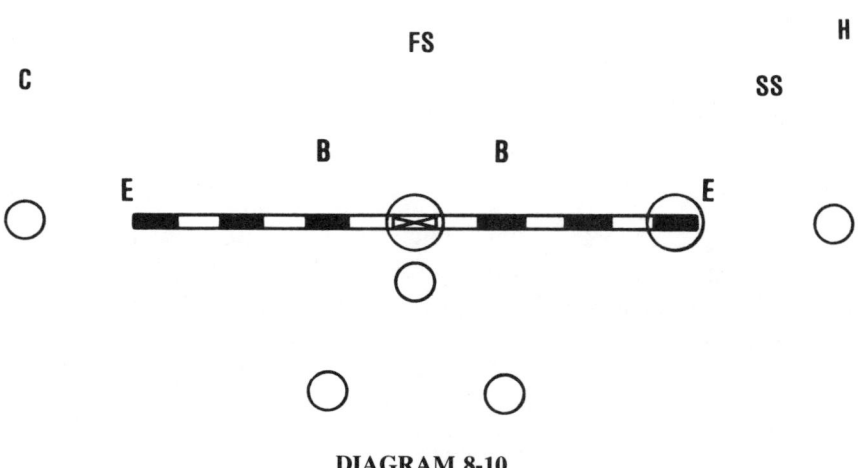

**DIAGRAM 8-10**
**Skeleton Pass Scrimmage Drill**

*Coaching Points:* A center should be used to help create the proper sense of timing of the pass play. A competitive game can be made of the drill awarding five points for a deep completion or touchdown, three points for a medium distance completion and one point for a short distance completion. The defense is awarded five points for an interception, three points for a knockdown of a pass and one point for an incompletion or pass that is not delivered in a set amount of time. A stopwatch must be kept on the quarterback to ensure that the pass is released within a certain time period (i.e.—3.5 seconds). It must be kept in mind that the drill can be a defensive pass coverage drill as well as a passing drill helping to add to the competitiveness and game-like action of the drill.

# nine

# Coaching Backfield Pass Receiving Techniques

Writing a chapter on backfield pass receiving techniques is an extremely difficult task to accomplish when one takes into consideration that so much of backfield pass receiving technique is dependent on the designs of the pass patterns and the assignments of the backs in the pass patterns. As a result, the major focus of this chapter will be concerned with pass receiving and separation techniques and the practice and drilling of such techniques.

## CATCHING TECHNIQUES

Catching techniques for a back are no different than they are for any other receiver. The back is concerned with four catching techniques; catching a ball above shoulder level, below shoulder level, pocket catching and one-handed catching. On all of these techniques, it is important for the back to separate the catching action of his upper torso (hands, arms, shoulders, head and even the chest and stomach area) from the running action of the lower body. Thus, one portion of the body is running to put the other part of the body in the best position to receive the pass. The upper torso body parts attempt to be in a relaxed position to allow for a soft, cushion-like catch of the ball. The fingers are well spread to help form as wide a basket-like target as possible for the ball to fall into. The fingers should be thought of as pincers which softly engulf the ball to snatch it out of its flight path. The arms and shoulders should act like shock absorbers to lessen the impact of the ball and the fingers enabling the soft catch. A properly caught ball should not make a harsh, sharp sound as a result of the ball's contact with the back's hands. Instead, a soft catch should produce almost no sound at all.

Concentration is also a key factor in all of the four catching techniques. Such concentration must be so great that the back should see the finger tips engulf the ball. Holding the hands out in front of the body upon reception helps produce the hand-eye coordination necessary for such a skill. In addition, holding the hands out in front of the body helps the receiver to actively "go get" the ball rather than passively wait for the ball and allow the defenders the split second amount of extra time to possibly make a play on the ball before it is caught.

Catching the ball above the shoulders utilizes the thumbs-in technique. The thumbs should come close to making contact as the fingers are, again, well spread. The fingers can really take on their pincers role in this technique. The hands must reach out for the ball. Such a reaching out for the ball allows the back the greatest opportunity for hand-eye coordination as the hands will be in an excellent position for the back to actually sight the ball into his hands. The thumbs-in above the shoulders catch technique is shown in Figure 9-1.

**FIGURE 9-1**
**Thumbs In Above the Shoulder Catch Technique**

Catching the ball below the shoulders utilizes the pinkies-in technique (many coaches will refer to this as the thumbs-out technique). In the pinkies-in technique the hands form a basket for the ball to fall into much in the same fashion as when the back is attempting to catch a toss or some type of pitch. The near hand forms the bottom of the basket. The back must be sure that the fingers, especially the thumb, are hyperextended backwards so that they do not interfere with the ball in its effort to fall into the basket-like hold of the hands. The farther hand acts as the back stop of the basket. The elbows should be fairly close together to facilitate such a positioning of hands. The pinkies-together technique does not allow for a reaching out type of action as does the thumbs-in technique. However, the back should raise the basket-like positioning of the hands as high as possible so that a soft, giving action can be executed to cushion the ball as the hands break the flight of the ball to produce a soft catch. The pinkies-in below the shoulders catch technique is shown in Figure 9-2.

When the ball is thrown low (below the knees or at knee level), the back may be forced to scoop the ball in an attempt to trap it to his body using the pinkies-in technique. Such a technique actually forms a

**FIGURE 9-2**
**Pinkies In Below the Shoulder Catch Technique**

basket in which the fingers, palms of the hands and inside of the forearms form one side of the basket, the elbow junction of the arms forms the bottom of the basket and the stomach and chest form the other side of the basket. By scooping we mean the attempt of the back to get his hands underneath the ball before it hits the ground by using his finger tips to tip the ball upward and into the basket so that it becomes trapped in between the hands, arms, stomach and chest.

If the ball is close to the ground, the back will have to fall or dive to the ground to ensure the best chance of making the reception. When such a commitment to going down to the ground is made, the back must be sure not to fall on his elbows as this will only tend to jar the ball loose. Instead, the back must execute a rolling action as he comes in contact with the ground to lessen the impact that could produce such a jarring loose action. The scoop technique to catch a low ball is shown in Figure 9-3.

**FIGURE 9-3**
**Scoop Tchnique to Catch Low Ball**

The pocket catch is the safest, most secure technique to use since the ball is almost totally secure upon the reception of the pass. The pocket catch is the best technique to execute when the ball is thrown directly at the back and a pinkies-in technique is awkward to execute. It is also an excellent means of catching a wet ball. The pocket catch allows the ball to spin into the natural pocket formed by the armpit, the upper arm and the side of the rib cage. The sides of the ball are actually trapped by the arm and the rib cage as the nose of the ball attempts to hit the armpit. As contact is about to be made, the hands simply engulf the ball to help draw it into the pocket so that the ball is secured upon impact. The back must be sure that the fingers of both hands are spread and hyperextended away from the pocket so that they do not interfere with the flight of the ball and, instead, help form a funnel-like positioning of the hands for the ball to enter.

The most difficult aspect of the pocket catch is body positioning to line up the back's pocket with the flight of the ball. The back may have to speed up or throttle-down to accomplish this task. The pocket catch technique is shown in Figure 9-4.

**FIGURE 9-4**
**Pocket Catch Technique**

The one-hand catch technique is utilized whenever a pass is so far away from the body that a two-handed catch technique cannot be utilized. A proper one-handed catch does not attempt to tip or bat the ball back towards the back's chest in an attempt to trap the ball. Instead, the one hand is used in attempts to execute a normal basket-like catch in which the one hand forms a one-handed basket. The fingers are, again, well spread. The middle finger forms the backstop of the basket as the pinkie and thumbs and the rest of the fingers are spread to form the sidewalls. The palm of the hand forms the bottom of the basket. The back must attempt to reach up for the ball and, as in the two-handed pinkies-in technique, use his arm to lower the hand as the ball makes contact with the hand to help create the cushioning effect. As the ball is lowered and control is started, the other hand is brought up to the ball to help secure the catch. If the back is forced to fall or dive out towards the ground, he must be sure not to fall on his elbows and, instead, roll, upon contact, to help absorb the blow and prevent the ball from jarring loose. The one-hand catch technique is shown in Figure 9-5.

**FIGURE 9-5**
**One-Hand Catch Technique**

## THE IMPORTANCE OF POSITIONING

Positioning of the body to make a reception is of utmost importance to the success of a pass play. The basic concept behind such proper positioning is that the back must be under control so that he has something left to either react to the flight of the ball or move to the most open area of his assigned route. Such a concept is similar to coming under control as a back is about to deliver the blow of a block. A back who is sprinting at top speed as he makes his final break may find that he cannot adjust to a poorly thrown ball that is slightly off the mark. Or, such a back may find he is overrunning the open area where he is most open to receive the pass.

Divorcing the upper torso in its efforts to receive the pass from the lower body run action necessitates correct body positioning. It is especially important that the back keeps his inside shoulder open to the quarterback to increase the range of the upper torso in its reaction to the ball.

Reacting, or moving to the ball is also an important part of body positioning whenever there are defenders behind the receiver. Such action cuts down on the time the defenders have to react to the ball as well as increasing the distance they have to pursue.

## BACKFIELD RECEIVER SEPARATION TECHNIQUES

Separation techniques refer to those skills which enable a back to disengage from the coverage of a defender and allow him to become open to receive a pass from the quarterback. The following will be a brief discussion of the separation techniques a back can execute. It is important to understand that the design of the pass pattern and the route

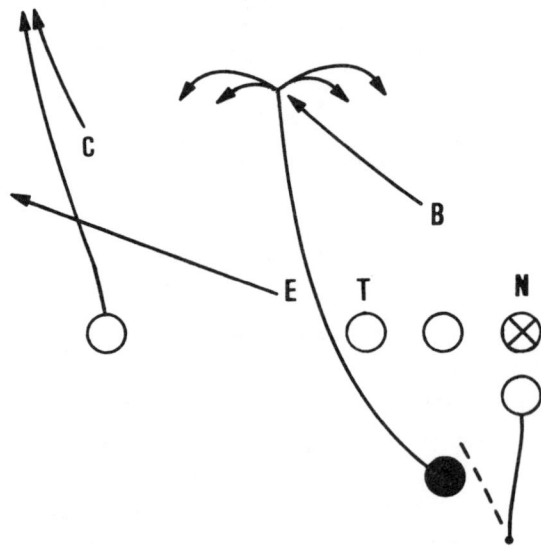

**DIAGRAM 9-1**
**Separate to Get Open**

the back is assigned to run will often dictate what separation technique the back must use if he is to use a separation technique at all. Diagram 9-1 shows a weakside halfback isolation pattern in which the back can execute any separation technique possible to get open. The play is designed to use him as the prime receiver as he separates to get open off the movement of the pass coverage.

Diagram 9-2, however, shows how the strict design of the flood pass pattern has the back on a strictly designed flat route of 5 yards deep with expansion as the major emphasis of the route. The design of the pass pattern attempts to create the open receiver by pitting two receivers on one defender. Thus, strict placement of the receivers in two areas which cannot be covered by one defender is the key to the play's success—not the effort to get open via the separation techniques.

The 90 degree angle turn separation technique is often one of the most commonly used separation techniques for backs due to the fact that backs are often used as complementary receivers at short to medium level depths. The 90 degree angle turn simply attempts to

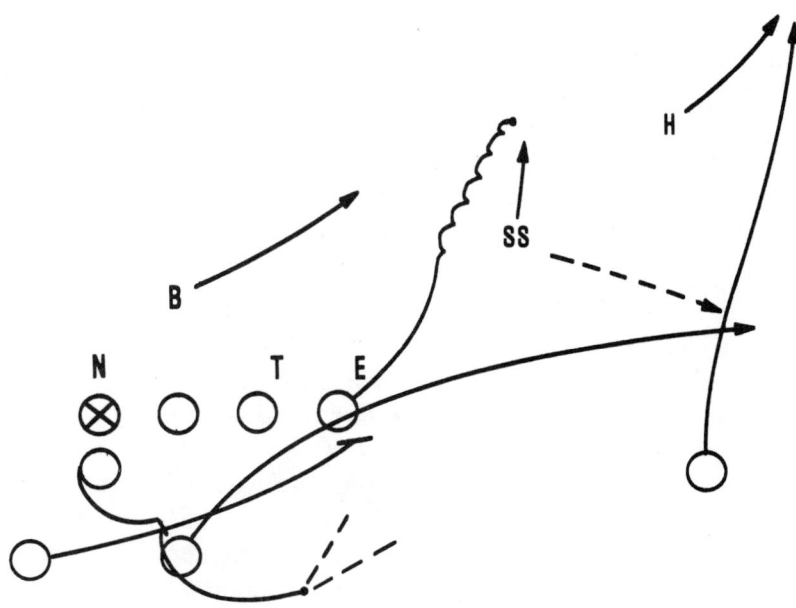

**DIAGRAM 9-2**
**Area Assignment of Routes to Create 2-on-1 Mismatch with No Separation Techniques**

redirect the back's movement from a north-south to an east-west plane. The separation technique is initially executed by bringing the body under control and taking a 45 degree angle step with the foot to the side of the intended separation. The forward body weight is brought back so that a major portion of the weight is over the top of the initial 45 degree angle step. The second step is both a break step and a plant step from which the third or final step is initiated. The second step is a slight crossover step in which the cleats are firmly planted. The third step is now executed in the intended 90 degree plane by ripping the third step foot out as the back pushes or drives off the second planted step.

The sharpness of the 90 degree angle is, of course, what helps separate the receiver from the defender. To execute such a sharp break another common separation technique can be applied. Snapping the head around to the passer as the elbow to the side of the head snap is whipped, or snapped, back to the quarterback helps to sharply disengage the receiver from the defender. Such separation techniques can be aided via the use of head faking or even faking the 90 degree angle cut in the opposite direction before the final break is made.

Speed in itself is a major concept of separation. By varying his speed for specific separation actions, the back can have something left to disengage from a defender at the desired time. Releasing into a route at less than top speed is the first of such speed separation techniques. Showing a defender a less than full throttle release may lull him into using defensive play geared to such a speed. As a result, a quick burst of speed on the back's final move will help the back disengage from the defender at the desired time. Releasing at less than full speed also enables the back to have his body under control so he can best execute his final separation move.

The change of pace separation technique is another popular speed separation technique. The concept behind the change of pace separation technique is that a receiver who throttles down usually does so to execute some type of lateral or back to the quarterback separation move. The defender reading such throttle-down action has a great tendency to cut down the pad of his coverage (distance he keeps between himself and the back) to play the back tighter. The change of pace separation technique is executed by shifting the body backwards over a plant type of step as the second step is dragged or suspended to help influence the defender to think a lateral or backward separation move is to be executed. A turning of the head back towards the quarterback can help to set up such an influence. The third step is simply an acceleration step back to full speed in an attempt to burst past the defender. It is important for the back to open up his strides to try to put distance (separation) between him and the defender.

Flat out speed is one of the most effective separation techniques. This is especially true in situations where a speedy back is a mismatch for a slower defender who is covering him. Deep or sideline patterns help to exploit such a weakness. What the back must understand is that he must use his flat out speed to separate from the defender. Once he is open via such separation, he then opens to the passer. Far too many backs will look up for the ball before they have truly separated and do nothing more than slow themselves down enough for the defender to be able to catch up and cover them.

Maintaining one's speed on a deep route is an excellent means of separating oneself from a defender. Similar to a back who looks up too soon for the ball, a back who beats his man but slows down once he looks up for the ball only allows the defender the opportunity to catch up. The back must learn to maintain his separation by continuing to burn deep (maintaining his speed) when he looks up for the ball. Any slowdown or lateral action will only distract from the north-south separation effort. In the same vein, reaching for the ball too early, fading too early or closing in on the ball too early will also detract from such north-south separation. The major concern the back must concentrate on is that he must maintain his full throttle, opened-up strides regardless of his upper body actions. This reverts back to the concept of disengaging the upper torso from the run action of the lower body.

Faking deep action by bursting deep before snapping off some type of lateral or back to the quarterback separation action is also an excellent speed separation technique. Almost all secondary philosophies start with not getting beat deep. The greater the north-south pressure (a speeding north-south receiver is the greatest north-south pressure) the greater the retreating action by the defenders to maintain their pad. Setting a secondary defender or linebacker back on his heels with a deep threat coupled with some type of 90 degree angle cut action will usually produce a wide open receiver.

Weaving is an excellent separation technique. Weaving is often combined with speed separation techniques to provide highly effective separation moves. The concept behind a weave is to tightly attack one side of a defender (actually his hip) in an attempt to force him to turn his hips to allow a run action with the receiver as he is threatening deep and then to sharply break tightly off the defender's other hip. Such action forces the defender to cross his legs and/or execute a difficult crossover action which puts the defender at a great disadvantage if the back opens his strides and utilizes his speed to separate himself from the defender.

Tight weaving is the key. Too much of a lateral fake means it will take more time to break back in the desired direction and, thus, more time for the defender to react and stay with the back. The weave separation technique can actually be combined into a series of two and three consecutive weave moves to produce a zigzag type of separation action. (Actually zigzag is a poor phrase that is commonly used in football coaching since players commonly associate zigzag action with the lateral action that makes it ineffective.)

A come back type of action is executed in much the same fashion as the 90 degree angle turn separation technique. The major difference is that the third step off of the second plant foot step is made in a sharper direction. Head and elbow snap greatly aid such action as well as a greater degree of throttle-down so that the body weight is gathered over the first and second steps aiding the redirection efforts of the third step.

The shoulder drive separation technique is an excellent technique to use against a defender who is playing the back tightly. The technique simply has the back drive up tightly north-south into the defender similar to a faking deep action except that the back uses his shoulder to drive up under and through the defender to the spot where he wants to separate. Such a shoulder driving action is usually met with an effort by the defender to fend off the shoulder drive and maintain some type of a pad. Such defensive action coupled with a separation action such as a 90 degree angle cut usually results in great separation.

A 270 degree angle cut separation technique complements the commonly used 90 degree angle cut separation move well. The back sets up the move by driving at the hip of the defender opposite the final cut in an attempt to influence the defender to turn his hips. The back then throttles-down to shift his weight back over the plant foot—the foot to the side of the cut. The back simply plants his foot and whips back the opposite elbow to execute a 180 degree plus second step with the opposite foot. The third step is simply a crossover step with the original plant foot. The back attempts to open up his strides starting with the crossover step to put separation between himself and the defender.

There certainly are many other techniques that can be utilized to put separation between the back and the defender. What is important for the coach and the backs to realize is that any of these separation techniques can be used individually or they can be combined into a series of separation technique moves. Hand signals can be effectively used to tell a quarterback which way a back is going to break his cut or even when such a cut will be made to help develop pinpoint timing. The use of a shoulder drag in which the back begins to turn his shoulders to the quarterback to fake some type of lateral or backward move to influence the defender to throttle-down as the back continues speeding north-south is another effective separation technique. General concepts such as running on a backpedaler and releasing on an angle against a slider are all utilized to help the back separate from the defender to get open to receive the pass.

There are also separate pass receiving skills that can be associated with the separation techniques to help the receiver to get open and yet properly react to the ball to make the reception. Fading inside or outside on a deep ball when it is thrown over the opposite shoulder is a difficult skill to master since it is quite an unnatural action. However, proper practice helps to develop this important skill. Staying inbounds on the sideline or at the end line is another important skill. The catching action of the upper body must be disengaged from the stretching, reaching back, dragging action of the feet and legs as the arms and hands stretch out to reach for the ball and make the catch. The use of peripheral vision as the back approaches the endline or sideline helps to adjust his body action properly.

## BALL SECURITY AND NORTH-SOUTH KNIFING

In any action which handles the ball, ball security must be of utmost concern once the reception is made. Ball security actually begins with the looking of the ball into the hands in an attempt to see the fingers engulf and make contact with the ball. Once such catching action is executed, the back combines the giving-with-ball arm cushion action with a drawing of the ball to the armpit whose side of the body is away from the upfield attack. The back should think, catch, tuck and go. Although a combined psychomotor pattern will be developed in which the back will react to execute the catch, tuck and go action, the coach must be sure that the ball is secured immediately and that the back does not start his upfield knifing action before he begins such ball security action. Actually, they will start to take place in an almost simultaneous fashion. Ball security demands utmost coaching concern as violent tackles immediately upon reception are a common cause of the ball being jarred loose.

Knifing north-south is of major importance to gaining north-south yardage. A sharp north-south action is executed by lowering the upfield shoulder to initiate the turn. Once such a redirection action is executed, the back must attempt to open his strides towards the goal line to put distance between himself and rear pursuers, and threaten any defenders in front of him with his north-south open field running techniques.

## BACKFIELD PASS RECEIVING PRACTICE AND DRILLS

Backfield pass action in which backs are called upon to act as receivers often produces a pass pattern's least efficient execution. Whatever the reason may be—lack of sufficient practice time, an improper emphasis on the role of the back as a receiver, the fact that the backs are the weakest pass catchers or that the backs have the poorest execution of the separation techniques—it must be kept in mind that a chain is only as strong as its weakest link. Even though a back is usually a complementary receiver and not the prime receiver, this does not mean the back is a less important receiver. Careful studies of team reception statistics will often surprisingly show a back to be the team's second or third leading pass catcher. The reason? Deep zone coverages leaving open the short zones that backs' routes often occupy, man-to-man coverages isolating quicker backs on slower linebackers, coverages which are bent at shutting off wide receiver threats or the threat of a great tight end—whatever the rationale may be, statistics do show that backs play a far more active role in pass receiving than most coaches realize.

Pass receiving is only a part of the valuable role of a back in a pass pattern. A flood pattern, such as the one shown in Diagram 9-2, can only be successful if the back performs a precise execution of his assignment. Whether it is a proper vertical or horizontal spacing of receivers, a crossing action, flood action, isolating action or any other combined action of two or more receivers of which a back is a part for the pattern to be a success, the back must execute his assignment precisely. This is true whether the back is the prime receiver, a complementary receiver or assigned to influence or clear out a defender.

Keeping in mind the importance of precise backfield execution in the pass patterns as well as the problem a coach has in having to allot his limited practice time not only to the pass game but to the run game as well as blocking, practice of the backfield pass game must be as concise as possible. To enable such concise practice, the coach must

*Coaching Backfield Pass Receiving Techniques* 177

again go to the playbook rather than the drillbook. The coach must be sure to practice and drill those aspects of the pass game that the backs must actually execute in the offense used.

An important concept of such game-like practice is to be sure the backs thoroughly understand both their role in the pattern and exactly how to execute that role. Thus, the back must understand enough of the pattern principal to know the purpose of his assignment. Seam control as shown in Diagram 9-3 refers to influencing the outside short zone defender to honor and play the halfback's seam control pattern by running up the alley between the tackle and the split-end's weak-side out route. He must understand the importance of horizontal spacing so that the outside short zone defender cannot cover the back and the split-end. He must understand the importance of depth so that he cannot be covered by a safety as the outside short zone defender covers the out pattern. The back must understand why he must hold his seam control pattern whether he is covered or not. Such understanding does more to help the back execute his assignment than any precise designation of where he should be and when. Knowing the whys helps the

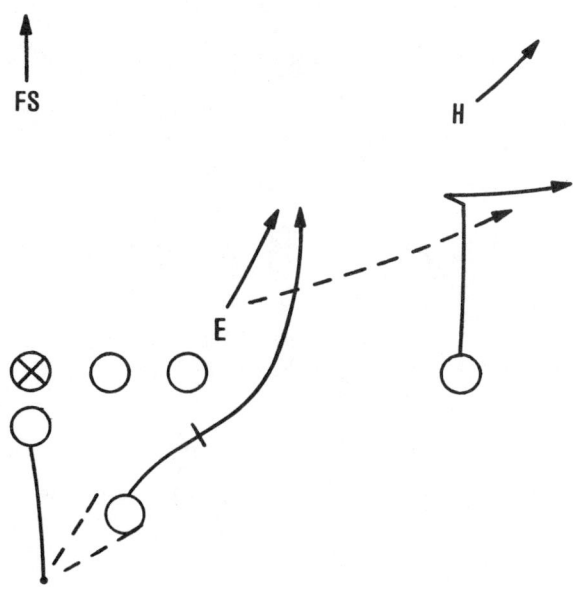

**DIAGRAM 9-3**
**HB Seam Control Route**

178    *Coaching Backfield Pass Receiving Techniques*

back to properly adjust to those abnormal situations where rules seem to fail.

Some of the following drills are pure pass catching skill drills. Others are drills which can be absorbed into the back's needs for execution of the passing portion of the offense by breaking down specific parts of the pass patterns into true game-like drills. The Boundary Drill can be practiced and drilled off of some type of out or flat route action that the back must actually execute in the pass offense.

**Drill #1: Around-the-Clock**

The Around-the-Clock Drill is an excellent warm-up type drill which helps to check proper hand positioning, sighting of the ball, finger pinching action on the ball and arm give for a cushioning effect. Two receivers stand approximately 12 yards apart and throw and catch the ball at positions "around-the-clock" as shown in Diagram 9-4.

**DIAGRAM 9-4**
**Around-the-Clock Drill**

*Coaching Points:* Note that "X's" are drawn at the armpit areas so that the back can practice pocket catching. Throwing the ball dead center also helps to create the pocket catch situation. The coach must check for proper hand positioning and finger spread as well as hand-eye coordination concentration. The backs can finish with "burn-outs"—firing the ball around-the-clock as hard as they can throw the ball. A contest can be made of the burn-outs—how many out of ten, or who is the first to miss a catch? Another alternate means of executing the Around-the-Clock Drill is to have the backs throw knuckle-balls to each other at the various points on the clock helping to develop the intense concentration needed to execute the knuckle-ball catching skill.

### Drill #2: Spin

The Spin Drill is an excellent drill to help develop quick catching reactions to a football that is located by the back's vision only when the ball is right on top of him. The drill is executed by having a back face away from the coach at a distance of approximately 12 yards. The coach throws a hard pass at the back at any point around-the-clock as in the Around-the-Clock Drill. As soon as the ball is approximately one yard from the coach's release hand, the rest of the backs in line yell "Ball!" This signals the back to spin around and react to the ball to make the catch wherever it is. The drill is shown in Diagram 9-5.

*Coaching Points:* The coach must be sure to vary his throws to the

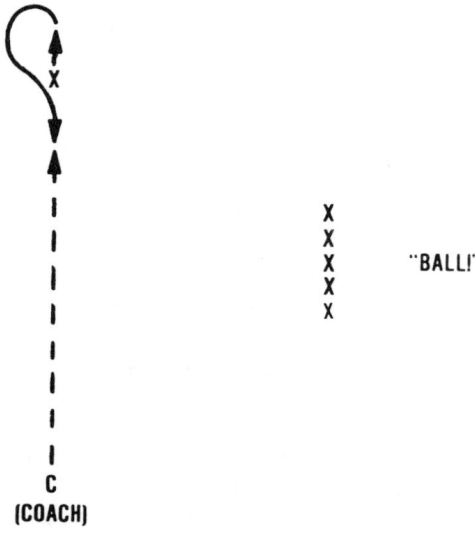

**DIAGRAM 9-5**
**Spin Drill**

various positions around the clock including at the armpits and dead center to force pocket catching. The coach must be sure the back is not signaled too early by the line of waiting backs.

### Drill #3: Catching on the Move

The Catching on the Move Drill enables the backs to practice catching a ball while moving across the passer's face or while running directly at the passer. The coach, or passer, must be sure to vary the throws so that the back can learn to adjust to the flight of the ball. Diagram 9-6 shows the two actions (lateral and back at the passer) off of two possible route actions the backs might have to execute.

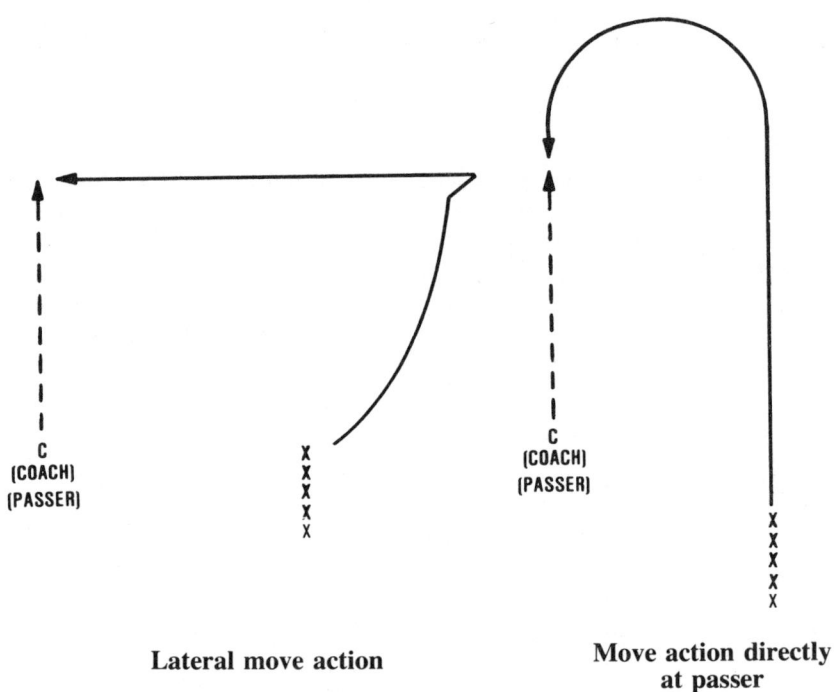

Lateral move action　　　　Move action directly at passer

**DIAGRAM 9-6
Catching on the Move Drill**

*Coaching Points:* The backs must be sure to work both left and right. When working back at the passer, the backs must learn to realize that the speed of the ball increases as they move closer to it.

### Drill #4: One-Hand Catch

The One-Hand Catch Drill helps to develop one-hand catching skills by forcing the back to concentrate on catching the ball and securing it under the armpit with only one hand. The drill can be executed by having the backs run laterally across the field and directly at the coach (the first section of Diagram 9-7) as well as towards each flag and straight upfield (the second section of Diagram 9-7).

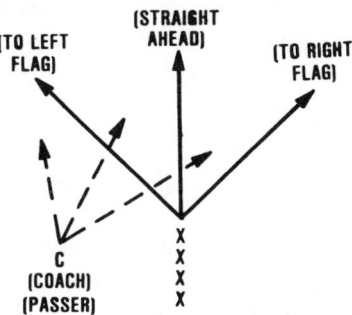

**DIAGRAM 9-7**
**One-Hand Catch Drill**

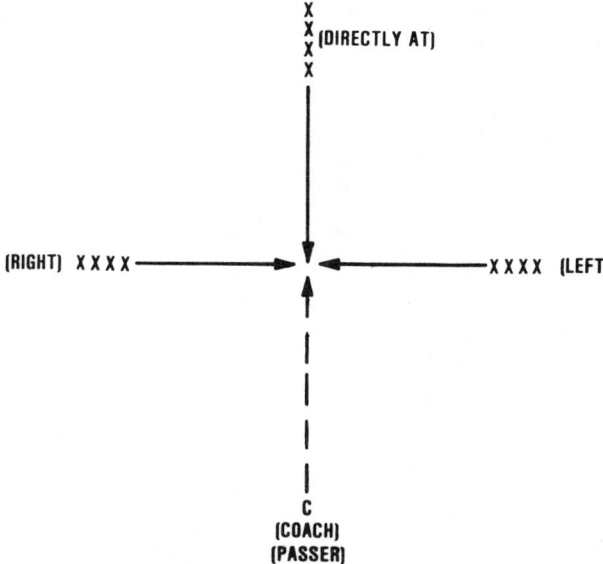

*Coaching Points:* The coach should lead the back far enough in front of the back so that he extends out for the ball in a similar fashion to an actual one-hand catch situation in a game. He must also be sure to alternate right-handed as well as left-handed one-hand catching.

**Drill #5: Bad Ball**

The Bad Ball Drill is set up in exactly the same fashion as the One-Hand Catch Drill. However, the backs practice two-hand catching of poorly thrown balls—too high, too low, short, long, wide, behind the back, etc. The backs must learn to be under enough control to enable them to react to a ball that is not well thrown, and must also learn that they must do whatever is necessary to make the reception—dive, jump, lunge, etc.

*Coaching Points:* The coaching stresses the ability to keep oneself under control so that the back can properly react to the ball. Actually, such drills as the Catching on the Move Drill and the Bad Ball Drill can easily be combined into one drill to make better and more efficient use of practice time.

**Drill #6: Dive**

The Dive Drill helps the backs to practice scooping balls that are low to the ground as well as proper rolling action so that the backs do not land on their elbows, a position in which the ball could possibly be jarred loose. The drill is set up in the same fashion as the One-Hand Catch Drill in which the backs work laterally across the passer. The balls are thrown very low to force the backs to execute their proper pinkies-together scooping action. Diagram 9-8 shows how the Dive Drill can be practiced off an out route action.

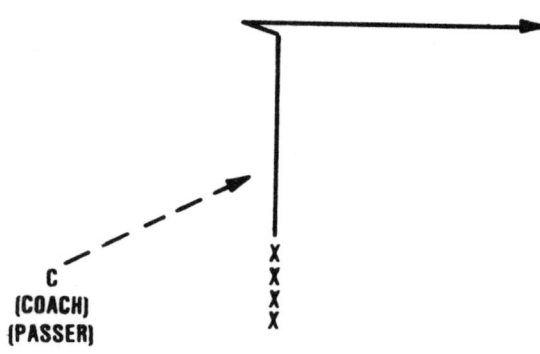

**DIAGRAM 9-8**
**Dive Drill (Off Out Route Action)**

## Drill #7: Deep

The Deep Drill helps the backs to practice catching deep passes. The backs must be forced to practice closing in and fading adjustment techniques by the coach throwing the ball side to either side of the back.

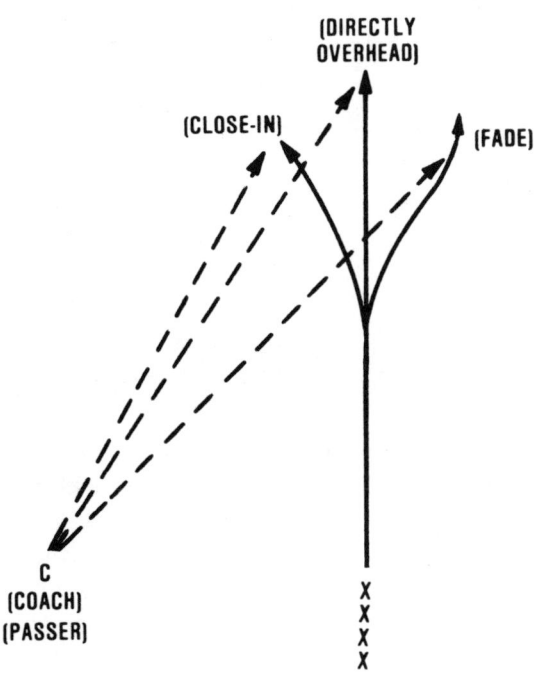

DIAGRAM 9-9
Deep Drill

*Coaching Points:* The coach must be sure to alternate the flights of the ball to practice closing in and fading skills. Extra emphasis can be placed on the more difficult fading action. The ball can also occasionally be thrown short to force the receiver to adjust back to such an underthrown pass.

## Drill #8: Pressure Drill

The Pressure Drill helps to develop the concentration necessary to catch the ball in a crowd and hold onto the ball once the defenders hit the back. The drill is executed by simply having the backs run a particular route (circle route used for example in Diagram 9-10) while

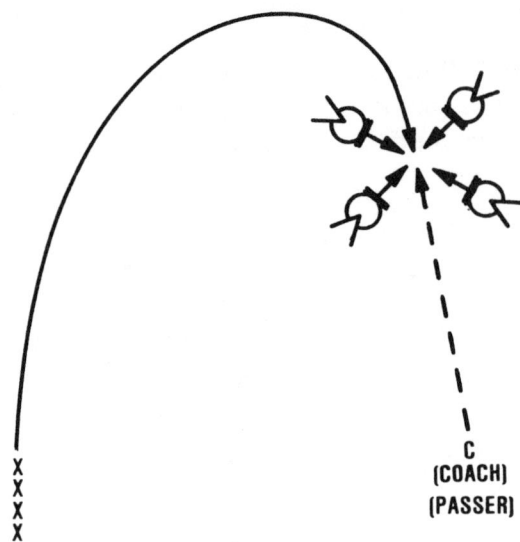

**DIAGRAM 9-10**
**Pressure Drill (Off Circle Route Action)**

four extra backs wait for them in the reception area. As the ball is in flight, the extra backs try to distract the receiver with hand and air bag waving action. One back can even run in front of the receiver across the path of the ball. As soon as the receiver touches the ball, all air bag carriers slam the receiver high and low in an attempt to jar the ball loose. One extra back can even forget the use of the bag and just utilize his hands in an attempt to strip the receiver of the ball.

*Coaching Points:* Distractions as the ball is in flight is a key to the drill. A waving bag or even an air bag thrown into the air helps to create such a distraction. The coach must be sure to check for proper ball security once the catch is made.

### Drill #9: Double (Triple) Hop

The Double (Triple) Hop Drill helps the backs to learn to catch the ball despite the interference of foot coordination problems. The backs run any of the short, across the field routes. Two (three could be used) bags are placed in their paths approximately four feet apart. The coach (passer) fires a pass at the back anytime during the hopping action whether the back is straddling a bag or is in between two bags. The back must make the reception of the ball and yet maintain enough foot

# Coaching Backfield Pass Receiving Techniques

balance to hop over the remaining bag(s). The drill is shown in Diagram 9-11 using three bags.

*Coaching Points:* The coach must mix the timing of the passes to create different foot coordination problems for the backs as well as mix the varying flight angles of the pass (high, low, wide, behind, etc.).

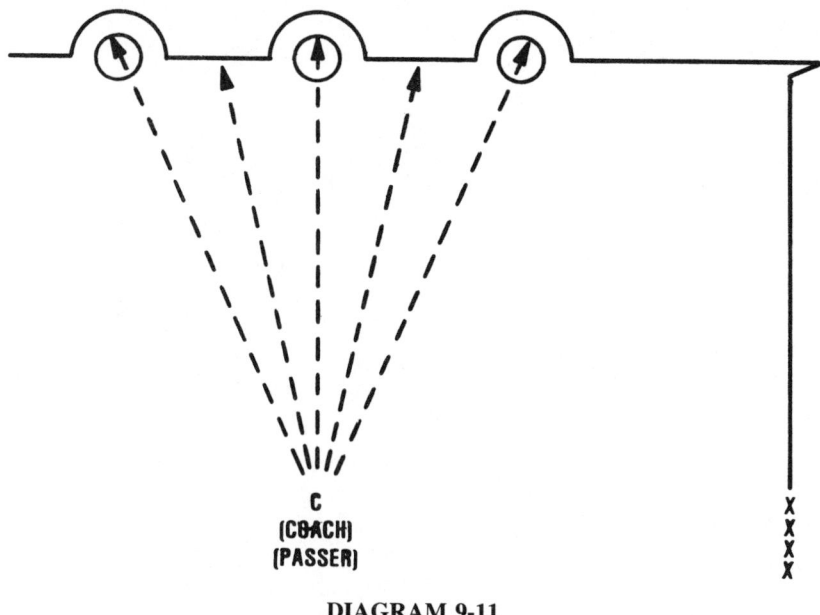

**DIAGRAM 9-11**
**Double (Triple) Hop Drill**

### Drill #10: Boundary

The Boundary Drill helps the backs to practice their skills of making a reception and keeping in bounds whether it is the sideline or the endline. The backs sprint to the boundary (Diagram 9-12 shows the use of a flat route sprinting to the sideline), make the catch and either knife upfield or keep one foot in bounds.

*Coaching Points:* The coach must be sure to practice endline boundary work as well as sideline. On the sidelines, the back must be sure to attempt knifing up the sideline if he can. It is important to stress the back's use of peripheral vision so that he knows where the boundary line is as he approaches it so he can maintain eye contact and concentration on the ball.

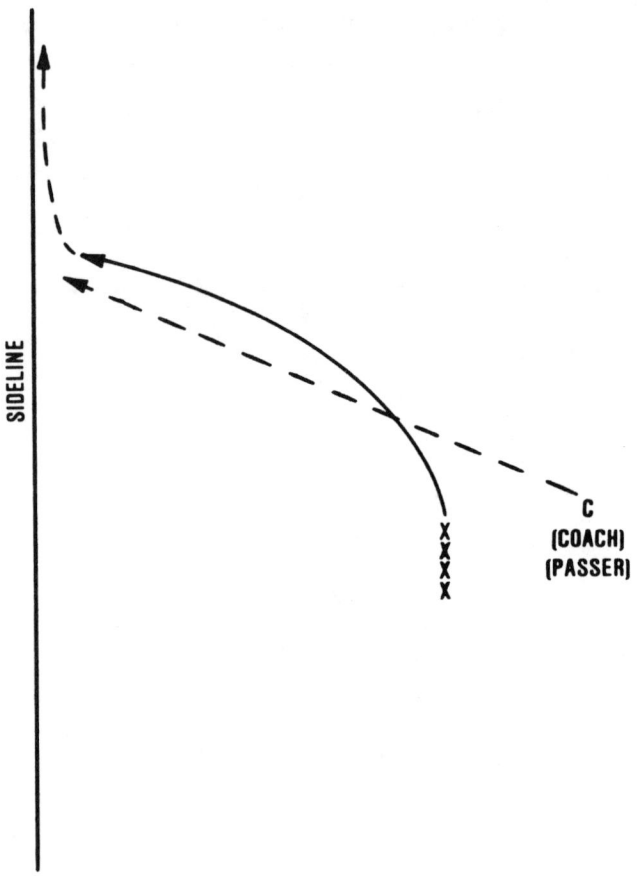

**DIAGRAM 9-12**
**Boundary Drill (Sideline Used for Example)**

## ten

# Installing the Added Dimension of Faking

Backfield faking often takes on two negative aspects. Either it is overlooked by not receiving enough coaching attention or the backs overexaggerate the faking action rendering such action useless. Both aspects are equally detrimental to effective backfield execution. The benefits of effective backfield faking can be extremely valuable. An unblocked defensive tackle who closes down to tackle a faking diveback, a linebacker who steps up to honor a diveback's fake on a play action pass or option action, such actions can eliminate defenders without having to block them. What is often so beneficial about such faking action is that as little as one step up forward towards the line of scrimmage by a linebacker is all that the influence of the fake may need to prevent such a defender from getting to the hook-curl zone on a pass drop to cover a curling flanker or getting to the perimeter to help support an option play.

The key to effective backfield faking is to simply make the faking action look like normal play execution. There must be no overexaggerated action of the faker that gives away such faking action. A quarterback who holds the ball up in the air as he drops back to execute a draw hand-off may as well yell "Draw!" to the defense. Such action does nothing but give the defense a definite key to initiate proper defensive reaction.

## QUARTERBACK HAND-OFF FAKING

The degree to which a quarterback can fake a hand-off to a faking back certainly depends on the design of the offensive play. What will be described here, therefore, will be the optimal hand-off fake whether it is a one-handed or two-handed fake of the hand-off. The speed of a play's execution may require the quarterback to give less of a fake.

A two-handed fake of the ball by the quarterback provides the best opportunity of influencing defenders. The reason for this is that the ball is placed in the faking back's pouch and ridden towards the line of scrimmage (or at least in the direction of the faker's course) until such a ride would interfere with the quarterback's ability to draw the ball out of the faking back's pouch. Such a fake best simulates the play action that the faking action is trying to emulate. The quarterback moves to the mesh point as he would on the normal hand-off action that the faking action is simulating. He keeps his shoulders parallel all through the faking action as he would on a normal hand-off. The ball is extended to the faking back's pouch and ridden on the faker's course. The ride should go no further than to the belt buckle of the quarterback on the plane that the front of his body is facing. Any ride further than this will result in the possibility of the faking back's pelvis bone interfering with the removal of the ball from the faker's pouch. Once the ball is ridden to the quarterback's belt buckle, it is simply drawn back to the quarterback's stomach—his third hand. Dive fake execution on option plays are prime examples of the need for never faking beyond the quarterback's belt buckle. Such two-handed faking action is shown in Figure 10-1 using a halfback dive fake as the example.

Many coaches prefer a one-handed hand-off fake as they feel it better helps protect the ball and helps facilitate quicker movement into the play action after the fake. One-handed fakes are most commonly used on play action passes to help facilitate the necessary drop back action to set up for the pass delivery.

On a one-handed hand-off, the quarterback positions the ball just above the seam or junction of the top of the leg and the bottom of the stomach. Actually, the ball sits on the soft of the bottom of the stomach as it is not hindered by the legs' movement. The quarterback must be sure it does not rest on the pelvis bone as it will not be well protected if he is tackled from behind. Actually, by sitting the ball on the pelvis bone a harder surface is created, aiding the jarring loose of the ball rather than its protection in the soft of the stomach.

Installing the Added Dimension of Faking

Ball in pouch

Ridden to belt buckle

Drawn back to stomach

FIGURE 10-1
Two-Handed Fake Action by QB

The free hand is what is placed in the faking back's pouch. The hand can actually be ridden in the pouch as long as the body movement away from the mesh point can facilitate such a ride. The quarterback can actually initiate the movement of his body away from the mesh point as soon as the faking back clears the quarterback's intended path. Two common errors on the one-handed hand-off fake must be avoided by the quarterback. First, the quarterback must not raise up too high in the carry of his body as the one-handed fake action will often cause him to do. He must attempt to keep his shoulders as parallel as possible to the initial level of a quarterback's shoulders in his pre-snap stance. Second, the quarterback must be sure to execute a good one-handed ride and not pull out too quickly in his effort to carry out the rest of the play's action. The one-handed hand-off fake is shown in Figure 10-2.

## QUARTERBACK PASS ACTION FAKING

The quarterback's faking action of a pass for such plays as a draw or a screen is simply executed by carrying out his normal drop back or sprint out action and by not overexaggerating the fake. The ball is carried as it would be in a normal pass drop action—in front of the

Positioning of ball
on soft of stomach

One-hand fake

**FIGURE 10-2
One-Handed Fake Action by QB**

breast to the side of the carry. The ball must not be held up high for the defense to see as this is only a dead giveaway that it is screen or draw action. One of the best things the quarterback can do to influence pass drop action by the defenders is to "look-them-off." By looking-them-off we mean that the quarterback stares into the secondary as long as he can (often this will only be for the first few steps) as if he were reading the secondary's drop movements. Such action will often influence the linebackers and deepbacks to drop off quickly into pass coverage to help set up the draw or screen action.

The fake of pass action after a hand-off of the ball to a running back takes on some specific coaching points. First, the quarterback can initially help influence defenders to honor his fake by accelerating at top speed from the hand-off mesh. A burst of speed can often cause enough concern to hold a defender in his alignment or even force him to flow in the acceleration direction. Second, the quarterback must attempt to hide his hands as they fake the carry of the ball. This can be accomplished by slightly turning the upper torso away from the line of scrimmage as if to hide the hands with the back of the quarterback's shoulder. Third, the quarterback must not hunch over such faking action with his head down. Instead, the quarterback must keep his head

**One-hand ride**

**FIGURE 10-2 (continued)**

up and attempt to look the linebackers and secondary defenders off. Such a carry of the upper torso and hands plus a sprinting acceleration towards the launch point of the false pass play will do much to cause defensive concern. Such a carry of the upper torso and the hands is shown in Figure 10-3 as the quarterback fakes a bootleg type action.

**FIGURE 10-3**
**Quarterback Pass Fake**

## OTHER QUARTERBACK FAKING ACTION

There are certainly other types of faking action that a quarterback may have to carry out in the execution of his particular offense. The important concept, again, is that the quarterback execute the faking action as closely as possible to the action used if the action were not faked, and that overexaggeration is not applied. Faking a toss or a quick pitch is a prime example. In the fake of a toss or pitch, the quarterback carries his body in the same way and on the same plane that he would if he were actually delivering the ball. All toss or quick pitch action such as follow-through, eye concentration, etc., should be executed. The ball must not be lifted up high to exaggerate the fake as this will only create a definite key for the defense that the action is a fake.

Executing an option fake of the keep-pitch key is another common quarterback faking action. The faking concepts are identical. Thus, the quarterback accelerates from the hand-off mesh, at top speed, stares at the keep-pitch key defender and brings his hands to the normal pitch position. Even though the defender may quickly see that the quarterback does not have the ball, such action will usually delay him long enough to prevent his pursuit of the ballcarrier. In addition, such option fake action will often force interior defender pursuit, further helping to influence defenders away from the ballcarrier.

A concentrated effort on a coordinated movement of the free hands once a hand-off is made is also a key action in helping to influence defenders to the faking action. This concept was thoroughly discussed in Chapter 4 in the explanation of the quarterback hand-off technique.

Whatever the faking action is, the quarterback must be sure to carry out his faking assignment and not stop to watch the ballcarrier. Nothing provides a better defensive key than for the quarterback to discontinue his faking action and point out the ballcarrier to the defense by watching his run action.

## RUNNING BACK FAKE OF HAND-OFF

The running backs execute the hand-off fake in the same manner as they would execute an actual hand-off. The faker creates a normal hand-off pouch. The bottom hand is just off the belt buckle with the fingers hyperextended down towards the ground. Thus, the "V" shaped carry of the arms allows for the ball to be freely placed in the faker's pouch and withdrawn without any interference from the faker's arms and hands.

To facilitate noninterference with the quarterback's faking action of the ball, the faker should hold his arm positioning for a split second longer than he would if he were receiving the hand-off. Actually, he should wait until he feels the ball being drawn out of his pouch before he begins to fold over the faking action.

The actual faking action simply has the faking back fold his arms together from the "V" shaped pouch positioning so that the hand of the top arm folds underneath the elbow of the bottom arm. The hands are flatly pressed against the side of the rib cage as the arms press against the stomach. As a result of the folding action, both hands are hidden underneath both elbows. Such a folding fake action enables the fake to create as much hand and arm surface over the pouch as possible, which helps to hide the fact of whether or not the ball is in the pouch. This action is diametrically opposed to a hard clamping action of both arms, which does little to sell a fake and actually gives the defenders a key to read since the clamping action is not used to receive a hand-off.

There are two important concepts tied in with such a folding of the arms faking action. First, hunching over the faking action with the faker's head down is a dead giveaway that the faker is faking the carry. A ballcarrier would never run with the ball this way so why would he use such a hunching over action and give the defense a definite key to read? The faker must keep his head up and eyes open as if he were looking for daylight. Second, the faker must accelerate at top speed as he rolls over his fake, just as he would if he was carrying the ball. In contrast to the poor faker who hunches over with his head down, an explosive acceleration as the folding over faking action is being carried out with one's head up is what will force a commitment to the faking action by the defenders.

## OTHER RUNNING BACK FAKING ACTIONS

The key for other running faking actions coincides with the key for faking itself. Carry out the normal execution of the action being faked, accelerate and do not use exaggerated actions which tip off that the back is actually just faking. The faking of a pitch or toss reception action is an excellent example. The back must not throw his arms up or perform some other type of overexaggerated action. Instead, the back must accelerate into his proper course, form his normal basket-like carry of his hands and stare at the quarterback's hands as if the ball were to be released. Such action mirrors identically the normal pitch reception action and creates the best chance of the faking action holding defenders in position so they cannot pursue the actual ballcarrier.

## BACKFIELD FAKING PRACTICE AND DRILLS

Backfield faking is afforded numerous opportunities for practice and coaching all throughout a practice session. Every time a play is run in timing drills, unit work, team work, scrimmages and even individual drills, there is almost always some type of faking assignment involved for either the quarterbacks or running backs. A poor dive fake on a predetermined keep pitch option offers the coach an opportunity to correct, teach and coach a vital and important facet of offensive execution.

Drilling fake action is usually coordinated with the drilling of other actions. Such a concept exists not to lessen the importance of faking action, but to help combine faking into a coordinated pattern of psychomotor skill development with the other skills or drills that go hand-in-hand with the faking action. Thus, quarterback option faking is difficult to execute unless it is combined with the dive hand-off action it develops from. Such a combination of faking action with other skills that it is associated with in a drill not only helps to create a game-like practice situation, but also helps to create an efficient use of practice time.

### Drill #1: Hand-Off Pouch and Fake

The Hand-Off Pouch and Fake Drill is actually nothing more than the Hand-Off Pouch and Reception Drill discussed in Chapter 4 with the exception that the backs execute a folding fake action rather than receiving a hand-off.

*Coaching Points:* The coach is looking for the folding, pressing, against the stomach faking action with the hands pressed to the sides of the rib cage underneath the elbows. The backs must keep their heads up and eyes open. The coach must be sure they don't overexaggerate the action via a harsh clamping action or a hunching over action.

### Drill #2: Hand-Off Pouch and Fake Circle Drill

The Hand-Off Pouch and Fake Circle Drill is actually nothing more than the Hand-Off Pouch and Reception Circle Drill discussed in Chapter 4 with the exception that the backs execute their folding fake action rather than receiving a hand-off.

*Coaching Points:* The coaching points are the same for the Hand-Off Pouch and Fake Circle Drill as they are for the Hand-Off Pouch and Fake Drill.

There are many other drills that practice faking action as well as other skill actions. The Timing Drill and the Breakdown Drill as described in Chapter 4 also offer the coach an opportunity to drill the faking on specific plays while allowing for a maximum number of repetitions of such faking action. A fun type of challenge can be added to this drill by telling the quarterback to run any play of a particular continuous series (i.e., the sprint draw or the sprint draw play action sprint out pass of the sprint draw series) without the coach knowing what the particular play is. The coach stands in front of the drill approximately 10 yards away and rates how well the particular play was disguised and how well the faking action was carried out. In other words, how well does the faking action "fool the coach"? In this manner, not only are the play and the subsequent faking practiced, but in addition, a firm understanding of coordination of the similar actions of series concept is established.

## eleven

# Developing Backfield Run Blocking Techniques

Backfield blocking is often the weakest area of offensive blocking. The fact that backs are usually selected for their running ability and not their blocking ability coupled with the number of blocks the backs must master is usually the rationale for such poor blocking. However, if total offensive execution is to be achieved, backfield blocking cannot be a weakness. The off-tackle kick-out play in which a 5-2 defensive tackle is eliminated by an excellent double team block by the tackle and tight end is of no significance if the blocking back cannot execute his kick-out block.

The only way effective backfield blocking can be developed is to make such blocking high priority skills. The backs must be made to believe that the only way they can become good backs is to become good blockers. A coach could even go so far as to say that if you can't block, you can't play. In practice, however, such a concept may be easier to establish than to carry out due to personnel considerations. Certain backfield sets may enable the weaker blocker to be placed in a position where he will have to block less. The "I" formation tailback spot is an example.

Another possibility is to substitute a strong blocking back for a weak blocking back when a particular backfield position is assigned a key blocking assignment. Such a concept, however, does have its limitations since a definite and easy-to-spot defensive key will be created.

Effective backfield blocking can, without a doubt, be developed.

A back is often at a size disadvantage in regard to the defenders he is assigned to block. However, he is able to couple the advantage of his speed plus the knowledge of whom he is going to block (the defender, of course, is at the disadvantage of not knowing who will block him, when he will be blocked or what technique will be used to block him) to nullify the defender's size advantage. In addition, backs are often among that best athletes on the field. Since blocking is as highly skilled a fundamental as any other football fundamental on the field, a back is often able to rely on his fine athletic ability to help him execute his required blocking assignments.

This chapter concentrates on backfield run blocking techniques. The chapter will not cover blocking concepts particular to a specific offense. Instead, the various types of blocking techniques necessary to execute all such particular blocking concepts will be the chapter's focus. Chapter 12 will discuss backfield pass blocking techniques.

## THE ISOLATION BLOCK

The isolation or "ice" block derives its name from the isolating, or leaving alone, of a linebacker by the design of the line's blocking scheme so that a back may block him one-on-one. The keys to the isolation block are an explosive and aggressive take-off and approach, the use of the "freeze" technique and an attitude of forcefully "making-it-happen!" The back explodes from his stance in a low and powerfully gathered approach. His elbows should be kept in close to his body to avoid standing up or wasted body action. The aiming point of the isolation block is a point which is dead center on the linebacker and just under the shoulder pads. As a result of using the "freeze" technique, as mentioned in Chapter 5, the isolation blocker does not have to fear over-aggressiveness. Instead, he can "take-it-to" the linebacker with maximum speed and power in an attempt to "make-it-happen." Diagram 11-1 shows two examples of an isolation play utilizing an isolation block from two different backfield sets versus two different defenses.

The block is executed by ripping up through the center of the linebacker with contact under his shoulder pads just as the back starts stepping on the toes of the linebacker. The back attempts to punch up under the shoulder pads simultaneously with his fists and forearms in a slamming action. Such an action will form a "V" shape of the arms in which the back tries to envelop the linebacker. As contact is made, the back rolls his wrists inward to pronate the thumbs so they point down

*Developing Backfield Run Blocking Techniques*

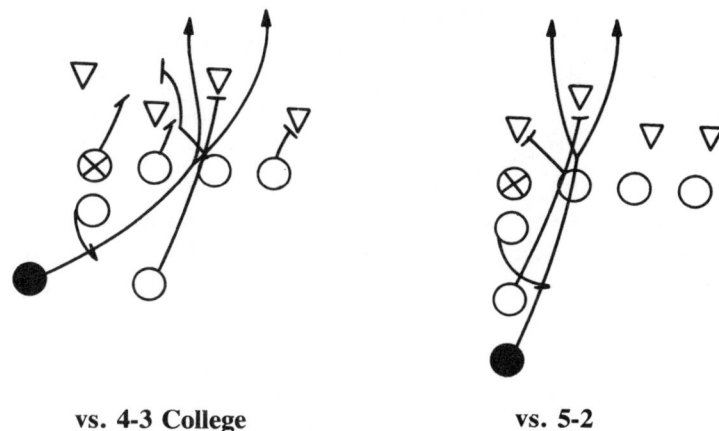

vs. 4-3 College          vs. 5-2

**DIAGRAM 11-1**
**Examples of Isolation Block from Split Back and "I" Sets**

to the ground. Rolling the wrists or pointing the thumbs downward helps the back to arch his back and roll, or snap the hips up under the blocker to help start the proper follow-through action.

It is extremely important for the back to throttle-down slightly just before he is to deliver the blow of the block. The throttling-down action helps the back to bring himself under control, drop his tail and widen his base so that he is in the most powerful and balanced stance from which to uncoil his block.

The contact spot of just under the shoulder pads allows the lifting action of the follow-through drive. The follow-through attempts to drive up through the upper torso of the linebacker as if the back were trying to lift the linebacker up or attempting to drive up on a 45 degree angle towards the sky. Whether or not the ideal lifting situation in which the back can totally control the linebacker exists, the back must, at least, attempt to drive the linebacker north-south by maintaining the press of the block keeping the linebacker caught up in the "V" of his arm positioning.

An important coaching point is that contact and follow-through should be thought of as one continuous action. It is not rip and then drive. Instead, it is one simultaneous action in which the back attempts to blow through the linebacker to rip up through him on the desired 45 degree lifting angle.

All body action is premised on a north-south thrust of the body power with all body parts working north-south. Another way of stating this would be for the blocker to be squared up to the linebacker so there is no loss of power in the thrust of the block. Any turning of body parts off this north-south plane will only result in a loss of power and a lessening of the back's blocking surface. An example of a non-north-south working of all body parts would be a dropping of the head or shoulder or a twisting of the entire upper torso off such a plane.

If, upon contact, the linebacker goes backwards, the isolation blocker continues driving up the center of the linebacker in an attempt to prevent the linebacker from regaining his base. If, upon contact, the linebacker slides to one side or the other, the isolation blocker rips north-south through the opposite breast of the linebacker as the ballcarrier cuts opposite the linebacker's direction. The emphasis on ripping up through the breast opposite the direction of the linebacker's flow in a north-south direction allows for maximum power and thrust as well as a maximum blocking surface and base as the back hits the linebacker. Such action will forcefully wall off the pursuit course of the linebacker. To attempt to go under the back's block would, of course, totally eliminate the linebacker's ability to get to the speeding north-south ballcarrier.

The back never attempts to gain an inside-out or outside-in positioning on the linebacker in attempt to shield the linebacker from the ballcarrier. Such a shielding action is extremely passive allowing for little, if any, power of contact, explosion and follow-through. If the linebacker tries to pick a side prior to contact, the isolation blocker simply adjusts his course to rip through the breast opposite the direction of the linebacker's pursuit angle.

If the linebacker tries to overpower the isolation blocking back by an attempt to run over the top of the back, the blocking back has to break down sooner in his approach and worry about colliding with the linebacker through the middle and up under his shoulder pads rather than with any follow-through techniques. Such action will produce a less effective isolation block. However, it will at least save the play by preventing the linebacker from jamming the blocking back into the ballcarrier.

Another important concept is that the back must not lunge at a linebacker who is retreating from the line of scrimmage in an effort to avoid contact. If the linebacker retreats in any way, the back continues to attack him and does not attempt to deliver the blow of the block until he is stepping on the linebacker's toes.

## THE LEAD-DRAW BLOCK

The lead-draw block is similar to the isolation block in that it does isolate the linebacker for the block of blocking back. However, it differs in that it develops off of a quick drop back pass action fake and the back is not able to utilize the "freeze" set-up technique as in the true isolation play. Instead, the lead blocker may be faced with a multitude of possible blocking situations varying from the linebacker who has bought the pass fake and has already dropped into his pass protection drop for three or four steps, to a linebacker who has read the play well and is plugging the hole and on to a fully blitzing linebacker. What is similar, however, is that the lead blocker, upon contact, will carry out the same technique on the execution of the lead draw block as he does on an isolation block.

The initial movement of the lead blocker is to quickly fake pass block set-up by lifting into a two point pass block stance and immediately locate the linebacker he has to block. After the initial quick lifting action to fake pass block, the lead blocker explodes at the isolated linebacker and executes an isolation block technique according to the reaction of the linebacker.

If the linebacker flies out into a pass drop and has positioned himself out towards the hook-curl zone area, the lead block will use a much more controlled type of isolation block in an attempt to wall the linebacker out in the direction he has flowed. The lead blocker attacks the linebacker in his normal low, powerfully gathered approach emphasizing the elbows tight to the body to avoid any standing up or wasted motion. The aiming point for the block is the inside breast of the linebacker. As the lead blocker approaches the linebacker, he is careful to bring himself under control to be sure he does not overextend or lunge into the block. The lead blocker must remember that the linebacker is the person out of position in this case. All the lead blocker really has to do in this situation is keep his body between the linebacker and the ballcarrier. An isolation block action is still used rather than a stalk type block, due to the fact that a linebacker is the type of player who usually has the physical tools to overpower a stalk block. The back is, however, more concerned with proper contact than he is with follow-through since such action is all that is needed to wall off the linebacker's pursuit to the ballcarrier on this type of linebacker reaction. This action is seen in Diagram 11-2.

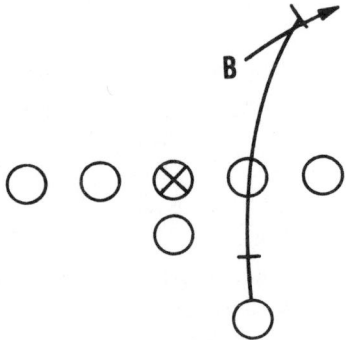

**DIAGRAM 11-2**
**Lead Draw Blocking Action vs. Linebacker Dropping to Hook-Curl Zone**

If the linebacker drops back over the middle short zone area, the lead blocker treats the action as a retreating defender. The lead blocker simply attacks the middle of the linebacker and does not break down to deliver the ripping up action of the isolation block until he can step on the toes of the linebacker. Once the blow is delivered, the lead blocker drives through the breast opposite the direction of the linebacker's effort to get to the ballcarrier with the same north-south follow-through action. This action is seen in Diagram 11-3.

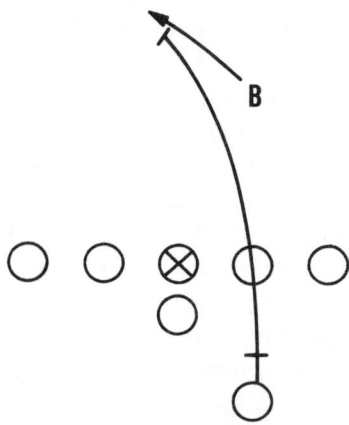

**DIAGRAM 11-3**
**Lead Draw Blocking Action vs. Linebacker Dropping to Short Middle Zone**

## Developing Backfield Run Blocking Techniques

If the linebacker does not buy the pass fake and sits in his original alignment, the lead blocker executes a normal isolation block. The only real exception to executing an actual isolation block is that the lead blocker must remember that the ballcarrier will not be able to help set up the block as he does on an actual isolation play since his approach to the linebacker is not directly behind the lead blocker due to the play's design. The linebacker will not necessarily be "frozen" in his efforts to determine the route of the ballcarrier since the ballcarrier is usually breaking off the block of a covered lineman rather than the isolation block of the linebacker. As a result, the lead back has to be a bit more cautious and can not "sell-out" as aggressively on his lead draw block, fearing lunging out at the linebacker while the linebacker side steps the blocker to step up and make the tackle.

If the linebacker blitzes, the lead blocker executes the same type of technique as he would on an isolation block. He breaks down sooner in his approach and worries more about colliding with the linebacker through the middle and up under the shoulder pads than any follow-through type action.

If the linebacker crosses the face of the lead blocker in his attempt to pursue the ball, the lead draw blocker rips through the opposite breast of the linebacker in relation to the direction he is flowing, in the same north-south fashion of the isolation block. This blocking technique attempts to blow the linebacker across the hole by taking him in the direction he wants to go. This technique is the same as on an isolation block on a linebacker who picks a side in his attempt to get to the ballcarrier. This is shown in Diagram 11-4.

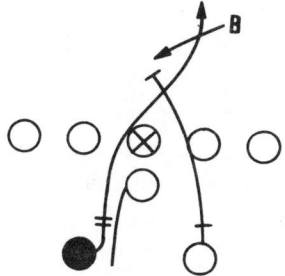

**DIAGRAM 11-4**
**Lead Draw Blocking Action vs. Linebacker Who Crosses Face of Blocker to Get to the Ballcarrier**

## THE KICK-OUT BLOCK

The kick-out block is derived, of course, from the kick-out blocking assignment on the defensive end, or end defender on the line of scrimmage, to allow the running back to cut up inside of the kick-out block by having been provided with an inside running lane. The kick-out block is shown in Diagram 11-5 to provide an off-tackle run lane.

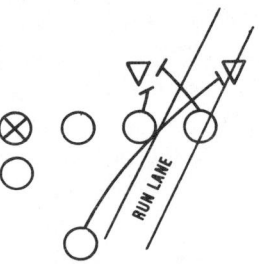

**DIAGRAM 11-5**
**The Kick-Out Block**

The key to the block is an explosive take-off in an attempt to attack the defensive end with speed and aggressiveness before the defensive end has time to properly read and react to the play. A back can easily see that there is almost always a physical mismatch between him and the defensive end. However, if the blocker takes advantage of the offensive weapons he has, he can whip the defender.

The blocker must keep in mind that he knows where the point of attack is, whom he is going to block and on what count the play is going to start. The defensive end knows none of this. Here lies the blocker's great advantage. The defensive end must initially take the time to read the play action to determine his necessary defensive reaction. In addition, the defensive end is often given "jamming" type assignments on the tight end while attempting such reads. At best, the first few steps are shuffle or jabbing-type steps in an effort to read and/or jam and be in a position to react to all possible types of situations. Thus, the blocker, by exploding out of his stance at maximum speed directly at the defensive end, has the ability to explode into the defensive end with his block before the end can charge back. The size and power of the defensive end is therefore overcome.

The kick-out blocker is also aided in his ability to explosively attack the defensive end through the "freeze" technique in which the ballcarrier runs directly at the defensive end in an attempt to set up the block. By not "tipping-off" where he will be cutting until the block is thrown, the ballcarrier helps put the defensive end in a "freeze," forcing him to sit and read the route of the ballcarrier. A sitting, reading defensive end is certainly easier to block than one who knows where the ballcarrier is going and as a result can forcefully attack the point of attack of the play.

The actual execution of the kick-out block is accomplished by exploding out of the blocker's stance and approaching the defensive end at top speed with a low, gathered, explosive carry of the body. The most important concept on the take-off is to take an inside-out route to ensure that the blocker will be able to ensure the inside-out blow necessary to produce a kick-out block. The inside-out angle of approach is shown in Diagram 11-5. Keeping the elbows in tight to the body will help produce a tightly gathered powerful approach and help avoid any standing up. The block is delivered by ripping up through the inside breast of the defensive end. The actual techniques for contact and follow-through are the same for the kick-out block as they are for the isolation block. The back uses the same north-south press of the block in which the back attempts to envelop the defender in the "V" of his arms. Actually, the proper terminology for the thrust of the block is north-south to the flag. Therefore, once the kick-out blocker makes contact up under the shoulder pad of the inside breast and continues on a north-south follow-through drive to the flag, he will cut off the defender's pursuit ability to the ballcarrier. Even if the blocker does not cut off such a pursuit angle, a continued press of the block via proper follow-through should enable the ballcarrier to escape up inside of the block as he hugs the double team block.

Another important reason for the inside-out approach of the kick-out block is that such an approach will allow the blocker to form a good base upon contact. A poor inside-out approach often means a cross-over-the-midline-step by the blocker, which eliminates the good blocking base necessary for the block's success since the positioning of the feet will be one in front of the other upon contact. The reason for such action is that the kick-out blocker is often forced to step across the midline of his body with his outside foot to get the proper inside-out angle that the block requires. This action is seen in Diagram 11-6.

Two major variations can take place as a result of defensive movement after the snap of the ball. The first is the defensive end closing down hard making a kick-out block virtually impossible due to

Proper inside-out angle with a good base

Improper inside-out angle resulting in cross-over-the-midline step and a poor base

DIAGRAM 11-6
Proper and Improper Kick-Out Approach Angles and Resulting Bases

the angle of attack of the kick-out blocker. When this action occurs, the kick-out blocker simply attempts to add thrust to the play by blasting over the top of the defender in an attempt to "make-it-happen." Such an aggressive action is the best reaction to the defensive maneuver, since such an aggressive blocking action will result in just that—making something happen. Usually, the something is positive. This is a far cry from what will happen if the kick-out blocker hesitates, slows down or attempts to kick-out without the proper inside-out angle.

The other defensive reaction to the kick-out block is the hard inside slant charge by the defender to be kicked-out resulting in a lock-on action by the tight end in his down blocking assignment. If this happens, the kick-out blocker hugs the lock-on action tightly and continues upfield in an effort to find a defender to block and add thrust to the play. Such a defender will often be a pursuing inside linebacker. This is seen in Diagram 11-7.

## THE FAKE AND BLOCK

The fake and block technique is just what the title says. A back fakes a ballcarry as discussed in Chapter 10, and in one fluid motion, continues on to block a defender. The back fakes the carry of the ball off of some type of inside run action and maintains the arm press of the fake against the body until he is stepping on the toes of the defender to be blocked. What the faker must realize is that a great fake of the

Developing Backfield Run Blocking Techniques 207

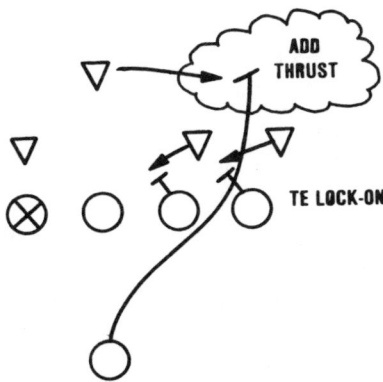

**DIAGRAM 11-7**
**Hand Inside Slant Change of Defender to Be Kick-Out Resulting in Tight End Lock-On Action**

ballcarry may make his second job easy. If, as a result of the great fake, the back can force the assigned defender to commit to his fake and tackle him, he eliminates the need and worry of making the block altogether.

The actual techniques of the block off the fake and block action can vary greatly. Such factors as the type of play fake action utilized, the positioning of the faker in relation to the position of the man to be blocked or whether the play is a run or a pass all help to determine what type of technique is needed to eliminate the assigned defender.

The first fake and block technique is simply the crash technique in which the back holds his fake course and does not veer off of it to get a good blocking angle on the defender. Instead, he relies on a great fake to hold the defender in his alignment and then crashes into whatever piece of that defender is in the path of his constant course. He may very well find that such action will seal the defender in the desired direction (inside or outside), or the blocker may find himself crashing through the defender's inside leg on an outside run play. However, if the fake is a good one and the crash is solid enough, there will be sufficient contact to slow the defender down enough to hinder his ability to pursue the ballcarrier.

The next fake and block technique is the legal clip. As the back comes out of his fake, he pursues the assigned defender until he is stepping on his heels. Once in this position, he simply takes the closest shoulder and drives it down through the back of the defender's knee area in an attempt to collapse the legs. Once the defender is on the ground, the back must whip his inside elbow tightly up and out to the sideline to propel the blocker's body into a series of three rolls over the back of the defender so that he is unable to regain his balance or get up and pursue the ballcarrier.

The shoulder drive technique is just the opposite of the crash technique. The faker breaks out of his inside run fake course to get good inside-out or outside-in positioning on the assigned defender. The same north-south thrust of the isolation block is utilized as the blocker drives his head in front of the pursuing defender and drives north-south as he catches the pursuing defender in the "V" of his neck and blocking arm. Continued north-south follow-through and a maintenance of the press of the block will seal the defender off from the ballcarrier.

If the blocker finds that the defender has pursued too quickly towards the ballcarrier to utilize any of the aforementioned techniques, he must pursue the defender until the defender breaks down in an effort to make contact and drive the defender in the direction of his pursuit across the face of the ballcarrier's path. Or, if the blocker already has made contact but cannot seal off his pursuit, he must maintain the press of the block, and attempt to drive the pursuing defender across the face of the ballcarrier's path. In this manner, the ballcarrier will be able to break for daylight off of such action.

The fake and block action on pass plays faces the problem of an offensive interference penalty if the blocker makes contact beyond one yard past the line of scrimmage on a pass over the line of scrimmage. The crash technique is usually the best technique to apply since the good fake is a prerequisite to the success of a good play action pass action, although the legal clip technique could be applied. The major problem is to be sure that the blocker plants a foot short of a yard past the line of scrimmage to halt his forward motion so he does not make contact and commit the penalty. A good teaching technique is to tell the back when in doubt about whether he is beyond a yard or not, stop—he probably is.

## THE LEAD BLOCK

The lead block, or the direct block of a back on an interior lineman with little, or no faking action, takes on the characteristics of both the fake and block action and the cut block to be discussed in Chapter 12. The basic difference of the lead block from the fake and block action is that the back is selling out for the block at the expense of the fake. There may be little difference between the lead block and the cutdown block as the same cutdown block technique to be discussed in Chapter 12 may be utilized as one of the techniques to execute the lead block. Thus, the lead block can utilize the crash and legal clip techniques of the fake and block or the cutdown block to eliminate an interior defensive lineman.

## THE ARC BLOCK

The arc block is part of a two man tandem unit in which a speeding ballcarrier is positioned just behind a blocker in an effort to get the ball to the outside on, say, some type of sweep or option action. The ballcarrier does not trail the arc blocker. Instead, he is positioned off the arc blocker's outside hip 1 yard by 1 yard to make it difficult for a defender to pursue the ballcarrier due to the shielding action of the arc blocker as a result of their relationship. An important concept to be taught is that the ballcarrier must remain in that relationship if he is to help set up a successful arc block. The ballcarrier is the key to the actual block. They must look like two jets in formation. As the arc blocker goes, so goes the ballcarrier until the contact of the block is made.

The basic premise of the arc block concept is that if the arc blocker runs a proper arc-shaped course forcing the defender to come to him, and if the ballcarrier and arc blocker remain in their proper relationship, the defender cannot make the tackle. If the defender tries to come in from behind, the arc blocker takes his block up sharply into the defender as the ballcarrier escapes to the outside. If the defender fights through the arc blocker's head, the defender will set up the best possible arc block situation for the arc blocker. If the defender overcommits to the outside while fighting through the arc blocker's head, the ballcarrier breaks upfield up under the block. If the defender forces the arc blocker so far to the sideline that a running lane cannot be ensured or if the penetration of the defender is so deep that the arc block cannot be executed, a reverse hip technique off of the normal arc block action is utilized as the ballcarrier cuts up inside. Diagram 11-8 shows the proper arc blocker-ballcarrier relationship.

The initial course of the arc blocker is of extreme importance. He must start his course toward a point where the line of scrimmage intersects the sideline. This enables the arc blocker to encompass *any* possible pitch support defender within his arc course, thus the *explicit* assignment of searching for the pitch support defender from outside-in! Once the pitch or sweep support defender has been identified, the arc

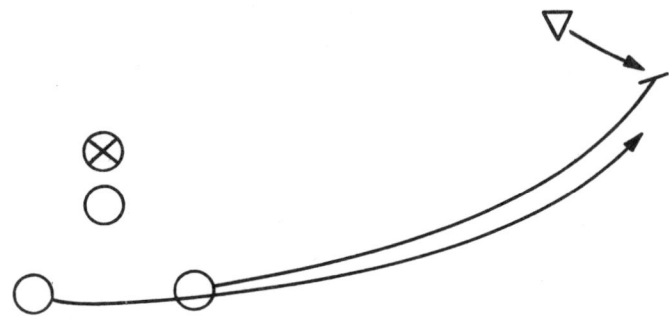

**DIAGRAM 11-8**
**Proper Arc Blocker-Ballcarrier Relationship**

blocker simply shapes his arc to a course where the blocker's inside shoulder can intersect with the defender's outside knee. Upon contact the arc blocker bends upfield at a 45 degree angle to maximize blocking surface and power to get a tight fit of the block. The arc blocker *must* strive to achieve the arc block at all costs until the extremes of either being too close to the sideline or too deep in the backfield exist.

The block is thrown with a ripping up action of the inside arm crashing through the defender in an attempt to get the head in front of and beyond the defender coupled with a slight turning of the inside hip up into the defender to give the block a broader surface. The important part of the block, however, is the striving for the initial body positioning creating the inside seal of the defender. Of equal importance to the block's development is that the arc blocker must not attempt to deliver the block until he is "stepping-on-the-toes" of the pitch support defender.

If the extremes of too wide a positioning of the defender to the sideline or too deep a positioning in the backfield exist, the reverse technique off the arc block action is executed by concentrating all thrust of the block into the hip, as the legs of the arc blocker are whipped around the defender and upfield. The reverse technique comes directly off the arc block look to help set it up. The arc blocker attacks the defender as if he were to throw a normal arc block. However, the initial ripping action of the inside arm becomes a decoy as the inside hip is simultaneously whipped around and the legs whipped upfield in an effort to seal the defender out the sideline.

There are definite coaching points for when to utilize the reverse technique off the arc block. When the defender to be arc blocked

*Developing Backfield Run Blocking Techniques* 211

penetrates so deep into the backfield that you can no longer see his outside leg, or would have to belly deeper to get to it, reverse arc block. When you feel that you are so close to the sideline (3 to 4 yards) that your block on the defender will do nothing but clog the running lane up the sideline, also reverse arc block. Diagram 11-9 shows these two problems.

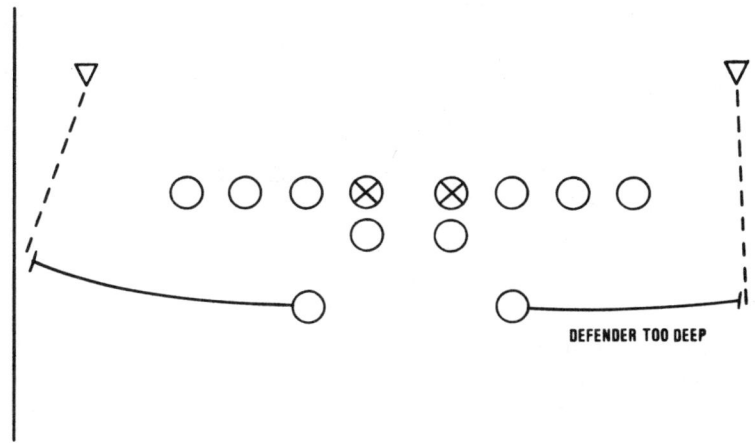

**DIAGRAM 11-9**
**Examples of Needs for Reverse Arc Block**

It must be kept in mind that the defender assigned to pitch support can come from many different alignments on many different pursuit angles from many different defensive actions. Walk-away ends, defenders in bump-and-go alignments on wide receivers, crash charges and cross charges—these are all examples of the type of actions the arc blocker (and the ballcarrier) must be ready to adjust to. The arc blocker has to take up the arc within the arc to get to the outside knee of the pitch support defender no matter how sharp or acute that arc within the arc may be. Diagram 11-10 shows various examples the arc block may have to shape to get to the desired contact point with the pitch support defender.

## BACKFIELD RUN BLOCKING TECHNIQUES
## PRACTICE AND DRILLS

As in the practice of any other backfield skill, the coach must set up the game-like drills which will help the back develop the actual

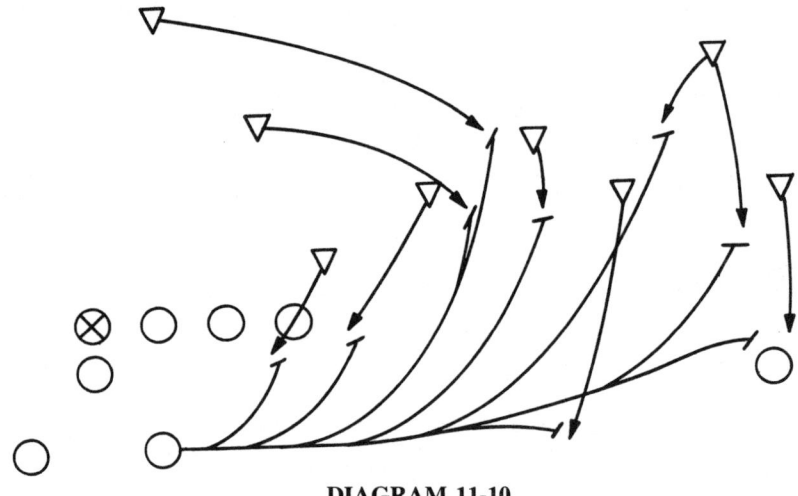

**DIAGRAM 11-10**
**Varying Arcs Taken by the Arc Blocker**

skills he will need in a game. The coach must again go to the playbook rather than the drillbook and break down actual portions of the offensive play as they will be performed on the field so that such game-like practice can take place. This does not mean that pure blocking drills will not be of value. Such a concept is far from true. However, any drill utilized must help the player develop skills he will need to execute his assignments, otherwise the drills will be artificial.

### Drill #1: Board

The Board Drill is certainly not a new drill concept. The drill helps to develop an explosive stance and take-off, a wide base, proper throttle-down action to help broaden the base by dropping the tail prior to contact, proper contact and proper follow-through. It is an excellent preseason drill when the most basic fundamentals are being taught or reviewed. The drill helps to develop the all-important drive block utilized on the isolation, lead draw and kick-out blocking assignments. The backs fire out, explode up into the dummies held by other backs and drive the dummies backwards off the boards via proper follow-through techniques. Two bevelled boards can be placed side by side to force the desired wide base. As on all blocking action, the block is maintained until the whistle is blown. The drill must be sure to practice drive blocking left and right as well as straight ahead. The drill is shown in Diagram 11-11.

*Developing Backfield Run Blocking Techniques* 213

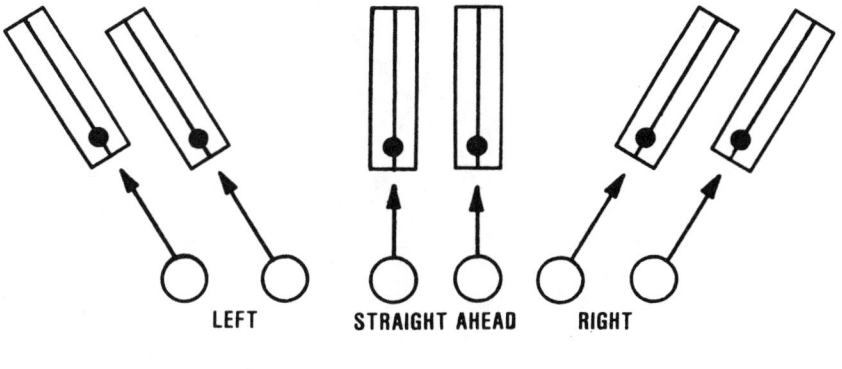

DIAGRAM 11-11
Board Drill

*Coaching Points:* All of the proper drive blocking techniques utilized on the isolation, kick-out and lead draw block must be taught. Special emphasis is placed on proper contact, base and follow-through.

### Drill #2: One-Man Sled

The One-Man Sled Drill helps develop the same skills that the Board Drill does. However, the action of the sled will help to heighten the practice of proper base and body balance during the contact and follow-through action. Actually, a one-man drive action on a two-man sled may be an even better drill than using a one-man sled since the drive of a two-man sled by one blocker requires a greater coordination of body balance, contact and follow-through. The backs must drive each side of the sled, so as to learn the use of both shoulders.

### Drill #3: Isolation-Lead Draw Block

The Isolation-Lead Draw Block Drill helps to develop the proper blocking techniques utilized on the isolation and the lead draw plays. Another back (a linebacker could actually be used in a semi-live type situation) holds a large shield and on the snap of the ball or starting cadence makes one of the possible reactions that a linebacker could make on a lead draw or isolation play in relation to the blocker attacking him. The drill and possible linebacker reactions are shown in Diagram 11-12.

*Coaching Points:* The coach signals to the linebacker what reaction he wants and calls out what type of blocking action he wants by the back

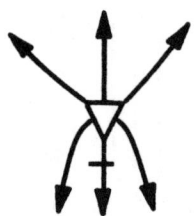

**DIAGRAM 11-12**
**Isolation-Lead Draw Block Drill**

(isolation or lead draw). All points for proper execution of the isolation and lead draw blocks are checked. The coach must be sure to vary the linebacker reactions for each blocker. The backs must be sure to practice the blocks from both sides.

### Drill #4: Kick-Out

The Kick-Out Drill is set up and run similarly to the Isolation-Lead Draw Drill. A back, or possibly a defensive end if live action is desired, holds a large shield and on a signal from the coach executes one of the three defensive maneuvers that the kick-out blocker might face as the back executes his proper kick-out action. The drill and possible end defender reactions are shown in Diagram 11-13. The backs must practice the blocking actions to both sides.

*Coaching Points:* As seen in Diagram 11-13, a tape or hose should be placed on the ground to help create proper alignment and positioning of the blocker and defender.

### Drill #5: Fake and Block

The Fake and Block Drill is also set up in the same fashion as the Isolation-Lead Draw Block Drill and the Kick-Out Block Drill except that a heavy bag is used if the simulation is that of a defensive lineman. All of the various techniques of the fake and block action (crash, legal

*Developing Backfield Run Blocking Techniques* 215

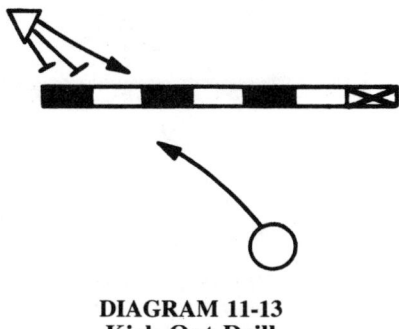

**DIAGRAM 11-13
Kick-Out Drill**

clip, shoulder drive or driving an overpursuing defender past the ballcarrier run lane) are practiced against all of the various reactions that blocker may see from the defender he is assigned to block. This is shown in Diagram 11-14.

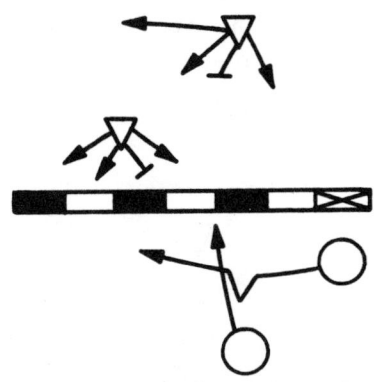

**DIAGRAM 11-14
Fake and Block Drill**

*Coaching Points:* A quarterback could be used to help practice the fake.

### Drill #6: Lead

The Lead Drill also simply enacts all the possible techniques and defensive reactions that might occur on a lead block assignment. A heavy bag is used to simulate a defensive lineman. The defensive reactions should be varied and the backs should practice the lead block to both sides. The drill is shown in Diagram 11-15.

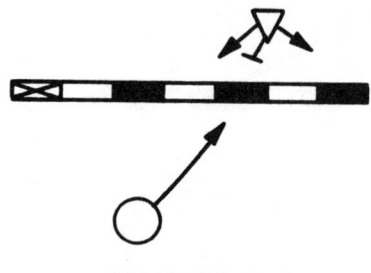

**DIAGRAM 11-15
Lead Block Drill**

### Drill #7: Arc Block

The Arc Block Drill enacts all the techniques and defensive reactions that might occur on an arc block assignment. The back simulating the defender carries a heavy shield. The action must be practiced to both sides. In addition, it is important that the arc blocking action be practiced with a ballcarrier since the relationship of the arc blocker and the ballcarrier is paramount to the execution of the block and helps the ballcarrier to practice his important role as well. The drill is shown in Diagram 11-16.

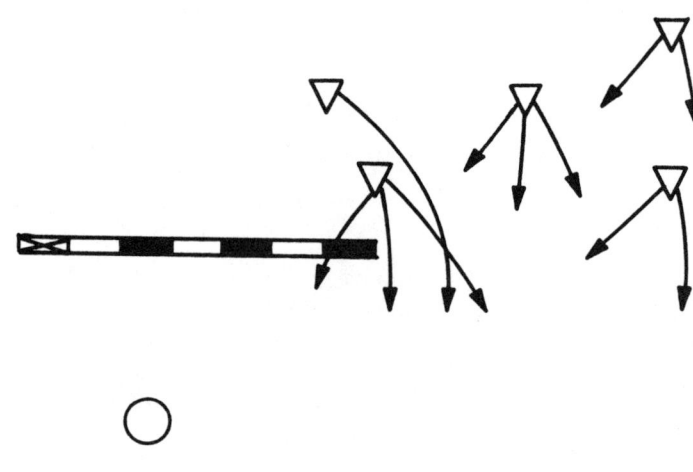

**DIAGRAM 11-16**

*Coaching Points:* As shown in Diagram 11-16, the back simulating the defender must vary both his alignment and his reaction. A strong safety, monster or corner back type defender could be used to create a live situation without a shield. It is important that the back is given reverse arc block situations in the drill so that skill can be practiced.

### Drill #8: Multiple Run Block

The Multiple Run Block Drill (actually pass blocking action can be added to simply make the drill a multiple block drill) is an excellent rapid fire drill which helps to create great variety of blocking assignments, technique execution and defensive reaction. The drill does, however, require a large number of service defenders to man the drill. A second coach may even be needed to help expedite the drill. The drill simply sets up all of the aforementioned situations of the Isolation-Lead Draw Drill, the Kick-Out Drill, the Fake and Block Drill, and the Arc Block Drill. Two backs work at the same time to accommodate more repetitions. A second coach can help to position the defenders properly and call for a variety of defensive reactions once the coach working with the blockers calls out for a specific blocking assignment. It is important to vary the defensive alignments as well as the defensive reactions. Diagram 11-17 shows a possible alignment of the drill, which can be varied according to the desired defense to be practiced against. The numerous individual reactions of each defender

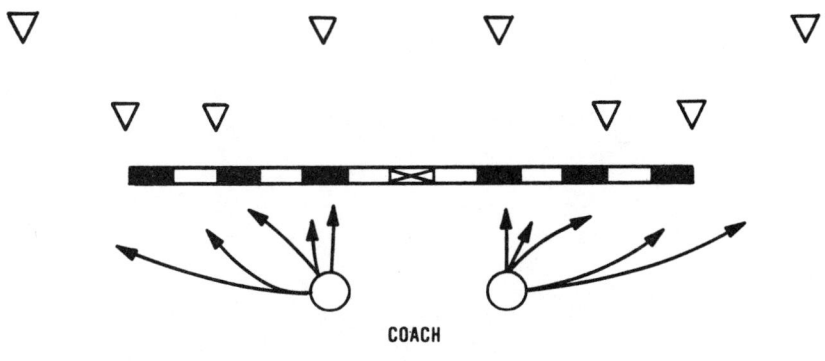

**DIAGRAM 11-17**
**Multiple Run Block Drill**

are not diagrammed to avoid cluttering the diagram (they have already been shown in Diagrams 11-12 to 11-16).

*Coaching Points:* Interior defensive linemen are simulated via the use of heavy bags as all other defenders use large hand shields.

On almost all of these drills, it was mentioned that it is important for the backs to practice their blocking to both sides. Actually, such practice to each side is needed only if the back actually executes blocks to each side. If, via the offense concept, his backfield alignment remains constant and, as a result, he only blocks to one side, then he need only practice his blocks to that side.

## twelve

# Developing Backfield Pass Blocking Techniques

There are basically two types of backfield pass blocking techniques to master—cut blocking and pass pro blocking. Cut blocking, although it may appear to be a difficult block, can become a high percentage block for the backs. Once they get the hang of this block, they will enjoy performing it because of its effectiveness in regard to the execution of the play and the demoralizing effect it has on the usually bigger and stronger defender who is being cut down.

Pass pro blocking, however, may be the most difficult blocking task for the backs to master. As a more passive block, it can take away the few advantages a back may have in blocking a large defensive lineman—speed, explosive power and surprise. However, diligent effort and concentrated practice on pass pro blocking can help to develop effective backfield pass pro blockers.

### THE CUTDOWN BLOCK

The cutdown block is a block which attempts to "cut down" (rip the outside leg or legs from under) the first defender outside the tackle's block or the end defender on the line of scrimmage, depending on the defensive alignment and the type of blocking scheme called. It can also be used in a run game block as a technique for the lead block (blocking an interior defensive lineman) or load or "H" block (to cut down the end defender on the line of scrimmage on a sweep or pitch play). Since they all utilize the same execution technique and are, in actuality, the same block, the discussion of the cut block has been saved for the pass game where it is most commonly used. Diagram 12-1 shows three types of uses for the cutdown block.

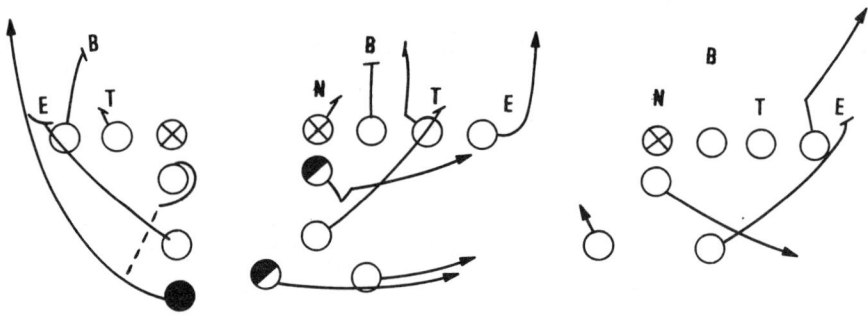

"H" or load block      Lead block      Cutdown on sprint action

DIAGRAM 12-1
Examples of Uses for Cutdown Block

On sprint-out or move-out type action, the cutdown block is utilized for a variety of reasons. The cutdown block gets the blocker to the defender fast with maximum blocking thrust and power and keeps the block away from the launch point with less possibility of interference with the passer. The cutdown block also denies the defender penetration, forcing him to make a more lateral move to avoid the block. The more the defender moves laterally, the easier it is for the quarterback to see the movement and adjust the launch point as needed. In addition, the cutdown block helps to keep the defender's hands down preventing any interference with the pass play as he tries to fend off the low blocking action of the cutdown block.

The blocker must understand that the quarterback's action will, in itself, help deny an inside rush route by the defender. Thus, the emphasis of the blocking is the effort to gain outside leverage on the defender's outside leg, denying both penetration into the backfield and lateral movement as the defender is actually sealed to the inside. Such an inside rush route does create a tougher technique problem for the blocker. However the blocker will be able to accomplish his task by shaping his approach up into the inside rush of the defender and utilize a shoulder block to bump the defender off his course. If the defender chooses to go outside of the block in an attempt to get around the blocker, he will be easily seen in the quarterback's peripheral vision and avoided by the quarterback's adjustment of the launch point. If the rusher attempts to jump over the cutdown block, the blocker can effectively combine his speed and power with as broad a block as possible to effectively protect the launch point. When the pass called requires the quarterback to move more than five steps to the outside, another back can be assigned to the outside knee of the rusher. Diagram 12-2 shows how the relationship of the quarterback and cutdown blocker helps to deny the possibility of an inside rush hindering the development of the play.

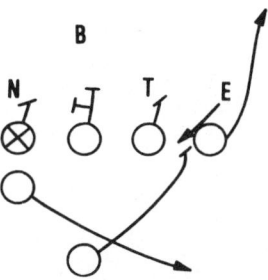

**DIAGRAM 12-2**
**Quarterback-Cutdown Blocker Relationship Denying Inside Rush from Threatening Play**

An explosive take-off is of utmost importance. As on the kick-out block, the defender must initially read the offensive action to properly react to the block. In addition, the defender is often on some type of "jamming" assignment. Thus, the blocker, by exploding out of his stance at maximum speed directly at the defender's outside knee, has the ablility to explode into the defender with the cutdown block before the defender can charge back into the blocker. Such action enables the usually smaller blocker to nullify and overcome the defender's normal advantage of size and power.

The aiming point of the block is the top of the defender's outside knee. However, three things are paramount to the success of the block. First, the blocker must not attempt to throw the block until he is "stepping-on-the-toes" of the defender. Such an action prevents a loss of contact and/or lunging-out. Second, the blocker must secure a tight fit on the defender to enable maximum blocking surface, power and contact. A tight fit is achieved by concentrating on driving the inside shoulder down through the defender's crotch as the blocker attempts to drive the shoulder through the top of the outside knee to rip the outside leg from under the defender. Third, the blocker must rip the block north-south through the defender's outside knee. Such action will in itself help to seal the defender to the inside. The major breakdown of a cutdown block is the east-west throwing of the block in which the inside shoulder and head of the blocker ends up being thrust towards the sideline. Such action enables the defender to play through the head of the blocker to the outside since the blocker loses both his contact and power.

If the defender tries to get inside of the blocker, the blocker just shapes his attack up into the defender, again north-south and puts a shoulder into the defender to enable the quarterback to escape to the outside. If the defender moves upfield or outside laterally, the blocker must remember the cardinal rule of not throwing the block until he is stepping-on-the-toes of the defender. Sooner or later, the defender will have to react through the blocker if he is to attempt to rush on the quarterback.

Follow-through via rolling is of utmost importance to the block's success. Cutting a defender down is of little use if he is able to get up and pursue to pressure the quarterback. The important concept of rolling to prevent the defender from regaining his balance is that the blocker must roll into the defender in an attempt to maintain contact as long as possible. The rolling action is initiated by whipping the outside elbow back into the defender immediately after the contact of the cutdown block. If the defender attempts to jump over the blocker after the block is thrown, the blocker must follow through by ripping, or lifting, straight up through the defender's crotch as the defender is jumping over or straddling the blocker underneath him.

When there are two backs assigned to cutdown one defender, two techniques can be utilized. In the first, the first blocker can set up the blocking by crashing down through the center of the defender with normal cutdown blocking action as the second defender cleans up with normal cutdown blocking action through the outside knee. The second technique has the first cutdown blocker attempt to cut the defender by himself through his normal cutdown blocking action, and the second blocker only "cleans-up" if needed.

Whether one or two backfield blockers are utilized, there is often the situation where the defender to be cutdown drops off into pass coverage leaving no one for the back to cutdown block. When this situation occurs, the back must vision such action as he approaches the line of scrimmage. As he sees the defender drop off into pass coverage,

# Developing Backfield Pass Blocking Techniques

he continues to a point out past the next blocker inside of his intended block, wheels to the inside and readies himself to cutdown block the first defender that comes free in pursuit down the line of scrimmage. This sealing type of cutdown block in which he helps block a defender who has slipped off a teammate's block or a linebacker who is pursuing close to the line of scrimmage is executed in the same fashion as a normal cutdown block. His aiming point is the top of the outside (upfield) knee of the defender to come free. This action is shown in Diagram 12-3.

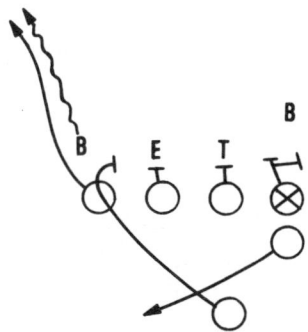

**DIAGRAM 12-3**
**Cutdown Blocker Turning Inside to Help Once His Assigned Defender Drops Off into Pass Coverage**

Two other points need mentioning. If the defender to be cutdown blocked feathers out down the line of scrimmage dropping off only 3 or 4 yards off the line of scrimmage, the cutdown blocker must slide along down the line of scrimmage and position himself between the defender and the quarterback. In this way, he will be able to protect the quarterback if that defender decides to put on a delayed rush. If the cutdown blocker turns inside to help prematurely and the defender puts on such a delayed rush, the quarterback will be unprotected. The key coaching point is that if in doubt as to what the defender is doing, stay in front of the defender to protect the quarterback—don't leave him unprotected by turning inside to help. This action is shown in Diagram 12-4.

The second point is coupled with the first. When in such a sit and wait situation, whether it be because the defender to be cutdown blocked neither drops off into pass coverage nor rushes, or because the blocker has turned inside to help and there is no one to help on the

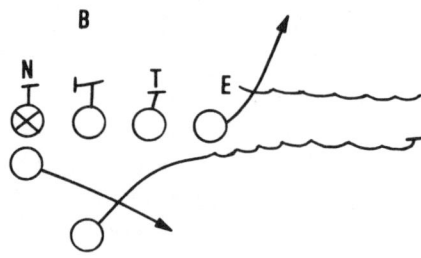

**DIAGRAM 12-4**
**Cutdown Blocker Staying in Front of Defender Who Neither Rushes nor Drops into Pass Coverage**

cutdown, the back must be ready for a possible "Go!" call by the quarterback. The "Go!" call will allow the back to release upfield to run block for the now running quarterback.

Another major problem of the cutdown block is that the cutdown blocker will often find that he is not able to get a tight fit of the block because the defender is feathering out away from him and, therefore, he is unable to rip out the outside leg of the defender. Such action usually results in the defender fending off the block with his hands and his legs are kept away from the blocker. If this situation arises, the back immediately goes into a scramble block technique in an attempt to prevent the defender from regaining the balance needed to slip to the outside and pursue the play. The back attempts to scramble into the defender's legs to tie the defender up until the whistle is blown.

## THE PASS PRO BLOCK

Body positioning and a controlled delivering of the pass pro block to the rusher are the keys to success in blocking an outside rusher. By body positioning we mean the fact that if the pass pro back is between the rusher and the quarterback, the rusher will not be able to get to the quarterback. Pass pro backs must be taught that utilization of proper pass pro techniques will prevent the pass rusher from being able to go over the top of the blocker. If the rusher tried to go around the blocker, the "riding-out or riding-in" techniques will lengthen the route of the rusher helping to buy time for the quarterback. The backs must understand that their assignment is not to attempt to knock the pass rusher down or backwards. Rather, it is to buy time for the quarterback. Each yard a blocker gives up grudgingly buys another second of time for the quarterback.

The pass pro blocker initially sets-up by taking a two step shuffle

*Developing Backfield Pass Blocking Techniques* 225

up and out towards the defensive end or end rusher to be blocked. This should position the back in the approximate area of the outside shoulder of the tackle. A major teaching point for the set-up is that the pass pro blocker should be taking a picture with his rear end of a spot one to one-and-a-half yards in front of the quarterback. Such an alignment will allow the rusher to see a rush lane through the outside shoulder of the blocker inviting the outside pass rush. However, the pass pro blocker will still be aligned so that his body is between the rusher and the quarterback. Such a set-up is shown in Diagram 12-5.

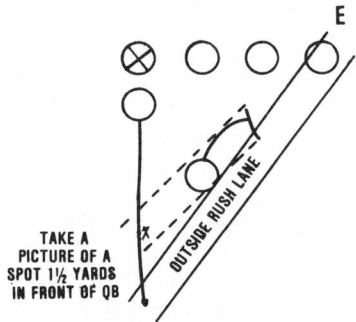

**DIAGRAM 12-5**
**Proper Back Pass-Pro Positioning for End Rusher**

The tail of the blocker is sunk low to ready him for the standing-the-rusher-up blow. The elbows are kept in tight to the body to allow for a low and powerfully gathered stance. The fists of the blocker are held in front of the blocker's breasts.

The pass pro blocker does not chop his feet up and down. This is unnatural and is always stopped when the blow is about to be delivered. At times the blocker can even be caught off balance while utilizing such a chopping motion. Instead, the blocker should have "floating-feet" which are ready to shuffle in any direction to maintain his inside-out alignment in the pass rusher's path to the quarterback.

The pass pro blocker MUST HAVE PATIENCE! If the pass rusher is slow in his approach, the blocker MUST NOT ATTACK! It must be remembered that the assignment of the pass pro blocker is to buy time for the quarterback. If the rusher is slow to approach, the blocker must wait for him—buying time all the while. Attacking a slow rusher, or any rusher, will only mean lunging and overextending the block—the death knells for a pass pro blocker.

The key to delivering the blow is to explode at a point half way between the center of the rusher and his inside breast up under the shoulder pads, when the rusher is so close that all the blocker sees is the number of the rusher in his face. The blocker then slams, or rips upward with his fists and forearms simultaneously, his elbows extending up and away from the body in an effort to stand the rusher up and stop his charge. During this technique, the blocker arches his back and snaps his hips up under the pass rusher. As previously mentioned, the blocker must not attempt to blast the rusher backwards for when the blocker's weight is out forward, he is unable to recoil and reset into his pass pro stance to deliver another blow. The additional power exerted in the delivering of the extended blow may be initially more successful on the first blow. However, it is usually the end of the blocker's efforts to buy time for the quarterback as the rusher uses the overextended position of the blocker to thrust himself forward to the quarterback. In addition, he must not attempt to blast the rusher upwards so extensively that he straightens and locks his legs. Such a straightening up and locking is just as dangerous as an extended blow. While extra force will be exerted, the straightening up and locking action of the legs will often mean the back has too much resetting to do and will not be able to accomplish it in time to deliver his next blow. Proper and improper delivering of the pass pro blow techniques are shown in Figure 12-1.

Once the pass pro blocker has "ripped-up" into the rusher and stood-him-up, he resets into his original pass pro-type stance by dropping off the rusher inside and back towards the quarterback. Thus, the pass pro blocker maintains his inside-out alignment and creates another outside rush lane to invite a continued outside pass rush by the defender. The back must be careful on his recoil not to leave his hands out in front of him as he drops off the rusher. He may in no way be holding. However, if the referee sees the arms extended and the hands (fists) in close proximity to the rusher, he will have no choice but to call a holding penalty.

The object of the pass pro technique is to deliver the blow, recoil, deliver the blow, recoil until the passer releases the ball. Keeping one's cool is extremely important each time the blocker recoils. He must again become patient and wait until the rusher's numbers are disappearing in his face. A common error of many pass pro blockers, whether linemen or backs, is that they will often attempt to attack the rusher early after they have recoiled once or twice, and risk the loss of the rusher by lunging or having their weight extended forward. Each time the pass pro blocker recoils, he must coolly start all over and buy time by grudgingly giving up ground.

*Developing Backfield Pass Blocking Techniques* 227

Proper set-up

Proper delivering of the pass-pro blow

Improper overextension of the pass-pro blow

Improper straightening up and locking of legs on the pass pro blow

**FIGURE 12-1**
**Proper and Improper Delivering of Pass-Pro Blow Techniques**

There are some adjustments in techniques to handle the several situations that can occur when blocking the rusher. If on a recoil set-up the pass pro blocker begins losing the rusher to the outside, he will drive his head in front of the rusher in a sealing effort and ride the rusher out to the sidelines. A general rule is used. If the blocker, in his recoil, realizes that the numbers of rushers are beginning to disappear due to the lateral bypassing of the pass rusher, he should seal block. The seal block is executed by bringing up the flipper to the side of the neck to make contact with the rusher and attempting to create as broad a blocking surface as possible to try to catch the rusher in the "V" of the neck and flipper. The object is to then press the block of the "V" up in the rusher. If on the seal block drive of the rusher to the sidelines the pass rusher tries to disengage by reversing out underneath the seal to gain an inside rush lane, the blocker immediately whips the legs around and reverse crabs the defender. A simple rule is used here. As soon as the blocker feels he is losing the rusher underneath while sealing, whip the legs around to reverse crab block.

If the pass pro blocker begins to lose his rusher to the inside, he will execute the same technique of seal blocking and possible reverse crab except that the seal block attempts to ride the rusher across the center of the formation and out toward the opposite sidelines.

If on a recoil set-up the pass pro blocker realizes he is being overpowered by the pass rusher, the blocker immediately whips down into a cutdown block and scrambles into the defender's legs or rolls into the defender to maintain a press of the block. In this way, he will prevent the rusher from getting up and continuing his rush on the quarterback.

An important concept to understand is that recoiling, so avidly discussed in the execution of pass pro blocking, is often impossible to carry out. To the contrary, a back will often find that he is locked on to a pass rusher after he has delivered a pass pro blow. By locked on, it is meant that the blocker is pressed into the defender as he attempts to maintain his positioning between the rusher and the quarterback in his effort to block the rusher. To attempt to recoil would only give the edge to the rusher. The blocker would not have time to reset to deliver a new pass pro as all advantage would shift to the defender's overpowering rush. Instead of such a recoiling attempt, the back "dog-fights" the rusher by attempting to maintain the press of the "V" up under the defender's shoulder pads as long as possible. The blocker will find that he will probably slide to a chest-to-chest confrontation as the action continues. The blocker's emphasis now simply switches to maintaining the press as long as possible, staying in front of the rusher and keeping a good foot base.

## PASS PRO BLOCKING A BLITZING LINEBACKER

When the back is assigned to pass block a linebacker, three techniques can be utilized. First, the back can carry out a normal pass pro action in which he sets-up in the linebacker's rush path as he blitzes. However, since he is forced to take the blitzing linebacker head on, he loses the advantage of an inside-out positioning and the ability to ride the pass rusher to the sideline. Any such effort to position oneself inside-out on a blitzing linebacker will just "open-the-door" for the linebacker in his effort to get to the quarterback due to the pursuit angle advantage the linebacker has. Therefore, the back utilizing the pass pro technique versus a blitzing linebacker is forced to drop straight back on his recoil action and, as a result, stands a greater chance of losing the blitzing linebacker to the inside or outside.

Another disadvantage of utilizing a pass pro block versus a blitzing linebacker is that any retreating and recoiling action may interfere with a drop back quarterback's launch point and also put the pass rusher in a good position to bat the ball down even though the back may be executing a proper pass pro technique.

The better technique to use against the blitzing linebacker is to simply isolation block the linebacker before the blitzing linebacker can get through the line of scrimmage. The rush lane is narrowest at the line of scrimmage due to the blocking and rushing action of the offensive and defensive linemen. This gives the back the best opportunity to attack the blitzing linebacker to deliver a violent isolation type block up under the shoulder pads of the linebacker. Just as if he were up against a blitzing linebacker on an isolation block technique, the back concentrates more on the contact than on any follow-through technique in an effort to stop the blitzer's rush and stand him up. After the initial contact, the back attempts to stay pressed to the blitzer in an effort to create a pileup at the line of scrimmage with the rest of the blockers and rushers.

If the blitzing linebacker is able to clear the line of scrimmage, the back will usually be at a strong disadvantage due to the "head-of-steam" that the linebacker will have on his blitz action. In this situation, the back does best to execute a cutdown block technique by securing a tight fit down through the crotch of the blitzing linebacker. After the cutdown block is executed, the back must carry out his normal rolling action follow-through to prevent the blitzing linebacker from getting up to continue his rush on the quarterback.

## BACKFIELD PASS BLOCKING TECHNIQUES PRACTICE AND DRILLS

The backs, due to their heavy assignment and execution loads (ballcarrying, faking, blocking, receiving, etc.) are almost always pressed for time on the practice field. Since pass blocking for the backs is often the toughest blocking technique to master, much practice time is needed. If the coach will examine his practice format, he will see that there are more opportunities to practice pass blocking and, for that matter, blocking in general, than he realizes. An excellent example of this is during a skeleton pass scrimmage. There is no reason why a manager can't hold a cutdown dummy (24" high) at the end of the tape so that the back assigned to cut the end defender on the line of scrimmage on a sprint-out action pass play can practice his cutdown block technique. The same concept could be utilized for a pass rush on a back who is pass pro blocking by having an extra player align in the defensive end spot with a large shield and put on a pass rush.

One of the greatest misconceptions coaches have is that blocking practice must be done live or at near full speed. Actually, the opposite is true. So much of blocking in general is proper technique. Technique can be practiced effectively through the concept of form blocking in which *proper* technique is emphasized rather than high speed live work. A player cannot develop a high degree of proficiency at a psychomotor skill by attempting to go full speed emphasizing an aggressive attack if he has not mastered the fundamentals of that action.

Form blocking at ¾ speed forces the back to concentrate on precise technique. During form blocking, all techniques of the skills are exaggerated to help the individual's concentration on such techniques. Form blocking can be practiced all through unit and team practice. A thud scrimmage in which a back attacks the defender he is to block, slows down as he approaches the defender and then stops his action is one of the biggest wastes of practice time on the practice field. The coach may not want excessive cutdown blocking action on the practice field in fear of injuries. However, there is no reason why the back who is assigned the cutdown block can't practice an explosive take-off, a proper outside-in approach on the outside knee of the defender, proper throttle action to drop the tail and maintain a proper base and an explosive north-south ripping action of the cutdown block by a simulated ripping up action of the inside arm north-south through the upper torso of the defender (avoiding the dangerous repetition of the actual cutdown block action). Thus, all the actual skills of the cutdown block can be practiced with a high degree of concentration and proficiency. This is a far cry from approaching the defender to be blocked, putting a hand on him to signify you have him and stopping. Again, such form blocking emphasis is by no means limited to pass blocking.

### Drill #1: Cutdown

The drill simply practices an explosive take-off, proper outside-in positioning, proper throttling-down action and the proper north-south ripping action of the cutdown block on a 24" high cutdown bag. The special low bag is of great significance in helping to develop the low contact point just above the defender's knee. The backs must practice the cutdown block to both sides. The drill is shown in Diagram 12-6.

*Coaching Points:* The person holding the bag must stand to the outside so that he can avoid the action of the cutdown blocker. It is important to emphasize the rolling follow-through action after the contact of the cutdown block.

Two blockers, as shown in Diagram 12-6, could easily go at the same time to produce a maximum amount of repetitions. As previously mentioned, this drill could be added to a drill such as the skeleton pass drill to help create extra cutdown blocking practice. It is also important to note that this same drill can be utilized to practice such run blocks as the "H" block and the load block, since the technique is all the same or at least quite similar.

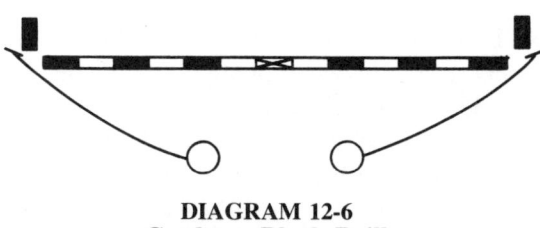

**DIAGRAM 12-6**
**Cutdown Block Drill**

### Drill #2: Big Bertha

Big Bertha is the name given to the monstrous sized pass blocking dummy hung from a frame. The Big Bertha Drill simply has a back take a normal stance on a 45 degree angle from Bertha, step up as on a normal pass pro blocking action to square up on Bertha and practice his normal delivering of the pass pro block and recoiling action. The back continues to rip up into Bertha and recoil until the coach blows the whistle. Big Bertha is shown in Diagram 12-7.

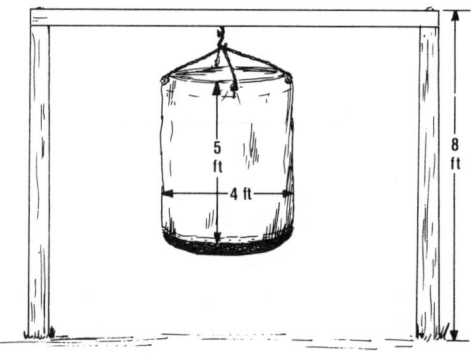

DIAGRAM 12-7
Big Bertha

*Coaching Points:* All the techniques of a proper pass pro block are stressed. Special emphasis is placed on the snapping under of the hips on the delivery of the blow and proper recoil action. The coach, or better yet a player so the coach can watch the blocker, helps to swing Bertha throughout the drill. On one of the recoil actions, the person swinging Bertha should hold her up and stop the swinging action to see if the blocker is waiting for the rusher to cover his face before he rips up into the rusher, or if he is lunging out at the rusher.

### Drill #3: Pass Pro Position

The Pass Pro Position Drill emphasizes proper body positioning of the back on his set-up, his positioning on the rusher as he rushes and as he repositions himself on his recoil technique. Such proper positioning forces the rushes to rush through the back's outside shoulder. The drill is a ¾ speed drill with little contact. It is similar to a mirror type drill in which the blocker is continually trying to maintain the proper positioning on the defender. The rusher utilizes all types of sharp cuts,

## Developing Backfield Pass Blocking Techniques

redirection of movement and changes of speed in an attempt to force the back out of proper position and open a better rush lane to the quarterback. The back continually readjusts his positioning to maintain the desired position. If the rusher gets close to the blocker's body, the block simulates an unloading of the pass pro blow by butting the rusher and then recoils in an attempt to maintain proper positioning. The drill is seen in Diagram 12-8.

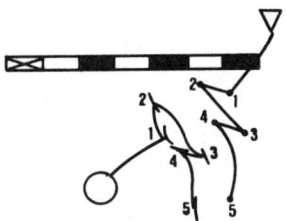

**DIAGRAM 12-8**
**Pass-Pro Position Drill**

*Coaching Points:* The coach is continually watching to see if the blocker is forcing the rusher to rush through his outside shoulder. The coach is checking for such proper techniques as foot shuffle (not crossing the feet), maintaining of a low, compact base and proper action for the delivery of the blow (in a modified sense since contact is not the focus of the drill) and proper recoil and reset action. Again, the focus of the drill and the technique is to keep the body of the blocker between the rusher and the quarterback forcing the rusher to rush through the back's outside shoulder.

### Drill #4: Pass Pro

The Pass Pro Drill is simply an enactment of a back executing his pass pro blocking techniques versus the various rush techniques of a defensive end type. The defender must vary his techniques. Two sets of blocker-rushers can be run at the same time providing they are spaced far enough apart so there are no unnecessary collisions. The drill is shown in Diagram 12-9.

*Coaching Points:* Diagram 12-9 shows the use of two tapes, or hoses, so that two sets of rusher-blockers are properly spaced avoiding any interference. The coach is, of course, coaching all of the various techniques associated with the pass pro blocking skills.

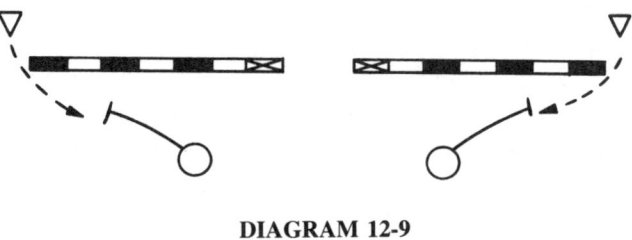

**DIAGRAM 12-9
Pass-Pro Drill**

### Drill #5: Pass Pro, Cutdown, Kick-Out

The Pass Pro, Cutdown, Kick-Out Drill is set up in the same fashion as the Pass Pro Drill shown in Diagram 12-8. However, the back practices the variety of his end of the line blocking techniques (pass pro, cutdown and kick-out) against a variety of defensive reactions. This drill is, perhaps, more realistic than the Pass Pro Drill since it creates more of a game-like situation and prevents the defender from uncommonly teeing off into an abnormally explosive pass rush.

*Coaching Points:* Again, the cutdown block can be practiced for both its pass blocking assignments as well as its run blocking usage.

### Drill #6: Ride-In/Ride-Out

The Ride-In/Ride-Out Drill is actually a breakdown of an important part of the pass pro block technique—the losing of a rusher to the inside or outside. Thus, the blocker is able to develop the proper techniques for riding the defender out to the sideline or across the formation to the opposite sideline by driving his head up in front of the defender to execute a seal block technique. The drill is set up by having a defender (another back could simulate a rusher) stand directly in front of the back. The back presses up against the rusher as if he has just delivered a blow up into him (the position he will be in just before he recoils). On a signal, the rusher blows past the back to the inside or the outside to simulate the situation of the back losing the rusher. The back now executes his proper seal blocking techniques to ride the rusher out to the sideline or across the formation towards the opposite sideline. The drill is shown in Diagram 12-10.

*Coaching Points:* The coach can further the value of the drill by having the rusher attempt to reverse out (spin out) under the seal blocking technique to force the back to execute proper scramble blocking techniques.

Developing Backfield Pass Blocking Techniques

**DIAGRAM 12-10**
**Ride-In/Ride-Out Drill**

### Drill #7: Scramble Block

The Scramble Block Drill helps develop the pass pro back's ability to scramble block the rusher from an unsettled and off-balance position. The scramble block is a last ditch effort when no other technique can be utilized. However, it is a very effective technique in keeping the rusher from the quarterback. The drill is set up by having the pass pro blocker take the unorthodox leaning position against a rusher as seen in the bottom left photo of Figure 12-1. On the signal of the coach, the rusher breaks away from the leaning back to cause him to lose balance and fall to the ground to help create the typical unsettled

**Starting position block**  **Rusher breaking away**

**FIGURE 12-2**
**Scramble Block Drill**

**Application of scramble**
**FIGURE 12-2 (continued)**

situation of a pass pro back losing the defender he is blocking and being in an awkward position. The back must immediately go into a scramble block by attempting to scramble up tightly into the legs of the rusher. The back continues the scramble action until the whistle is blown. The action of the drill is shown in Figure 12-2.

*Coaching Point:* The coach must concentrate on getting the backs to maintain a press of the scramble block up into the legs of the rusher until the whistle is blown.

# Index

## A

Air Dribble Drill, 33
Arc block, 209-211
Arc Block Drill, 216-217
Arc blocker and ballcarrier, relationship of, 86-87
Arm Wrestle Drill, 114
Around-the-Clock Drill, 178-179

## B

Backfield faking, drills for, 194-196 (see also "Faking")
Backfield option game, coaching, 119-143
    Counter Option Action, 133
    Counter Option Triple Option Dive Read, 125
    Inside Veer Option Action, 131-132
    Keep-Pitch Read Downhill Attack, 125-131
    Lead Option Action, 132
    Outside Veer Option Action, 134-135
    Outside Veer Triple Option Dive Read, 124-125
    practice and drills, 137-143
        Dive Read, 139
        Down-the-Line Pitch, 137
        Individual option, 140
        Multi-Option, 141-143
        Perimeter Option, 143
        Rapid Fire Option Pitch, 138-139
        Triple Option Read, 139-140
    Quarterback-Pitchback Pitch Ratio, 135-136

Backfield option game, coaching *(cont'd.)*
    Trap Option Action, 133-134
    Triple Option Dive Read, 119-124
Backfield pass blocking techniques, developing, 219-236 (see also "Pass blocking . . . .")
Backfield pass receiving techniques, coaching, 164-186 (see also "Pass receiving techniques . . . .")
Backfield stances and take-offs, 38-53
    practice and drills, 51-53
        Chute drill, 52-53
        Stance, Take-Off and Landmark, 52-53
    stances, 38-42
    take-offs, 43-53
        counter dive take-off, 47-48
        counter step take-off, 46-47
        dive take-off, 44
        end run take-off, 45-46
        off-tackle take-off, 44-45
        quick-pitch/swing pattern take-off, 48
        sprint draw tailback take-off, 51
        step technique, 43-44
        tailback "I" formation take-offs, 49-51
Backs, coaching to run for touchdowns, 76-108
    defender, dragging or carrying, 99
    dive concept, 77-82
    dive jump technique, 93-94
    dive squeeze technique, 94-96
    end-run techniques, 85-90
        arc blocker and ballcarrier relationship, 86
        Green Bay (pro) sweep, 89-90

*237*

Backs *(cont'd.)*
   freeze technique, 83-85
      effective on isolation play, 83
   open field running, 91-93
      north-south acceleration, 91-93
   practice and drills, 99-108
Burma Road, 105-106
   Carry, 107
      Dive, 99-100
      Dive Jump, 103-104
      Dive Squeeze, 103
      Drag, 106-107
      Flag, 102-103
      Nutcracker, 100-101
      Open Field Running, 107-108
      Seven Yard Line, 104-105
      Sideline, 101-102
      Stumble, 106
   spinning out technique, 96-97
   stumble technique, 98-99
Bad Ball Drill, 182
Ball Change Drill, 115
Ball-handling skills, developing, 31-37
   practice and drills, 32-37
      Air Dribble, 33
      Forward Finger Flip, 35
      Forward Hand Roll, 34-35
      Globe Trotter, 37
      Ground Dribble, 33-34
      Hand Circle, 36-37
      Iso Grip, 32-33
      Lateral Hand Roll, 35-36
      One Hand Finger Passing, 37
      One Hand Juggle, 37
      Two Hand Juggle, 37
      Two Man Tug-o-War, 33
   specificity, 31
   "tricks," 32
Ball Iso Drill, 114
Ball security, total, developing, 109-118
   carry, proper, 109-110
      elbow, key role of, 109-110
      two-armed, 111-112
   changing from one hand to another, 112-113
   practice and drills, 114-118
      Arm Wrestle, 114
      Ball Change, 115
      Ball Iso, 114
      Gauntlet, 117-118
      Monkey Roll, 117

Ball security, total, developing *(cont'd.)*
   practice and drills *(cont'd.)*
      Rapid Fire Double Ball Carry, 116-117
      Rapid Fire Two-Hand Carry, 115-116
      Two-Hand Carry, 115
   problem areas, 113-114
Ballcarrier pouch, 57-58
Ballcarrier reception of quarterback hand-offs, 57-58 (see also "Quarterback-ballcarrier exchange . . . ."
Ballcarrying, three aspects of, 38
Basket-type positioning of hands to receive pitch or toss, 69-70
Big Bertha Drill, 232
Board Drill, 212-213
Boundary Drill, 185-186
Breakdown Drill, 74, 195
"Bucket Day" practice, 27
Burma Road Drill for backs, 105-106

## C

Cadence snaps for center and quarterback, 29-30
Carry Drill, 107
Carrying of football, proper, 109-110
   changing from one hand to other, 112-113
   elbow, key role of, 109-110
   two-armed, 111-112
Catching on the Move Drill, 180
Catching techniques for backfield, 164-169
   concentration essential, 165
   one-hand, 168-169
   pinkies-in technique, 166-167
   pocket catch, 167-168
   scoop technique, 167
Center pump-skid action Drill, 28
Center quarterback exchange techniques, developing, 19-30
   center snap and quarterback reception, 21-23
   "goosing" for football, 24-25
   offside snap, 25
   practice and drills, 27-30
      Cadence Snaps, 29-30
      Center Pump-Skid Action, 28
      Closed Eye Ball Pump, 28-29
      Guess-who, 30
   problems, common, 23-24
   stances, 19-21
   wet ball snaps, 25-27

# Index

Change of pace separation technique, 172-173
Chute Drill, 52-53
Closed eye ball pump Drill, 28-29
Concentration essential for ballcarrier receiving toss, 69
    for catching techniques, 165
Counter dive action of quarterback, 62-63
Counter dive take-off, 47-48
Counter Option Action in coaching backfield game, 133
Counter Option Triple Option Dive Read, 125
Counter step take-off, 46-47
Cutdown block, 219-224
Cutdown Block Drill, 231

## D

Deep Drill, 183
Deep Passing Drill, 162
Defender, back's carrying or dragging, 99
Delivery of ball for pass, 147-150
Dive concept running, 77-82
Dive Drill, 182
    for backs, 99-100
Dive Jump Drill for backs, 103-104
Dive jump technique, 93-94
Dive Read, 139
Dive Squeeze Drill for backs, 103
Dive squeeze technique, 94-96
Dive take-off, 44
Double Kneel Throw Drill, 156-157
Double (Triple) Hop Drill, 184-185
Down-the-Line Pitch, 137
Drag Drill for backs, 106-107

## E

Elbow as key in proper ball carry, 109-110
End-run techniques of running, 85-90
    arc blocker and ballcarrier relationship, 86-87
    Green Bay (pro) sweep, 89-90
End run take-off, 45-46

## F

Fake and block, 206-208
    crash technique, 207
    legal clip, 207-208
    shoulder drive, 208

Fake and Block Drill, 214-215
Faking, 187-196
    backfield practice and drills, 194-196
        Breakdown, 195
        Hand-Off Pouch and Fake, 195
        Hand-Off Pouch and Fake Circle Drill, 195
        Timing, 195
    faking action, additional, 192-193
    overexaggeration, danger of, 187, 192, 194
    quarterback hand-off, 188-190
    quarterback pass action, 190-192
        "look-them-off," meaning of, 191
    running back actions, other, 194
    running back fake or hand-off, 193-194
Flag Drill for backs, 102-103
Foot Adjustment Drill, 159
Form blocking, 230-231
Forward Finger Flip Drill, 35
Forward Hand Roll Drill, 34-35
Freeze technique of running, 83-85
    most effective on isolation play, 83

## G

Game-like drills, meaning of, 31 (see also "Ball-handling skills . . .")
Gauntlet Drill, 117-118
Globe Trotter Drill, 37
"Goosing" center for football, 24-25
Green Bay (pro) sweep, 89-90
Gripping ball for pass, 145
Ground Dribble Drill, 33-34
Guess-who Drill for center and quarterbacks, 30

## H

Halfback option passing, 153-154
Hand Circle Drill, 36-37
Hand-Off Pouch and Fake Circle Drill, 195
Hand-Off Pouch and Fake Drill, 195
Hand-Off Pouch and Reception Drill, 71-72
    Circle Drill, 72

## I

"I" formation tailback, 49-51
"Ice" block, 198-200

Individual Option Drill, 140
Inside Veer Option Action, 131-132
Iso Grip Drill, 32-33
Isolation block, 198-200
Isolation-Lead Draw Block Drill, 213-214
Isolation play and freeze technique, 83-85

## K

Keep-Pitch Read Downhill Attack, 125-131
Kick-out block, 204-206
Kick-Out Drill, 214-215
Knifing north-south, 175-176

## L

Landmark, meaning of, 52, 57, 77
Lateral Hand Roll Drill, 35-36
Lead block, 208-209
Lead Drill, 215-216
Lead-draw block, 201-203
Lead Option Action in coaching backfield game, 132
"Look-them-off," meaning of, 191

## M

"Matador" reverse pivot action, 60-61
Monkey Roll Drill, 117
Move-Out Pass Ready Drill, 159-160
Move-Out passing, 151-153
Move-Out and Throw Drill, 160-161
Multi-Option Backfield Drill, 141-143
Multiple Run Block Drill, 217-218
90 degree angle turn separation technique, 171-172

## N

North-south acceleration, importance of in backs' open field running, 91-93
Nutcracker Drill, 100-101

## O

Offside snap by center, 25
Off-tackle take-off, 44-45
One-Hand Catch Drill, 181-182

One hand catch technique, 168-169
One Hand Finger Passing Drill, 37
One Hand Juggle Drill, 37
One-Man Sled Drill, 213
Open field running for backs, 91-93
   drill, 107-108
   north-south acceleration, 91-93
Option game, coaching, 119-143 (See also "Backfield option game . . . ")
Option-pitch of quarterback, 67-69
Option-Pitching on Knee Drill, 74-75
Outside Veer Option Action in backfield game, 134-135
Outside Veer Triple Option Dive Read, 124-125

## P

Pass blocking techniques, backfield, 219-236
   cutdown block, 219-224
   pass pro block, 219, 224-230
      blitzing linebacker, 229-230
      seal block, 228
   practice and drills, 230-236
      Big Bertha, 232
      Cutdown, 231
      form blocking, 230-231
      Pass Pro, 233-234
      Pass Pro, Cutdown, Kick-Out, 234
      Pass Pro Position, 232-233
      Ride-In / Ride-Out, 234-235
      Scramble Block, 235-236
      in skeleton pass scrimmage, 230
   types, two, 219
Pass Pro, Cutdown, Kick-Out Drill, 234
Pass pro block, 219, 224-230 (see also "Pass blocking. . . . ")
Pass Pro Drill, 233-234
Pass Pro Position Drill, 232-233
Pass receiving techniques, backfield, 164-186
   ball security and north-south knifing, 175-176
   catching techniques, 164-169
      concentration essential, 165
      one-hand, 168-169
      pinkies-in technique, 166-167
      pocket catch, 167-168
      scoop technique, 167
   positioning, 169-170
   practice and drills, 176-186

*Index*

Pass receiving techniques, backfield *(cont'd.)*
    practice and drills *(cont'd.)*
        Around-the-Clock, 178-179
        Bad Ball, 182
        Boundary, 185-186
        Catching on the Move, 180
        Deep, 183
        Dive, 182
        Double (Triple) Hop, 184-185
        One-Hand Catch, 181-182
        Pressure, 183-184
        Spin, 179-180
    separation techniques, 170-175
        change of pace, 172-173
        90 degree angle turn, 171-172
        shoulder drag, 175
        shoulder drive technique, 174
        speed, 173
        270 degree angle cut separation, 174
        weaving, 173-174
        zigzag action, 174
Passing techniques of quarterback, coaching, 144-163
    delivery of ball, 147-150
    follow-through, 150
    gripping ball, 145
    halfback option passing, 153-154
    on the move, 151-153
    practice and drills, 154-163
        Deep Passing, 162
        Double Kneel Throw, 156-157
        Foot Adjustment Drill, 159
        Move-Out Pass Ready, 159-160
        Move-Out and Throw, 160-161
        Set-Up and Throw Drill, 157-158
        Skeleton Pass Scrimmage, 163
        Trajectory Passing, 161
        Varying Foot Position Drill, 158-159
        Warm-Up, 155-156
    setting up, 145-147
    sidearm passing, 144
    trajectory, 150-151
Patience essential for pass pro blocker, 225,226
Perimeter Option drill, 143
Pinkies-in technique of catching, 166-167
Pocket catch technique, 167-168
Positioning to receive catch, importance of, 169-170
Pressure Drill, 183-184

## Q

Quarterback-ballcarrier exchange techniques, developing, 54-75
    ballcarrier receiving toss, quick-pitch or option pitch, 69
    concentration essential, 69
    counter dive action, 62-63
    draw actions, techniques on, 63-65
    hand-off technique, 55-57
    option-pitch, 67-69
    practice drills, 71-75
        Breakdown, 74
        Hand-Off Pouch and Reception, 71-72
        Hand-Off Pouch and Reception Circle, 72
        Option-Pitching on Knee, 74-75
        Timing, 72-73
    quarterback movement to exchange point, 54-55
    reception of hand-off by ballcarrier, 57-58
    reverse hand-off, 70-71
    reverse pivot, 59-61
        "Matador" reverse pivot action, 60-61
    sprint-draw action, 61-62
    stomach as "third hand," 54-55
    toss/ quick-pitch, 65-67
Quarterback hand-off faking, 188-190
Quarterback hand positioning, 20 (see also "Center-quarterback exchange techniques. . . .")
Quarterback pass action faking, 190-192
    "look-them-off," meaning of, 191
Quarterback passing techniques, coaching, 144-163 (see also "Passing techniques . . . .")
Quarterback-Pitchback Pitch Ratio, 135-136
Quick-pitch/ swing pattern take-off, 48

## R

Rapid Fire Double Ball Carry Drill, 116-117
Rapid Fire Option Pitch, 138-139
Rapid Fire Two-Hand Carry Drill, 115-116
Reverse arc block, 210-211
Reverse hand-off, 70-71
Reverse pivot action of quarterback, 59-61
Ride-In / Ride-Out Drill, 234-235

Run blocking techniques, backfield, 197-218
    arc block, 209-211
        reverse, 210-211
    fake and block, 206-208
        crash technique, 207
        legal clip, 207-208
        shoulder drive, 208
    isolation block, 198-200
    kick-out block, 204-206
    lead block, 208-209
    lead-draw block, 201-203
    practice and drills, 211-218
        Arc Block, 216-217
        Board, 212-213
        Fake and Block, 214-215
        Isolation-Lead Draw Block, 213-214
        Kick-Out, 214-215
        Lead, 215-216
        Multiple Run Block, 217-218
        One-Man Sled, 213
Running back fake or hand-off, 193-194

**S**

Scoop technique of catching, 167
Scramble Block Drill, 235-236
Seal block, 228
Security of ball, 175-176
Separation techniques, backfield receiver, 170-175 (see also "Pass receiving techniques. . . .")
Set-Up and Throw Drill, 157-158
Seven Yard Drill for backs, 104-105
Shoulder drag as separation technique, 175
Shoulder drive separation technique, 174
Sidearm passing, 144
Sideline Drill for backs, 101-102
Skeleton Pass Scrimmage, 163
    as opportunity for pass blocking practice, 230
Skidding of ball by center, problem of, 23-24
Specificity in practice drills, concept of, 31
Speed as major concept of separation, 172, 173

Spin Drill, 179-180
Spinning out technique for backs, 96-97
Sprint-draw action of quarterback, 61-62
Sprint draw tailback take-off, 51
Stance, Take-Off and Landmark Drill, 52-53
Stances, coaching, 38-42 (see also "Backfield stances . . .")
Step technique for take-offs, 43-44
Stomach as "third hand," 54-55
Stumble Drill for Backs, 106
Stumble technique for backs, 98-99

**T**

Tailback "I" formation take-offs, 49-51
Thumbs-out technique of catching, 166-167 (see also "Catching techniques . . . .")
Timing Drill, 195
Toss/ quick-pitch of quarterback, 65-67
Trajectory Passing Drill, 161
Trap Option Action in coaching backfield game, 133-134
Triple Option Read, 119-124
Triple Option Read, 139-140
Two-Hand Carry Drill, 115
Two Hand Juggle Drill, 37
270 degree angle cut separation technique, 174
Two Man Tug-o-War Drill, 33

**V**

Varying Foot Position Drill, 158-159

**W**

Warm-Up Drill, 155-156
Weaving separation technique, 173-174
Wet ball snaps, 25-27

**Z**

Zigzag type of separation technique, 175